Hey, That's My Music!

MUSIC SUPERVISION,

LICENSING, AND

CONTENT ACQUISITION

by Brooke Wentz

HAL•LEONARD®

Hal Leonard Books
An Imprint of Hal Leonard Corporation
New York

Published in 2007 by Hal Leonard Books
An Imprint of Hal Leonard Corporation
19 West 21st Street, New York, NY 10010
Printed in the United States of America

Cover design and layout: Stephen Ramirez

Editor: Patrick Runkle
Editorial assistance: Rick Weldon

Produced in association with Mike Lawson, Lawson Music Media, Inc.

Library of Congress Cataloging-in-Publication Data is available upon request.

ISBN-10: 1-4234-2212-0
ISBN-13: 978-1-4234-2212-9

www.halleonard.com

This book is dedicated to my best little friend, Gabrielle, and my mother, Dr. Lydia Seebach, not only one of the greatest woman doctors I know, but my biggest supporter and fan.

"What hath God wrought"
—Samuel Morse, 1844, first telegraph message

"What hath man wrought"
—Lyndon B. Johnson, 1967, comment upon signing of Public Broadcasting Act

Acknowledgments

Although my business, the Rights Workshop, is a culmination of a multitude of my experiences in the music and media businesses over the last 25 years or so, I have to thank a variety of colleagues and friends who have supported my efforts along the way. First and foremost thanks go to Mike Lawson, who was instrumental in making this book happen. It all started at a NARAS Nomination Party with colleague and fellow supervisor Gerry Gershman, who has been supportive of the project from the get-go. And to Hal Leonard for taking the leap of faith to publish this. As one with Minnesota roots, I hope to visit Winona some day and enjoy one of those cats at your local famous hotel.

To Charles Yassky for encouraging me to take a job at ESPN in Connecticut, where I would never have thought of working. He felt the experience would be with me forever; so far he's right. To my lawyer colleagues, Todd Gason at Zent Law Group, and George Rush and Cydney Tune at Pillsbury Winthrop, for reviewing the manuscript's legal verbiage. To my co-workers David Wurzburg and James Lynch III for reviewing sections of the manuscript and putting up with my wild and passionate ways on a daily basis. To colleagues Joei Alvarez, Amy Rosen, John Califra, Miriam Cutler, Marc Capelle, Sue Devine, Kevin Wilson, Noubar Stone, Andrew Stess, and David Katznelson.

To Byran Dale who transcribed the interviews, and Yvette Torrell who shot the Sound & Cinema Series from which the interviews are drawn. To director Varda Hardy for documenting my seminar in which the extractions kept my writing focused, and certainly to Paul Cowlings at Film INDependent who continues to invite me to speak!

Special thanks go to editor Patrick Runkle, who used his magic to pick up where the very helpful Rick Weldon left off. And last but certainly not least to all my diverse clients—from Argentina and Italy to Crested Butte and New York City—and especially my local clients (Nancy Kelly, Sam Green, Henry Rosenthal, Vicky Funari, Mark

Becker, Haskell Wexler, Bruce Conner, and many more), whose support has allowed me to live in Northern California.

On a personal note, I'd like to thank Julie Green for coming through with a computer when the wine slipped one late Stinson Beach night. To Katherine Cowles for her advice, support, and encouragement. To Alfredo Alias, who for years enriched my life about bridges and hooks. To my daughter for all her patience and understanding, and to all my friends who helped avail their time to allow me time to write this during my busy schedule. Enjoy.

About the Author

Brooke Wentz is a seasoned music supervisor and intellectual property rights executive who founded the Rights Workshop in 2002. Her entrepreneurial career and business are built on years of experience in music licensing and publishing, record production, and performing rights organization administration. Prior to founding the Rights Workshop, she spent six years as Music Director at ESPN, where she oversaw all music for the network, including music for the X Games, World Cup, and Sports Century telecasts. She also initiated the company's publishing efforts.

Ms. Wentz is an accomplished producer, having won a Billboard Award for the 4CD set *Global Meditation*; she went on to produce over 25 critically acclaimed recordings. She was Manager of A&R Administration for Arista Records and is co-founder of SynkLynk, a digital marketing tool. In 1999, she was chosen to be Music Producer for the New York City Millennium Celebration. She was also a longtime radio host on NPR, where she interviewed hundreds of artists, composers, and musicians. Many of her interviews have been transcribed for publication. Ms. Wentz is a frequent speaker and teacher on content acquisition, digital rights, and the future of media.

A native and current resident of San Francisco, Ms. Wentz holds an MBA from Columbia Business School and received her undergraduate degree from Barnard College. She sits on the NARAS Board of Governors and is a board member of the Stern Grove Music Festival.

Ms. Wentz's film and TV credits as music supervisor include the following:

▶ *The Unforeseen*, Two Birds Films, January 2007

- *When the World Was Green*, Sea Glass Productions, 2007

- *My Brother*, Gregory Segal, March 2007

- *Pray For Me: The Jason Jessee Film*, David Rogerson, January 2007

- *Audience of One*, Michael Jacobs, March 2007

- *Who Needs Sleep?*, Haskell Wexler, 2006

- *Romantico*, Mark Becker, October 2006

- *Push*, Matchstick Productions, October 2006

- *Have You Heard From Johannesburg*, Clarity Films, December 2006

- *Salud!*, Clarity Films, December 2006

- *World Salsa Championships*, Salsa Seven Productions, 2006

- *Ballets Russes*, Geller/Goldfine Productions, October 2005

- *The Devil and Daniel Johnston*, Jeff Feuerzeig, winner 2005 Sundance best director award (Feb 2006 release)

- *Three of Hearts: A Postmodern Family*, Susan Kaplan, 2004

- *Up for Grabs*, Michael Wranovics, 2004

- *Boricua*, Marisol Torres, 2004

- *Voices of Iraq*, Eric Manes, produced by Mark Cuban, 2004

- *To You Sweetheart, Aloha*, Leo Chiang & Mercedes Coats, 2004

- *Paternal Instinct*, Craig Harwood & Murray Nossel, HBO, 2004

- *Happily, Even After*, Hotbed Media, 2004

- *Sumo East & West*, Ferne Pearlstein, 2003

- *Freestyle: The Art of Rhyme*, Kevin Fitzgerald, VH1, 2003

- *Imelda*, Ramona Diaz for Cinediaz, 2003

- *Loss of Nameless Things*, Bill Rose, 2003

- *The Weather Underground*, Sam Green & Bill Siegel, 2003 San Francisco Best Documentary, SF Film Festival

- *Soundz of Spirit: The Creative Process in Hip Hop Culture*, Joslyn Rose Lyons, 2003

- *Confessions of a Burning Man*, Hotbed Media, 2003

- *Underground Zero*, Jay Rosenblatt, HBO, 2002

- *Heart of the Sea: Kapolioka'ehukai*, Charlotte Lagarde, 2002 Audience Award for Best Documentary SF Film Fest.

- *Britney Baby, One More Time*, Ludi Boeken, 2001

- *Amandla!*, Lee Hirsch, 2001

- *Mule Skinner Blues*, Steel Carrot, Stephen Earnhart, 2001, Sundance Channel

- *Sounds Sacred*, Out of the Blue Films, Barbara Rick, 2001

- *Just Me and Mom*, Illumina Films, Yvette Torell, 2000

- *An American Love Story*, (10-hour doc) Jennifer Fox, American Playhouse/PBS, Fall 1999, Special Presentation at Sundance 1999

- *Not for Ourselves Alone*, (2 part series) Ken Burns/Florentine Films, Soundtrack Producer, Fall 1999

- *Rumi: Poet of the Heart*, Haydn Reiss, Magnolia Films, 1998

- *Snow Days*, Kip Marcus, 1998/1999

- *Killing Zoe*, Quentin Tarantino and Roger Avary, 1993

Contents

Preface

The new millennium has brought on an explosion of information and content through new media formats such as satellite radio, online games, podcasts, and cell-phone downloads. These new media platforms seek content supplied by established producers of music, art, text, and film, but they also encourage end users to create their own content.

YouTube, the most recent high-technology sensation, would not exist if it were not for user-uploaded content. But what all these new-media companies are quickly learning is that most of the content they have or want is filled with copyrighted material. If they don't acquire licenses to use this content, lawsuits will grow like weeds. In fact, as of this writing in early 2007, lawsuits from Hollywood studios are pending against YouTube after licensing talks have broken down.

Unfortunately, some media companies have become like Wooly Mammoths plodding along the frozen tundra. It has become increasingly more difficult to secure licenses because the larger publishing houses and record labels are inundated with requests, and yet they maintain strict guidelines for clearance that prolong the process. Furthermore, they find it difficult to effectively police unauthorized uses of their content. Therefore, it is crucial for musicians and song-writers themselves to understand what rights they own and control, and how to manage and earn revenue from those rights.

No one knows this better than a dear friend of mine, the grand-son of songwriter Edward Hammond Boatner. Boatner wrote many arrangements of early twentieth century gospel tunes, including "Go Down Moses," "Wade in the Water," and "Deep River."

Boatner was a struggling musician who had transcribed his arrangements as sheet music. His grandmother had cancer, and, as she lay on her death bed, Boatner gave up the rights to some of his arrangements to a publishing company. Although Boatner was able to pay his grandmother's medical bill, it wasn't a very fair deal. One of the copyrighted arrangements he sold, and lost his rights to, was "When the Saints Go Marching In." Although the song is a traditional gospel hymn, Boatner's arrangement is the one we all know.

Too many stories like this one abound where artists don't know what their copyrights are worth, don't register them, and/or sell them for nothing. They give them away for a Chinese dinner. That may be fine if you are hungry, but don't complain that the MSG has left you wanting more.

The following pages will help guide musicians, songwriters, future music supervisors, and anyone wanting to use music content through the licensing process for film, TV, ads, games, and online entertainment. You will discover how complex the clearance process is and how important it is to work with someone who knows this process.

After 25 years of working in the music business, teaching, lecturing, and, most importantly, working closely with thousands of artists, I can honestly say licensing music in the United States has become more complex than ever before. It has become a process that makes me want to join the call for a reform to the copyright system. Yet there's a big side of me that values the creative process too highly to change a system that has given the world so much great music.

In 1993, I produced a 4CD set called *Global Meditation*. We licensed 64 tracks of music from 25 different countries. Although there were bumps along the way—one company didn't want to participate because of the title, another company refused because there were white people involved—the project was tremendously successful. It garnered accolades and amazing critical acclaim, winning a *Billboard* Music Award and ultimately spawning more world-music projects.

At that time, we were able to license the tracks for a few hundred dollars each. It took a few months, a few phone calls, and many faxes. Today, the process would take about nine months and the cost would be prohibitive. Because of the proliferation of red tape at the record labels, even since 1993, as many as ten people are needed to sign off on the use of one track. Numbers have to be met by the various departments and they must keep about a mile of paperwork for documentation. Even when a deal in place, and you request them to issue a contract, it can take up to one year to receive it.

My business, the Rights Workshop, is based on music supervision and licensing, and I can tell you that the process has become more insane than ever before. As a result, I have compiled in this book some real-life examples of how this business works. We live under a copyright cartel that has made life relatively difficult for anyone wanting to use copyrighted material: filmmakers, producers, creative advertising executives, game companies, corporations, or anyone else. This book will help you get a grasp of the ins and outs of licensing and give many helpful tips to grease the wheels of progress. Hey, many things may change in ten years, or maybe two years, but one thing will remain the same until the courts or legislators say otherwise: You must license copyrighted material and pay artists and their owners!

CHAPTER 1

In the Beginning There Was ...Copyright?

So you've started making music. Or you want to get into the business end of music. Unless you're just noodling around in your friend's garage—and chances are that if you bought this book, you're a little more serious than that—you will soon start to consider many important questions related to the business. Foremost among them is the notion of ownership and copyright. Without the ability to control what they create and own, musical artists and record companies would not be able to maintain an industry based on the use of their music.

Never has this been more true than today. In the past, the concept of copyright barely registered in the mass consciousness, mainly because copyright infringement in the analog world was more difficult and less profitable than it is today. With the explosion of digital media now all around us, however, the rules have changed. Not only has copying other artists' works become easier, but there are also many more outlets in which musical works can be used and consumed by the public. Accordingly, copyright issues are now discussed regularly in the news, and copyright is quickly becoming part of the vocabulary of today's youth culture.

In October 2006, the Los Angeles Area Council of the Boy Scouts of America unveiled its new Respect Copyrights Activity Patch, which can be earned by Boy Scouts throughout Los Angeles. The Associated Press reported, "Scouts will be instructed in the basics of copyright law and learn how to identify five types of copyrighted works and three ways copyrighted material may be stolen."

A brief glance through any major newspaper will find articles about media and technology, and many of the legal cases involve copyright issues. Specific topics can vary widely, from infringement cases and ownership issues to copyright extension, catalog valuation, and purchasing. Moreover, you may have heard about a select number of grandmothers, teenagers, educational facilities, community organizations, filmmakers, websites, and game companies who have been sued for either copyright infringement or illegal downloading. Napster, Metallica, the RIAA, the MPAA: Do any of these ring a bell?

In response to the constantly evolving ways that entertainment is created and consumed, copyright owners are shifting the ways in which they control their product. Some are increasing licensing fees for the use of their material in new media formats, waiting to see what the market will bear. Others have instead opted to give away their works for free in exchange for exposure or credit. The entertainment industry is entering a phase where artists have more direct control over how their art is used, reused, distributed, recreated, and imitated.

The extreme breadth of copyright law has caused unending legal, ethical, and intellectual discourse. Its innumerable facets keep lawyers busily researching and billing hours to their clients, with every content provider and user trying to be attentive to the ever-changing rules and circumstances that could bring cease-and-desist letters, hefty settlements, or even court proceedings. Before I get into the meat of what I do and how I clear songs for use in movies and TV, I want to give you a brief introduction to the legal framework of music copyright. This is by no means comprehensive and I encourage you to seek out more information if you are interested.

What Is a Copyright?

Any original piece of work, whether it is a book, a movie, a painting, a sculpture, a piece of music, or an architectural work, is considered the product of a unique creator. The creator can be an individual, a corporation, or a group of people. In a visual work of art, such as a painting, sculpture, or drawing, the person who conceives the artwork is often the same person who creates or realizes it. There is one artistic entity that manifests the work by using whatever tools are needed. Likewise, most literature is the product of a single author who puts pen to paper and writes a story. In music and other more technological media, however, there are often two or more people involved in the creation of a work. In music, this can take several forms: songwriting partnerships, combinations of composers and performers, and so on. In the composer/performer scenario, each entity holds a copyright that covers its contribution.

In U.S. copyright law, a work qualifies for copyright protection as soon as it is "fixed in a tangible medium of expression." With visual art, the creation of the piece constitutes this fixation. With text, the work must be written in words of a particular language. With music, the work can be recorded, or it can be notated on sheet music. Once the work is fixed, the copyright owner immediately acquires ownership of a number of important rights over that work.

A Bit of History

United States copyright law is based, like most of our legal system, on British law. In 1790, Congress enacted the first U.S. copyright statute, which was authorized by a clause in the Constitution. The term of protection at that time was 14 years, with a possible renewal of another 14 years. There have been many changes since then, and we now live under a copyright framework established by the 1976 Copyright Act, which went into effect in 1978. This framework has been amended and the term of protection extended since then, but many principles of the 1976 Act still stand.

For a majority of works created after 1978, the term of copyright protection is the life of the author plus 70 years. Works made for hire, which covers works that were created and are owned by corporations, have a different standard: either 95 years from publication or 120 years from date of creation, whichever expires first. Determining whether something is still covered by copyright is difficult and has many complexities based on the date of creation or publication.

In 1887, the Berne Convention for the Protection of Literary and Artistic Works (signed at Berne, Switzerland) defined the scope of international copyright protection. (The Convention was initiated by a group of authors, artists, publishers, and others led by Victor Hugo.) Under the terms of the Convention, reciprocal copyright protection was granted automatically to all creative works from member countries. In 1908, the Convention was amended to add 50 more years to the life of a copyright. The United States did not participate in the Berne Convention for over a hundred years, due in part to domestic opposition and the drastic changes it would have needed to make in its own copyright law. However, the United States at last became a party to the Convention with the Berne Convention Implementation Act of 1988.

In 1989, the Convention established that an author is not required, as a condition of copyright protection, to register or otherwise apply for a copyright. As soon as the work is "fixed"—recorded on a physical medium, such as words written on page, music recorded onto tape, and so on—its author is automatically granted exclusive rights to the work until the copyright expires. It is important to note, however, that registration in the United States does have benefits; it makes proof of copyright ownership easier, and it provides attorney's fees for a successful lawsuit. Although also no longer required by law, it is a good idea to include a copyright notice on any copyrighted work as well; the copyright notice is the familiar © symbol, which is often followed by the year of release.

Various aspects of copyright law change as courts and regulatory agencies clarify the scope of protection. This book focuses on the permissions that must currently be obtained by those who want to use another entity's copyrighted material. I've heard too many times from writers and musicians who discover their music has been incorporated into new works without their permission. The aim of this book is to turn the phrase "hey, that's my music!" from a cry of anguish into a happy recognition of this potential new revenue stream for an artist's music.

Music Rights

Compared to other copyrights, clearance of music rights tends to be a more complex and unwieldy procedure. This is due to the fact that there are generally at least two different entities to contact for the clearance of any given piece of recorded music. The first copyright is on the song itself, meaning the intangible words and music. The second copyright is on the specific recording of the song that you want to use.

Although there are some cases where both copyrights are controlled by the same company, the two will usually be separate. For example, Smokey Robinson and Ronald White are the writers of the song "My Girl," which is owned by Jobete Music and controlled by EMI Music Publishing. The most famous recording of "My Girl," by the Temptations, is controlled by Motown, a record label that is part of the Universal Music Group. In order to use this recording of "My Girl" in a movie, TV show, or video game, both copyright owners need to grant a license. The understanding of these two different rights is at the crux of music licensing.

Songwriters are generally represented by publishers, to whom they grant rights in their songs, whereas recording artists are represented by record labels, to whom they grant rights in their recordings. Note that "copyright control" is used to designate a song that is controlled by the writer or copyright owner; the rights have not yet been transferred to a publisher. In order to use a piece designated as such, one has to obtain permission from the songwriter directly.

The correct permissions depend on who owns the rights to the song, and on the medium in which you will be using the song. You need to evaluate what rights you need and who can give them to you. Let's take a closer look at the relationships between the various kinds of artists that help to realize the music we all know and love.

COMPOSERS, LYRICISTS, AND RECORDING ARTISTS

Recorded music comes to fruition in all sorts of different ways. Singer-songwriters such as Bruce Springsteen, Paul Simon, James Taylor, Ani DiFranco, and Dave Matthews write and record their own music. Performing artists such as Aretha Franklin, Diana Krall, Michael Jackson, Hilary Duff, and Yo-Yo Ma often do not write their own music. They are hired for their technique and style in realizing a composition.

Often, the artists who compose music and write lyrics go unnoticed by the public: Norman Whitfield and Barrett Strong, Linda Perry, and Rod Temperton, for instance. These are the creative forces behind the songs "I Heard It through the Grapevine," "Beautiful," and "Rock with You," respectively. They are individuals who write prolifically; other artists then realize the songs through their own recordings.

Over the years, there have been many famous songwriting teams: Ashford and Simpson, Lieber and Stoller, King and Goffin, Williams and Hugo (otherwise known as the Neptunes), and many others. Today, there are very few examples of popular music written by a single individual. Producers and co-writers (and sometimes even engineers) often claim a portion of the writer's share. Take, for example, "Yeah!" recorded by Usher. The song is credited to seven writers: Sean Garrett, LaMarquis Jefferson, Robert McDowell, James Elbert Phillips (LRoc), Jonathan Smith (Lil' Jon), Patrick J. Que Smith, and Christopher Bridges (Ludacris).

Cover songs and sampling can further complicate matters. Some songs have been hits over and over again in different versions. A famous example is "All Along the Watchtower," written by Bob Dylan and first released in 1967 on the album *John Wesley Harding*. In 1968, guitarist Jimi Hendrix recorded his legendary version and included it on his album *Electric Ladyland*. It became a hit once again in 1974, when Dave Mason released his version on his eponymous album. The Grateful Dead also captured a version of the song in 1989, which was included on their live album of Dylan covers, *Postcards of the Hanging*, released in 2002. In 1998, Dave Matthews covered the song on the Australian release of his single *Ants Marching*. There are more than 200 versions of this song available in the marketplace to purchase today.

Similarly, the song "I Will Always Love You," written by Dolly Parton in 1974 and recorded on her record *Jolene*, has been performed and recorded more than 350 times. Whitney Houston re-recorded it in 1992 for use in the film *The Bodyguard*. It became an enormous worldwide hit; this re-recording of the song illustrates the magnitude of popularity a song can attain years after its initial recording.

COPYRIGHT CLEARANCE

In terms of copyright, each of the aforementioned recordings has a unique copyright independent of the underlying musical composition, so when seeking permission for the use of a particular performance, it is absolutely necessary to know which performance is to be used. This is important because you must correctly identify what record label or entity owns the rights, pay the necessary fees, and give the proper attribution. When Pearl Jam included a cover of the Beatles' "I've Got a Feeling" on the Japanese release of the album *Ten*, for instance, they released a new version of an older song. The owner of this specific recording is the new copyright holder, and the new copyright is designated on the back cover of the Japanese release by a ℗.

Even though I have already used this term generally, I want to introduce "copyright clearance" as the specific phrase for the process of requesting and obtaining copyright licenses. An interchangeable term is "content acquisition," and these terms apply whether one is attempting to license a single work of art or a bundle of compositions. The process can be difficult and timely; the costs involved are based on numerous factors surrounding the nature of use, term of use, and territory of distribution. Music copyright fees are intangible, ephemeral, subjective, and dependent on what the market will bear, as perceived by the publisher or owner. Sometime it feels like purchasing a rug at a Turkish bazaar!

Copyright Formalities

Once an original work has been created, its copyright should be filed with the U.S. Copyright Office in Washington, D.C., so that a proof of ownership exists. At this point, it is given a title or number to identify it. The copyright grants its holder the "exclusive legal right to print, publish, perform, film, or record material." It is the mark of ownership of a unique creation that identifies the maker of the work. Remember, however, that a creator owns the copyright to a work whether or not the work has been registered with the U.S. Copyright Office.

Filing a composition or original work has become increasingly easy thanks to the Internet. Anyone can go to the website (www.copyright.gov) and follow the very simple steps necessary to register musical works (Form SR), literary works (Form TX), visual works of art (Form VA), performing arts (Form PA), or periodicals (Form SE). The fee is currently $45 per registration for music; you can file one song or sound recording at a time, or submit a group of compositions on one CD. (The latter is considered a single filing.) Simply complete the form and mail it in along with $45 and a copy of the material, and you're set. See Appendix D for examples of copyright forms.

POOR MAN'S COPYRIGHT

Some people attempt to save money with a "poor man's copyright." This is when you put your material in the mail and send it back to yourself. Once you receive the piece in the mail, you leave it unopened. The postage date confirms the date of origination. Then, should you ever have to go to court to prove the date of origination, you can produce the material in court. This is not the wisest way to copyright your work, but it can provide some limited protection.

PUBLIC DOMAIN

After a certain period of time—and it varies depending on what year the work was created—copyrighted works fall into the public domain. When a piece of music is in the public domain, it is considered communal property and can be used freely without permission. Many traditional and religious songs are in the public domain as well as some classical music.

Some "traditional" songs that you would expect to be in the public domain are not. Warner Chappell owns the 1935 work-for-hire copyright to "Happy Birthday to You," which will expire in 2030. "Sloop John B.," made famous by the Beach Boys, is a public domain song. Brian Wilson's specific arrangement of "Sloop John B.," however, is owned by New Executive Music. It is important to check whether the particular arrangement of a public domain work that you and your client want to use is itself copyrighted.

Moreover, don't get your hopes up for works entering the public domain. Because of the extremely long duration of copyright law, most popular works from the latter half of the twentieth century will not enter the public domain during our lifetimes. In addition, Congress passed and President Clinton signed a 1998 copyright term extension act that extended copyright protection retroactively for all registered works for another twenty years. The Walt Disney Company and the Gershwin estate exerted a lot of pressure to get this legislation passed, due to the fact that certain Gershwin songs, as well as Mickey Mouse himself, were about to enter the public domain. The Mouse is safe from the public, for now at least.

A very thorough chart on copyright duration and the public domain can be found online at the following address:

http://www.copyright.cornell.edu/training/Hirtle_Public_Domain.htm

To conclude, here's an entertaining exchange that took place between two characters on the late 1990s Aaron Sorkin show *Sports Night* about public domain works:

Mallory: During your broadcast on September 5th you sang "Happy Birthday" to your partner, Casey McCall?

Dan: Yeah, but I can explain that it... wait, but it was his birthday, why do I have to explain that?

Mallory: You sang "Happy Birthday" on the air?

Dan: Dana cleared it.

Mallory: Who's Dana?

Dan: Dana Whitaker's the producer of the show.

Mallory: Oh, well yes, but my predecessor didn't clear it.

Dan: Who's your predecessor?

Mallory: Marty Shinebaum.

Dan: Who's Marty Shinebaum?

Mallory: My predecessor.

Dan: Look, I don't have a whole lot of time…

Mallory: Listen, I think it's sweet that you and your partner sing to each other on television. Others may think it's vaguely gay, but I disagree.

Dan: Thank you.

Mallory: Nonetheless, you can't do it anymore.

Dan: Why not?

Mallory: It's against the law.

Dan: It's against the law to be vaguely gay?

Mallory: It's against the law to sing "Happy Birthday" on television.

Dan: That doesn't sound quite right to me.

Mallory: It is.

Dan: You went to law school and everything, right?

Mallory: Yeah.

Dan: You took the bar?

Mallory: Three times.

Dan: It's against the law to sing "Happy Birthday" on television?

Mallory: Federal copyright law.

Dan: "Happy Birthday" is protected material?

Mallory: Yes.

Dan: Who holds the copyright to "Happy Birthday"?

Mallory: The representatives of Mildred and Patty Hill.

Dan: Mildred and Patty Hill?

Mallory: The authors.

Dan: The authors.

Mallory: They wrote it.

Dan: They wrote the song?

Mallory: Did you think that song just happened?

Dan: Well, yeah.

Mallory: It didn't.

Dan: Live and learn.

Mallory: Yes, indeed.

Dan: Would they be happy with an autographed hat?

Mallory: Yes, they would.

Dan: Great (gets up to leave).

Mallory: Along with 2,500 dollars.

Dan: I'm sorry?

Mallory: They've billed the network 2,500 dollars.

Dan: Twenty-five hundred dollars to sing "Happy Birthday"?

Mallory: Yes.

Dan: Ouch.

Mallory: Intellectual property, dual morale, fair use, royalty structure. These things may not mean anything to you, but I assure you they mean a great deal to me and they meant a great deal to my predecessor.

Dan: Marty Shinebaum.

Mallory: Marty Shinebaum.

Dan: You know what? From now on I am only singing songs in the public domain.

Mallory: That'll teach 'em.

Dan: I'm not kidding.

Mallory: Go knock 'em dead.

CHAPTER 2

Permissions Needed

In Chapter 1, I discussed the concept and ownership of copyrights of various types of works. Below are the general types of permissions you need to incorporate parts of copyrighted works into a new work:

▶ ART WORK: 1) permission from copyright owner of the art work, which may be the artist, and sometimes 2) permission from the owner of the physical work of art;

▶ LITERARY WORK: 1) permission from the author and/or the book publisher;

▶ MUSICAL WORK: 1) permission from the owner of the song (music publisher), and 2) permission from the owner of the sound recording of the song (typically the record label).

Each license grants rights to use the given work within the terms negotiated between the licensee and the owner. Common usage restrictions to a license include territory, which is the geographical region in which you may use the copyrighted work, and time, which could be in months, years, or perpetuity. At the conclusion of a license, you are obligated to return the property to its owner, just as if you were borrowing a book from the library. The intended medium and the manner in which you want to use the piece of music are crucial factors used to determine what sorts of permissions are needed when licensing pre-existing music.

As a music supervisor, I am usually talking about licensing a given piece of music to appear in, say, a movie. But it doesn't end there. The filmmakers need to get a license to play that movie in theaters, and if the movie is going to home video, that use must be licensed as well. When I talk about securing a license for "all medias," that means that I am getting a license to put a given song in a given movie no matter how that movie will be distributed. This concept will become clearer as we go through the licensing process in Chapters 4-6.

The Entities

There are several important entities involved in the creation and ownership of any commercial piece of music. Of course, you already know about the songwriters, the performers, and the musicians. But, in business terms, there are also the publishers, the labels, and the master owners. Sometimes they may all be the same entity; many times they are not.

PUBLISHING COMPANIES

As I've said, the owner of most commercial songs—the music and lyrics—is a publisher. The publisher may be controlled by the songwriter, or it could be a third party that purchased the rights to the song from the songwriter. A publisher can be a single individual or it can be a huge conglomerate, such as EMI Music Publishing, Universal Music Publishing Group, Warner/Chappell, and Sony/ATV. A publisher, whether an individual or a large company, performs four basic functions: It controls the copyright, exploits the copyright, protects the copyright, and collects the income generated from the use and exploitation of the copyright.

Understanding how the publishing industry developed, and what the large publishing houses do with an extremely popular song, gives you a good idea of how the system works and all the possibilities for commercial music exploitation.

The concept of music publishing came to the forefront in the 1880s with the start of Tin Pan Alley. This once referred to a specific place in New York City, West 28th Street between Broadway and Sixth

Avenue, where numerous publishers and songwriters had offices and wrote mainly for Broadway stage productions. The publishers literally printed and published sheet music, and the legendary songwriters of the time were Irving Berlin, Hoagy Carmichael, George Gershwin, Jerome Kern, and Cole Porter.

The Brill Building's famous entrance as it looks in 2007.

The first reproductions of music for a mechanical device were player-piano rolls. A fee was paid to the songwriter per mechanical roll that was sold, hence the term "mechanical royalty." The term "mechanical rate" is still used in current terminology to designate the fee paid to the publisher of a song for each recorded version of that song, whether it is mechanically reproduced on vinyl LPs, cassette tapes, compact discs, or via digital download. More on that later in this chapter. When sound recordings and radio began to be widely popularized, publishing concerns also began collecting royalties for the public performances of recorded songs.

Publishers have always been powerful forces in the industry. In the 1960s, the Brill Building (located at 1619 Broadway in New York City) was the industry's songwriting hotspot, and included such talents as Carole King, Gerry Goffin, Doc Pomus, Mort Shuman, Jerry Leiber, Mike Stoller, and Neil Diamond. The Brill Building at this time was a classic model of vertical integration. Without leaving the building, you could write a song, then make the rounds and meet with various publishers until someone bought it.

You could go to another floor, get a quick arrangement and lead sheet for $10, have some copies made at the duplication office, book an hour at a demo studio, hire some of the musicians and singers that were loitering around the building, and finally cut a demo of the song. Finally, with demo in hand, you could go around the building to the record companies, publishers, artist managers, even the artists themselves. If you made a deal, there were radio promoters available to sell the record.

RECORD LABELS

Record labels originated to produce records and own masters of their recordings. They often came from humble beginnings, often as recording studios such as Sun Records (Jerry Lee Lewis, Roy Orbison, Johnny Cash, Carl Perkins), Motown (Stevie Wonder, Marvin Gaye, Smokey Robinson, the Temptations), Stax (Sam & Dave, Isaac Hayes, Booker T & the MGs), and Atlantic (Aretha Franklin, Ray Charles, John Coltrane, Eric Clapton). These studios captured the many styles of talent that came through their doors, but they not only recorded the music, they pressed it on vinyl and worked to get the songs played on radio as well. Those lovely 7- and 12-inch discs brought the music to the masses.

These studios took great risks by making financial investments, not just in equipment but also in the talent—the performers whose recorded songs the labels ultimately owned and sold. Over time, these humble recording studios either turned into record companies themselves, or were bought by larger, more established labels or media corporations. Today there are only four major labels (Sony/BMG, Universal, Warner, and EMI) and countless independent ones, although many smaller label imprints are owned by one of the four majors. Here is a short table of labels now controlled by the four conglomerates:

Major Label Subsidiaries			
Sony/BMG	**Universal**	**Warner Bros.**	**EMI**
RCA	Interscope	Lava	Blue Note
RCA Victor	Island/Def Jam	Atlantic	Capitol
RCA Nashville	Geffen	Reprise	Chrysalis
Arista	Lost Highway	Rhino	Virgin
Ariola	MCA	Nonesuch	Liberty
Jive	Mercury	Elektra	Astralwerks
J	Verve	Rykodisc	Manhattan
Milan	A&M	Sire	
Windham Hill	Polygram	Bad Boy	
Zomba	Motown	Blacksmith	
Columbia	Decca	Maverick	
Epic	RMM		
Legacy	Verve		
Jet	Motown		

Labels as Master Owners

The finalized sound recording is commonly referred to as the master. The labels often own the masters, and therefore control the copyright of the sound recordings. As owner of a master, the job of the label is to control the master, exploit the master, protect the master, and collect the income resulting from the use of the master copyright. If any other label or entity wants to use a master for a compilation album, in a film, in an advertisement, or as a sample, permissions must be granted by the label that owns the original work.

The process of obtaining permission to use master content has become more complex as more media is introduced and the means of distribution have increased greatly. In addition, due to industry expansion, licensing departments today are bombarded by licensing requests. These changes and developments have created new opportunities for record labels to license their masters, creating new revenue streams in the process. This source of licensing income (sometimes referred to as "ancillary income") has grown substantially. In the early 1990s, the major record labels initiated new departments to tap into so-called "special markets." These departments handle any and all licensing requests, including but not limited to compilations, synchronization licenses for films and TV, grand rights for theatrical performances, and any other requests.

Warner Music Group's licensing division grew out of its business affairs department. "Warner Special Products used to handle calendars, T-shirts, and record compilation licensing," recounts Bill Bishop, VP of Film, TV, Commercial, and Video Game Licensing, who has been with the company for 16 years. "The company was looking to develop more ancillary income, and there were individuals in the business affairs area who were visionary enough to see the potential business. In the mid '90s, we mostly focused on film and television. In 1993, we started doing commercials, then video games, then Internet licensing," Bishop continues. "We have people who pitch, who go out and create business. We have a music-clearance staff and a contract department to generate the contracts. Our biggest current growth areas are video games and new overseas opportunities. Advanced as it is, the Internet is still just getting off the ground. Today, Warner Special Products has become a significant generator of income after record sales."

Today, these divisions generate revenue by licensing master content for use in films, television, advertisements, in-flight listening, Internet streaming, video games, at corporate conventions, in kiosks, for product demonstrations, and released on other compilation albums or soundtrack albums. If you're looking to request a license for this kind of use, this is the department to contact.

Some big record labels only have two persons handling all the requests. Karen Lamberton, VP of Music Licensing for RCA, Arista, and J Records, has seen an expansion in her department. "There has been increased importance for exposure, and therefore growth, of music in film, TV, and advertisements," recounts Lamberton. "There are more medias to compete with because radio is difficult to get exposure for new artists. Licensing for TV has become so much more important. There is a quicker turn around and a singer-songwriter can get in front of millions of kids. But as this area has become more important, it has become harder to get placement." With the plethora of new media and requirements by various sites, the clearance departments at the record labels and publishing concerns have had to expand staff in order to maintain the level of requests.

"The big difference today is a willingness by artists to write for film and TV," explains Lamberton. "When an artist is writing for a specific production it allows the artist to step out of their space and be creative in a different way, like Avril Lavigne did for the film *Eragon*. When young artists see their icons like the Rolling Stones and Bob Dylan licensing music, they see that writing for a different media can be fun and hip."

Because there are no set rules or rate sheets for licensing outside of the statutory mechanical license, fees are entirely subjective. Just like a piece of art at auction, the sky's the limit. Factors such as the "hit value" of a song, its *Billboard* chart placement, its potential use and frequency of use, and the temperament of the artist all affect the fee. Some artists could care less what your project is about, they just want money. Some are pickier, and may only license to, say, independent films. Still others don't even consider requests, or will only authorize use of their music if they feel passionate about your work. More on that in later chapters.

While artists and managers remain a fickle lot, there is always the chance of a positive response, which makes everyone's day brighter. As a music supervisor Sue Jacobs's duty is to secure the necessary music for a film's soundtrack. Recalling one early experience, she said, "There was a tiny movie I was hired to do, it had a budget of just $1 million," reminiscences Jacobs. "But it had an indie hipness, and I got Page Hamilton of Helmet to do the score. The director also hired me to put in temporary music. They told me I could pick anything and not think about cost. The first song we went for was a Pearl Jam song. It worked so well it looked like it was made for the movie."

The movie was 1998's *Chicago Cab,* and she knew that the industry-standard clearance fee for the Pearl Jam song, "Who You Are," from the album *No Code,* would prevent its use in the film. Ultimately, she gave a copy of the film to Eddie Vedder, and he liked it so much that he gave them the song for free. He even threw in the unreleased Pearl Jam rarity, "Hard to Imagine," which is on the *Chicago Cab* soundtrack. Although Pearl Jam's label was a bit upset, Jacobs says, "I love that sometimes it's about the artists and it is not about money."

Two "Sides"

As I discussed in Chapter 1 and previously in this chapter, there are two copyrights for pre-recorded music, and hence two permissions that must be acquired when intending to use a given piece of pre-recorded music. One is from the publisher, the second from the master owner who controls the rights to the recorded performance of that song. Exceptions include compositions in public domain, and new recordings of existing songs.

Let's say you want to use Carlos Santana's well-known version of the song "Oye Como Va" (from the 1970 album *Abraxas*) in a television production, you must secure two permissions. The first is from the music publisher, EMI Music Publishing, who controls the estate of the writer of the song, Tito Puente. The second must be secured from the owner of the master recording of this song, Columbia Records, which is now controlled by Sony/BMG.

If you decide you want to use another version of the same song, this time by Joe Cuba Sextette, you would still need to secure permission from EMI Music Publishing. However, as to the master, you would now need to obtain permission from Pazzazz, the record label that is the copyright owner of Joe Cuba Sextette's performance of Tito Puente's song. Either way, permission must be granted prior to using the song in a new production.

The two points of contact—publisher and master owner—are called "sides." Both sides must agree to the use of the song before the requesting party can move ahead. If either denies permission, you may not use the particular recording that you have in mind. Let's look at some examples.

CASE A: TWO COPYRIGHT HOLDERS, ONE DENIAL

I was the music supervisor on the film *The Devil and Daniel Johnston*, a recent feature-length documentary about indie music legend Johnston. During the course of clearing the music for the film, we received one permission and one denial for the same song.

Toward the end of the film, director Jeff Feuerzeig wanted to show the relationship between Daniel and his father, Bill. As stated in the film, Bill had read the biography of Brian Wilson, and Feuerzeig hoped to use 35 seconds of the Beach Boys song "Wouldn't It Be Nice." Permission was granted by the record label, but not by the publisher. We tried reaching out to the publisher to overturn the denial, but in the end the director decided to substitute the song with a soundalike. This is when one performer or group legally records a new song in the manner and style of another (more well-known) performer or group without violating the previous song's copyright.

CASE B: ONE COPYRIGHT HOLDER FOR BOTH SIDES
In some cases, the publishing and the master are controlled by the same entity. This happens more frequently when dealing with independent labels. The forthcoming film *Audience of One* featured the songs "Devotchka!" and "Dark Eyes" by Devotchka. The band controlled both the master and the publishing rights to the songs. When director Michael Jacobs needed to secure permission for the use of the song in his film, he had only to contact one party to secure both the synchronization license and master use license. As you might guess, this one-stop shopping is tremendously attractive to music supervisors because it is one less point of contact that needs to be made.

CASE C: THIRD-PARTY LICENSING
Another sort of license arises when an entity wishes to use a piece of music from a compilation album. Usually, the record label that released the compilation record does not own the master recording. Upon request, they may instruct you to secure a license with the original master holder, or they may be able to provide you a license through third-party licensing. This circumstance sometimes arises with international music, where the original master holder does not have a contact in the United States and does not have experience granting permission for rights in a country of non-origin. Hence, the original record label will give the compilation company the ability to provide a third-party license for the music, or essentially act as a representative for all licensing negotiation. In turn, the label generally charges a percentage for administering the fees.

CASE D: RE-RECORDING

When a song is re-recorded, no master license is necessary, only permission from the publisher; hence, re-recordings are a great way to save money and try new talent. Advertisement agencies do this all the time, as do filmmakers. There are definite advantages to making a new recording of a known song: the contractor tends to have more control over the use of the song, and ultimately owns the master as well. They can, in turn, use their new recording in as many media formats as they want for as long as they want.

In the film *I Am Sam,* when director Jessie Nelson discovered how impossible it would be to secure the master rights for all the Beatles songs she wanted to use, she decided to include re-recordings of all the songs in the film. The same goes for the documentary film *The Guitar Man* by director Eric Paul Fournier. Because the film focuses on the life of a guitar collector, the chosen songs were all classic guitar songs, and they were all re-recorded: Hendrix's "Fire" was done by John McLaughlin, Duane Eddy and Lee Hazlewood's "Rebel Rouser" by John Popper, Doc Watson's "Call of the Road" by David Grisman, Albert Collins' "Frosty" by Lenny Wayne Shepherd, and Van Halen's "Ain't Talkin' 'Bout Love" by Linda Perry.

CASE E: NEW ARRANGEMENTS

When a writer radically rearranges a song, he may be able to publish that particular arrangement and participate in any income it generates. This happens most commonly with songs in the public domain, especially traditionals, hymns, and various classical works. Of course, in the case of a work originally in the public domain, no permissions from the songwriter are necessary. The song "Elijah Rock," for instance, is a traditional spiritual that the famous gospel singer Mahalia Jackson recorded in 1962. Raymond Myles has since rearranged and recorded the song in 2003, renaming it "Elijah's Rock."

It can be the job of the music supervisor to make sure that the person who did a new arrangement for a film, if that arrangement is an independent copyrightable work on its own, gets appropriate compensation and credit. Sometimes this doesn't happen, as with a recent popular film about the urban music industry. An actress in the film sings a song she arranged herself during a pivotal scene where the main character decides to turn his life around. The actress registered her arrangement of the song with BMI. The producer of the film, however, paid her just $200 for her work on screen and refused to acknowledge her arrangement as a copyrighted work. He gave her no credit in the film and on the cue sheets. Because of the producer's stature in the business, it would be very expensive and counterproductive for the actress to attempt to litigate the situation.

Copyright Rights and Licenses

As I've said, anyone who owns a copyright in a work has a bundle of rights that make up that copyright. Accordingly, there are various rights that must be secured for different uses and different media. If you want to secure content for a on a CD or for your Internet site, these are different rights than if you want to secure music for use with images. Let's look at the most important rights and licenses for music supervisors.

SYNCHRONIZATION RIGHT

The song publisher grants synchronization rights. A synchronization right is the authorization to use a composition locked with a moving image or other audio/visual work. Just like in synchronized swimming, where all the swimmers move in unison together, a synchronization right grants permission to use a composition in unison with an image, where the sound and the image are integrated.

Sometimes the publisher who represents the songwriter will deny a request if the song is to being incorporated with images that do not meet with their approval. Violence, drug use, war, religion, sex, and corporate or governmental affiliations can all be potentially contentious issues. Sometimes other factors come into play, such as budget. Final approval ultimately comes from the publisher, who represents the songwriter.

MASTER RIGHT

A master right, sometimes confusingly called a "master synchronization" right, is the right to use a master recording with a locked moving image or other audio/visual work. This right is secured through the master owner, or the entity that originally paid for the recording. Generally speaking, this will be a record label, but it may also be a production company (if you are requesting music written specifically for a prior film) or even the artist themselves (most likely if they released the recording on their own).

Note that these first two rights make up the two "sides" that I just discussed. On occasion, the master rights to a recording revert back to the artist. This is the case for much indie music released on small labels in the early 1970s. Many of these labels are defunct: Ralph Records, Factory, Subterranean Records, SST. For the documentary film *American Hardcore,* for instance, much of the music was secured by going directly to the band members themselves. Anthony Countey, manager for the Bad Brains, recounts his early deal. "We released our first album as a cassette on the ROIR label," he says. "The music was played once, recorded, and pressed. The deal was honest and creative and they paid from the first sale."

Labels like ROIR and others were interested in getting the music out there and participating in the income as it sold, not holding on to it forever. (Labels with this ethic exist today, as well.) This sort of scenario is portrayed in the film *24 Hour Party People.* While the film is a dramatic interpretation of real events, it well encapsulates the attitude and temperament of a label, Factory, which existed solely to support a scene. Factory held very loose contracts with its artists, ultimately leaving the label with no assets to sell. It presents a very different perspective on ownership and how music is valued in terms other than revenue.

MECHANICAL RIGHT

A mechanical right is the right to reproduce a song in a physical format such as on a CD, or in a digital format via download. Unlike most of the licensing that I will discuss in the coming chapters, the mechanical right is subject under U.S. copyright law to a compulsory license. This means that you can record a cover of any existing song and put it on your CD, and the copyright holders to the song (the publishers) can't do anything about it as long as you pay them as provided under the statute.

Under the compulsory mechanical license, the publisher is compensated according to a statutory rate incorporated and drafted into law set by Copyright Arbitration Royalty Panel (CARP). Keep in mind, however, that there is no compulsory license for sound recording copyrights, so even though you can cover a song and make a new sound recording of it, you cannot put the original recording of that song on a CD without a negotiated license from the master owner.

The statutory rate sets forth the monies payable to a publisher for each recording of its song. Since January 1, 2006, the statutory mechanical rate has been 9.1 cents per CD for cover songs five minutes or less, and 1.75 cents per minute or fraction thereof, if the song is longer than five minutes. For instance, a cover lasting 6 minutes and 35 seconds will cost you 12.25 cents per copy ($7 \times \$.0175 = \$0.1225$). This rate will remain in effect until the next schedule of mechanical licensing rates is determined.

The mechanical right is also, of course, licensed outside the context of the compulsory license. For instance, a mechanical license will be included in agreements to use a song in a film and then put that song on the soundtrack CD. In these cases, the publisher usually agrees to receive some fraction of the statutory rate. These are sometimes called "controlled composition" clauses, or "¾ rate." The ¾ rate is generally granted when an advance is provided. The technicalities of mechanical licenses are beyond the scope of this book, but you should be aware that they exist.

GRAND RIGHT

This is the exclusive right of a copyright holder to license a composition for use in live performance, such as theater, dance, and opera. This pertains to dramatizations generally performed on stage, such as a ballet choreographed to a piece of music. The music is combined with the live performance, and in essence becomes a new work.

A publisher grants these rights. Many times, a master use license is not required because orchestras and ensembles are present at the performance. Some performances, however, are set to pre-recorded music and would need to obtain master licenses.

What is interesting about a grand right is that it is essentially a license to create a derivative work. The collaborative work, combining the music and movement together, is considered a new work and can be copyrighted as such. Most grand right licenses provide that the song must be rehearsed and "woven into the storyline as an integral element of the plot." It must further the action and be every bit as essential as the dialogue, either lyrically or instrumentally.

PERFORMANCE RIGHT AND PERFORMING RIGHTS ORGANIZATIONS

The performance right is the exclusive right of the copyright holder to perform a piece of music in a public place. Although you have the right to sing "Losing My Religion" at the top of your lungs at home, you do not have the right to make a public performance of it unless the venue where you perform it has secured a license from the performing rights organization BMI, which represents the song's publishing company, Night Garden Music.

Securing such a license is not difficult; performing rights organizations grant so-called blanket licenses to radio stations, music venues, hair salons, clubs, restaurants, gyms, websites, convention centers, and any other outlet where music is played. (There are some statutory exceptions; churches, for instance, do not need to pay for licenses.)

The three organizations in the United States—ASCAP (American Society of Composers, Authors, and Publishers), BMI (Broadcast Music, Inc.), and SESAC (Society of European Stage Authors and Composers)—collect huge piles of money by issuing these licenses, then make distributions to their members based on how often they believe each member's songs are getting played.

The first performing rights society that came into formation was a group called SACEM in France in 1851. Rumor has it that a French composer heard his music being played at a café, and when it was time to pay for his cup of coffee, he refused to pay on the grounds that he had not bee paid for the use of his music. Similarly, the composer Puccini helped jumpstart the first performing rights organization in the United States, ASCAP. According to Edward Waters, former head of the music division at the Library of Congress, when Puccini visited the United States in 1910 for the world premiere of *The Girl of the Golden West*, he asked his U.S. publisher about the additional income he would earn by the public performances of his music. When he heard there was no such organization to collect performance royalties in the United States, he became upset and explained the situation to George Maxwell, who later got together with two colleagues and set up ASCAP.

Today, ASCAP represents more than 25,000 composers and lyricists, as well as about 6,000 publishers. Joining ASCAP or BMI is fairly simple, and both have easy-to-use websites that will guide you through the process. Once you join, you will need to register your compositions so that the organization can start looking for performances of your works as part of its monitoring efforts. Although independent musicians don't get a lot of money unless they have hits, you may be surprised at some of the places where ASCAP and BMI find your music being played!

DISPLAY RIGHT

The copyright owner also has the exclusive right to authorize "display" of the work. This is most often a right that deals with fine art; however, this right also means that the publishing companies control the display of their songs' lyrics in album booklets, karaoke machines, and other public exhibitions. So, although you can put a cover version of a Rolling Stones song on your CD if you pay the compulsory license fee, you can't put the song's lyrics in your album booklet without permission from the publisher.

CHAPTER 3

Sources of Content (Let Me Count the Ways)

In the previous chapters, I talked about copyright, and the types of rights that exist to license. Now it's time to put on our creative hats and think about what music is appropriate to license for different uses. This chapter is mostly aimed at content creators who are looking for music for their productions—whether it's a film, TV show, a video game, or even an exhibition. There are generally three sources that productions can look to: originally scored music, music production libraries, and pre-existing commercial music. There is nothing that makes one source inherently more or less successful than the others. Your choice of source should depend on your vision and budget.

Originally Scored Music

This source is often the least expensive route, if you are looking for music for an entire film. There is usually one price for both synchronization and master rights, and you can work with the composer to mold the music to your needs. The music should ultimately create an underscore for scenes and scenarios with the intent of adding emotion and smoothing transitions, ultimately enhancing the objective of the director. Legendary film composer Jerry Goldsmith once said simply, "The function of a score is to enlarge the scope of a film."

Marc Capelle conducting a live performance of music to film.

For a filmmaker, using the right composer can make all the difference in the world. This means that as a music supervisor, you should prepare thoroughly; make sure to budget the production's time and money realistically so your client can develop a mutually satisfying working relationship with the person who is going to help carry out his creative vision. For this chapter, I have talked to a number of working composers who agreed to share their thoughts on various parts of the process.

FINDING A COMPOSER

Start your journey by taking note of music in films you like that works effectively. Take note of the music credits, and seek out the composer or get a referral from colleagues and friends. Oftentimes, the famous composer you like may be too expensive, but there will be other composers who will be able to produce a similar sound for a lower price.

There are many composers advertising in industry magazines. Although many will like to give you reels with a variety of styles, it is best when you can find a composer who works well in a more limited number of styles that more appropriately fit your bill. It is easier to get a composer whose sound comes closest to what you want to achieve than to try to work with someone who you know may be good, but to whom you must constantly re-explain yourself. If you take a chance, not only will you save a lot of money, but you may also be pleasantly surprised at the results. Film composition is an unexpectedly cutthroat business; most young composers are eager and have something to prove.

Recording studios, music schools, and the classified sections of select trade magazines such as *The Independent*, *MovieMaker*, and *Release Print* are also great sources for finding composers. There is also Mark Northam's Film Music Network, which is a comprehensive Internet site and resource tool for scoring composers and music supervisors. The organization publishes *Film Music Magazine*, and has networking events and seminars in Los Angeles and New York. Its listing board allows anyone in need of finding a composer to submit listings; the organization will send the announcement far and wide for composers to submit their reels. You will be surprised at the number of demos you receive.

One important piece of cautious advice is that you must not get star struck. Many times a music supervisor or filmmaker gets excited about working with some sort of famous or semi-famous musician who used to be in a band, and has now decided he is a film composer. He may come at a surprisingly low price, most likely because he wants to get into film scoring quickly. This should be a big red flag. He may not understand the process of scoring, and you will ultimately be having nightmares with a "composer" who can't deliver a film score. Oftentimes, ghost writers will need to complete the score.

John Califra (*Tarnation*, *The Personals*), a New York City-based scoring composer who orchestrates and records in Eastern Europe, tells me that he was going to work with a member of a famous urban act to score a horror film. "Shortly after starting to work with him, we realized he had no ability to do a score. He didn't even create his own beats. My concern is that he would have contributed nothing but had a credit. And would have made the job more difficult for me."

"It is definitely something to avoid if you can," Califra continues. "On the other hand, if a [ghost writer] has a strong stomach it might be a way to advance his own career. But beware, the person may be well-known and incompetent and it will be difficult."

Unless an artist has true experience in scoring, orchestrating, writing for other instruments, communicating with other musicians, handling union issues, and producing recording sessions, you run the risk that delivery may not be what you need. If you do decide to travel down this road, please be cautious and make sure you have someone overseeing the recording and delivery, such as an experienced music supervisor, music director, or arranger.

Composer Marc Capelle (*Monumental, Lost in the Fog*), who works with many local Bay Area bands, expands on this thought: "Independent filmmakers are attracted to musicians who make independent music; they are of like minds and think they will mesh well. But many times what is missing is the basic mechanics for scoring a film. You cannot expect a person who is in an indie band writing songs to suddenly orchestrate music. You want them to know the weight of the timbres and the delicate balance of music to film."

So, finding the right person for your project is very important. It's like dating; if it wasn't meant to be, the break-up is hard, fast, and sometimes very painful. Yet finding the right person can ultimately take your project to the next level.

WORKING WITH A COMPOSER

You need to get along with the person to whom you are entrusting your musical expression. Understanding how you envision the score, and communicating it to your composer, are both crucially important. Do you want synthesized music, live musicians, a sparse jazzy ensemble, a rich orchestration, or a solitary dudek player? Do you need to see the composer every day in the same city, or can she deliver via MP3 and a few visits?

Director and music editor William Gazecki gives this advice: "Make sure you are working with a composer with whom you get along really well, particularly in terms of communication. Communication, the relationship between composer and director, is the key to a good score."

Hence, it is very important to understand your relationship and how you are going to work together. Los Angeles-based composer Miriam Cutler (*Lost in La Mancha, Absolute Wilson*) says, "Personality, working style, background, and experience are all part of what composers bring to the table. Even if you are drawn to someone's music, don't underestimate the importance of how you respond to one another as people. If there is a good rapport and a collaborative spirit—in addition to great composing chops—then you are more likely to have a productive creative experience."

Cappelle says that directors bring their experiences to your desires and temper your desires with those experiences. In the end, it is the director's movie. "The hardest thing is figuring out how many cues and styles of cues are needed because directors generally don't spot a film. Inexperienced directors have never worked with a composer. Some movies are over-scored and some are under-scored." The key is getting that right balance.

In the 2005 documentary *Ballets Russes*, composers Todd Boekelheide and David Conte were tasked with an unusual challenge. The film had 40 minutes of existing classical music, much of which was embedded in dance footage; the composers had to write another 40 minutes of chamber orchestra to contrast with the film.

Conte says, "When segueing into Stravinsky's 'Firebird,' we were conscious about the key relationships. Our music had to accompany the narration and interviews. It was challenging."

"We knew the styles of these pieces of music, and we had to make a seamless tapestry. Our music had to stand next to Stravinsky, Debussy, and Ravel, and make sense. We did not want it to sound jarring, but to have character. My style is more Franco-Russian American, and Todd's is more traditional American. We only had two weeks to do it, so we split the cues in half. We had a ball."

Timing

Starting early in choosing a composer is important. Capelle says that a common mistake among directors is that they don't spend enough time with their composer. "The more time they spend the better it will be. Directors need to get involved early on because it only helps make the process go faster and smoother. It is a real mistake if they go away for two months and like any relationship, communication is lost. While composing, there may be infinite possibilities for every note."

The most difficult situation tends to be with independent filmmakers. When they first talk to composers and music supervisors about working on a film, the schedule they have in mind is often completely fantastical. It is important for filmmakers to be as realistic as possible about the schedule and upfront with the composer. It is good to get a composer on board early but if the project is going to take years, it's not helping anybody.

Temp Scores

Many times a composer will work from a "temp score." This is a track of other film music or songs placed in temporarily to guide the filmmakers and composer, with the notion that the music will be substituted with composed music at a later time. The temp score is there to give a feeling of what the music might or should sound like.

The temp score is useful to explore what the director is thinking. It can be a helpful tool, but it is not without its problems. For one, the filmmakers can get too attached to it and not like what the composer writes. Cutler explains, "It is a process and with everyone I work with, we get through it. The goal of the temp score is to get you on the same page. That is where you have to be giving, honest, and open-minded."

Sound Design

Another important point Cutler touches upon is that the filmmakers should have the sound designer and mixer communicate with the composer so they don't waste time. If a sequence is going to be filled with helicopters flying at top volume, the music may need to be louder, more percussive, or maybe there doesn't need to be music at all.

Cutler feels strongly that it is important to have the sound people and the composer on the same page for technical reasons. "There have been problems lately, technically, where I have specs for my QuickTime, and sounds on separate tracks that don't meet my specs. Everyone is using different versions that may not be the right tools for the composer. They should try to do some technical tests, because you can lose a week or so."

Keeping Channels Open

It is important that everyone integrates well. Music supervisor Sue Jacobs gets involved in the composing process. "I get involved in score because I used to manage composers," explains Jacobs. "Seventy percent of films I work on, I help find a composer. A lot is about personality. Who you relate to and who you bring to the table." Once, she flew across country to meet with a director who didn't like certain aspects of a score but couldn't articulate it. "He really just needed to vent to someone about it," she continues. "I have to help someone hear what it is they are *not* liking and back them up. In this particular case it was the instrumentation."

There should always be a point person so communication can continue and be fluid. Many times a composer does not know how to interpret a filmmaker's language, and vice versa. If there is not a mediator or an interpreter, such as a music director or supervisor, there may be the end to the relationship. And if so, make sure there is a kill clause in the contract.

HIRING A COMPOSER

Composers are generally hired for a flat fee using a work-for-hire agreement. Similar to other skilled persons involved in a production, composers are hired for a certain period of time to deliver a designated amount of music. The scope of his or her work should include a list of cues, various instrumentations, and timings. The composer figures out how to deliver the music for the designated price in the designated amount of time. Under a work-for-hire arrangement, the production company becomes the copyright owner of the master when it is delivered.

This is often called a package deal. The composer gets a certain sum of money from which she extracts both her production costs and her fee. It is important to specify what is and isn't part of the package. Cutler explains, "All things are possible; they just aren't free. Additional musicians, rewrites, changes after the recording sessions have occurred, and picture changes after the final music mix all add up. Thus, delivering a great score on a limited budget requires lots of planning, as even the smallest detour can be expensive. Pick your priorities carefully and listen to suggestions from your composer. The better your working relationship with the composer, the more services you are likely to receive within the parameters of the package deal."

Publishing is the wildcard in a composer agreement. Generally, if a composer is paid well, the hiring party will want to retain a portion of publishing. This means that the production company will become owner or part-owner of the underlying composition and will control the publishing. If the hiring party is not paying very much money, it is more common for the composer to keep the publishing or a certain portion thereof.

Either way, the hiring party should make sure that all the delivered music can be used in any fashion in perpetuity within the context of the production and marketing of the film. This is very important! A producer does not want to find out later he can't use the music he is paying for in DVD extras, Internet downloads, or in promos. Any composer agreement that has been vetted by a competent entertainment attorney will give the producer these rights.

If the filmmakers want to retain a portion of publishing rights, they will have to set up a publishing entity. By taking ownership interest in the copyrights of music in their production, they are increasing their ability to make money in the future through performance royalties. This can be beneficial when a CD soundtrack is released as well as when a show is broadcast on television.

One final reminder: As I've said, a work-for-hire agreement where the production owns the master is the industry norm. This means that if another company wants to use the same music down the road, it will have to contact the original producing company to secure a license. However, some composers may exchange getting a lower fee with ownership of the master, so the composer can market the music elsewhere sometime in the future. (Limitations on this right can be secured by contract.) This type of situation works well for clients with very limited budgets.

COMPOSER AGREEMENTS

It is great to get along and become overly excited about jumping into a project, but just like the real world, be careful before you jump into bed with someone. Use protection and get yourself a contract! Both of you!

For some composers, credit is more important, for others retaining publishing is more important, and for the desperate few, a nice fat check is the primary concern. So make your choice and be happy with what you decide.

Although a producer can go into a project with the best intentions, things can happen that affect the situation. Prior to starting a project, the general terms should be discussed and a deal memo drafted that outlines the important negotiating points.

Composer Deal Memo

This is an agreement entered into as of this day_____of _____2007 by and between individual ("Composer") and ("Producer").

1. The Producer has commissioned Composer to compose original music and Composer shall produce, record and deliver a master recording of the Music (the "Master") suitable for synchronization for all medias by Producer in his production ("Production").

2. Composer grants Producer exclusive use of the composition and music for all rights in perpetuity. If composition is licensed out to third parties, 100% master monies are due Producer, and 100% publishing monies are due Composer.

3. The term of this agreement is for perpetuity.

4. In exchange for the services to be performed by Composer, as well as all expenses, incurred by Composer in connection therewith, and the rights

conveyed in this Agreement, producer shall pay Composer $____.00 at the commencement of work, and another $____.00 fee upon delivery. If additional changes or writing is needed after delivery, compensation will be afforded in good faith.

5. Composer shall indemnify and hold Producer harmless from any and all costs, losses, damages or expenses arising out of any breach of the foregoing warranties and representations.

6. Composer will receive a composer credit, provided that the producer provides credit. If credit is granted please provide the following: Music by

7. Producer has exclusive rights to the music in-context of the Production; Composer retains exclusive rights to the composition. Producer will provide a cue sheet to Composer upon delivery of the film to distributor.

This Deal Memo shall constitute the initial understanding between the parties with respect to the Project, and shall be amended only by a written document signed by both parties.

Background principles of contract law tell us that both parties should be operating in good faith. Even so, to provide for future disagreements, a contract might say something like: "While Composer maintains all rights of creative control, Composer will, in good faith, take into account Producer's opinions and beliefs regarding the Music."

Even if you plan ahead, unexpected contractual problems can happen: One of my director clients found a terrific songwriter and gave him money to begin writing and recording songs for a film before having a contract in place. A fee was paid out and the songwriter, so excited about the job, moved ahead and began recording. Ten songs were produced and then, after recording the songs, the songwriter divulged to the director that he had an exclusive songwriting contract with EMI Music Publishing. This is a big no-no!

The problem was that the exclusive songwriting contract meant that EMI owned the publishing of the songs the director just paid the songwriter to write and record. The director would have to license the compositions from EMI for a fee, the production would not be able to share in any re-use fees of the songs, and there was additional paperwork and delay on paying the composer his balance.

In the end, it all worked out, but this situation only reiterates the importance of having a contract in hand prior to working together. This conflict may not have been prevented by a good contract, but the resolution may have been put in the hands of the songwriter and not the director.

A good entertainment lawyer will be invaluable in the contract process, but you can get a jumpstart on the process by considering the following points, all of which should be included:

▶ Amount of music to be delivered: The running time of music to be delivered, or number of cues, or number of songs. Many times this will also include a list of instrumental cue styles such as guitar, violin, keyboard, etc.

▶ Fee: Amount of money to be paid to the composer. This will also include the payment schedule, and a provision for good faith payments if a production goes over a certain period of time.

▶ Kill fee: What the composer gets paid if the relationship goes sour.

▶ Delivery date: Self-explanatory, but many times rough demos are presented prior to finals and there should be a schedule assigned to this process.

▶ Creative control: A clause about how much control the composer may or may not have regarding placement of their music in the film.

▶ Production period: How long the period of retainer will approximately be.

▶ Medias and use: Any restrictions on media should be mentioned here, especially in-context or out-of-context promotion.

▶ Third-party payments: This is an indemnification clause that pertains to any musicians who perform on the recording. Most hiring entities will not care how many musicians it takes to achieve what they want delivered; they just want to know that no one else is going to come back to them later asking for money.

▶ State of jurisdiction: The state whose law governs the contract, should any conflicts or litigation occur.

Music Production Libraries

Music Production libraries are collections of numerous musical cues in many different styles for many situations and uses. Fees are much less expensive than using commercial music and songs, and the library is delivered in usable form with no copyright issues. The downside, of course, is that library music is not composed specifically for the production. However, the variety and quality of library music available today can make up for this limitation.

Music libraries originated at a time when television was transitioning from live broadcast to prerecorded sitcoms and dramas. Live orchestras were no longer necessary, and creating original music for each episode was expensive and inefficient. The first libraries, like Regent music in New York, came on 78 records and were used in shows like *Father Knows Best, Rin Tin Tin*, and *Superman*. The term "needle drop," referring to the kind of broad license that a library grants the end user, came from the period when the production assistant would literally drop a turntable needle down to designate the cue.

Cassie Lord, of music library 5 Alarm Music, recalls sending quarter-inch tapes to post-production houses. "There was not the sophistication we have now. I started in 1983 and it was all LPs that went to post-production houses. The records were pretty heavy to carry around. When CDs came around we even gave away CD players in 1988."

Today music libraries are enormous and much more sophisticated. Libraries buy music in many different genres from many different composers. They now deliver tracks to end users in many different formats: hard drives encoded with metadata, MP3 files searchable using iTunes, iPods encoded with metadata, or wave files that are searchable through a program called Soundminer. Clients can also search cues on various library websites. "We are not cutting back on our production of CDs," says 5 Alarm's Maddie Madson, "but we see a trend with about 25 percent of our client base who now only want hard drives and search online."

What is great about all libraries is the ease of access. They are one-stop shops where both master and publishing rights to the music are controlled by one entity. Hence, you can negotiate a single price for each piece of music. They have rate sheets that list what the fees are for various uses. Here are some example rates for library music:

▶ Feature Film, worldwide, all rights in perpetuity: $1,200—$3,000

▶ Cable, TV all media, excluding theatrical: $600—$1,200

▶ DVD only, buy-out: $650—$3000

▶ Podcasting under 4 minutes: $100/minute

Moreover, libraries are not just for instrumental music. Over the years the libraries have come to include genre-based songs with lyrics, hooks, and choruses. These are fantastic when, for instance, you can't clear the rights to a popular R&B song and you need to substitute an appropriate R&B track. The music production libraries always have something for every situation.

Library music can be very idiosyncratic, top-quality work. Libraries are now hiring lots of known musicians with great chops to write for them. Disbanded goth acts, defunct rock bands, and retired jazz musicians can be secretly heard on many libraries. "Musicians are realizing that this is good mailbox money," says Madsen. For instance, she has hired blues guitarist Johnny Lee Schell, who toured with Stevie Ray Vaughn and Bonnie Raitt, to create a CD of blues guitar cues. "The artists approach us," continues Madsen. "They want their music out there working for them and making money." Some libraries in the United Kingdom give writers a percentage of publishing but not much upfront. In the United States, libraries often buy more rights from the music creator for a larger upfront fee. Depending on the arrangement, both the writer and library can receive performance money.

There have been some drawbacks to the proliferation of the music-library business, however. With more people who don't understand music rights starting libraries, there has been a race to the bottom in terms of value. Some libraries will give away all rights for $400, which seems like an attractive proposition. However, low prices and indiscriminate blanket licenses are killing the industry and preventing more high-quality content—which is the lifeblood of any music library—from being created. It is important to see the value in the library industry and price the music rights accordingly.

FINDING A LIBRARY

Many post-production houses have already purchased numerous libraries for use by clients. Also, specific libraries can be found online at their own sites; once you become a client you can log in and get MP3 files. Furthermore, you can sample the library's music online upon signing up. This allows any user to have access to entire catalogs, and eventually download appropriate music for use in any production.

Some of the more famous libraries are:

▶ Killer Tracks

▶ FirstCom Music

▶ APM

▶ Extreme Music

▶ Non-Stop

▶ Manhattan

▶ 5 Alarm

▶ De Wolfe Music

▶ Groove Addicts

▶ Master Source

▶ Megatrax

▶ Non-Stop Music

▶ Wild Whirled Music

Commercial Music

The third source of music available to productions is commercially released, pre-existing music. Yes, those lovely tracks you purchase on a CD, or the files you download from iTunes or another service, are never too far from the minds of filmmakers who are intent on putting even the most famous Rolling Stones songs in their independent movies. In order to incorporate any of this music into your production, as I discussed in previous chapters, you need to get permission from both the publisher, who owns the song, and the record company, who owns the master. A good deal of my job, and much of the rest of this book, is about the process of asking for, negotiating, and getting permission for using commercial music.

Unlike hiring a composer or using a music production library, where you are essentially going to one source for music, when using commercial music all the related rights holders must be notified, and permission must be requested and granted. Then, a contract has to be drafted and signed. And paid. This can involve many dozens of companies and contracts. Most importantly, you need to keep in mind that pricing for commercial tracks, unlike library rates or composer fees, can be entirely capricious. If the publisher wants to charge $500,000 to use 10 seconds of "Honky Tonk Women," the publisher may do so.

As you might guess, the clearance process is very time consuming. I believe it should be done by a professional clearance house or music supervisor. At the Rights Workshop, we have clients who begin the clearance process, but find it so crazy that they ultimately come to us. Most indie filmmakers who have attempted to save money by doing the clearance process themselves will quickly concede that they will never do it again. I have heard numerous war stories, and I can only say that it is best to start from scratch with a clearance company. A good clearance company will know how to do it correctly from the beginning, and that will make for relatively smooth sailing.

To illustrate what can happen in the process, consider the following: A few years ago, a quote came in at $100,000 to use the Sam Cooke song "Shake" in a documentary production. After trying to negotiate with the copyright holder, we set up a meeting to have the director visit the publishing house and show them an excerpt of the film. They must have liked what they saw, because the price was reduced to $5,000 after the meeting.

In another example, a national department store chain wanted to use the Green Day song "Wake Me Up When September Ends" in a corporate piece that was being played to their staff at a one-day convention. Management informed the music clearance company verbally that the song was cleared, however the publisher then denied the request in writing. It came to light that the denial was based on the fact that this department store did not carry Green Day's album *American Idiot.*

Upon reconsideration, management waited to hear back from a label sales representative, who said that although it is true this particular retailer did not carry *American Idiot,* they did carry other Green Day recordings. Ultimately, the denial was reversed and permission granted.

Happy endings do not always happen, but in some cases where the song is truly instrumental to a piece, or used in a thoughtful, integrated way, it is best to give it your best shot and make sure you are being represented in the best light. Bear in mind, however, that the same song for one production could be free, and for another production $1,000,000. It just depends on how the copyright holder assesses the production.

While most of the negotiation with music production libraries and composers is one-on-one, with commercial music there are a variety of people involved. This can make the process drag on *ad infinitum.* Unless you are dealing with a very small copyright entity, there are about four levels of approvals, not to mention the artists or writers themselves. So, for example if you want to use a song by the Who, the record label must track down some of the surviving members of the band (or their representatives) and literally inform them of your request to obtain approval. If you don't have someone representing you, you may be waiting a long time or forever for that to happen.

Moreover, other factors out of your control can come into play, such as whether or not the writer has recouped his advance, and what sort of numbers the licensing department needs to make this quarter. This mainly occurs with the larger publishers (EMI, Warner Chappell, Sony/ATV, Universal, and BMG as well as Peer, BUG, and Famous) and major record labels. These concerns can adversely affect your schedule as well as the price you pay.

At the Rights Workshop, clearance constitutes a large portion of the work we do. Our clients have said nice things about us, and we hope that you will have similar experiences with your clearance company:

"The Rights Workshop has always completed our projects on time and under budget. That's important because a music licensing company without connections in the music world is like a race car driver without a car. They take a lot of the stress out of production."

Oscar-nominated filmmaker Sam Green says, "I cannot recommend highly enough for filmmakers to anyone else who needs help in navigating the difficult waters of licensing music. With my most recent documentary, *The Weather Underground*, Brooke was able to negotiate a slew of complex licenses and ended up saving me thousands and thousands of dollars. She knows her stuff. She's a pleasure to work with and she'll save you far more money in license fees than you will end up paying her for the service. My only regret is that I didn't start working with her earlier!"

CHAPTER 4

Music Supervision

Music supervision is a vast job that can include many different smaller jobs: music selection, clearance, budgeting, scheduling, composer delivery, and negotiation, to name a few. Music supervisors also need a healthy dose of business finesse and a hard shell against rejection. In many people's eyes, the job seems illustrious, hip, and fun. In reality, a music supervisor is a hard-working mediator who caters to the needs of directors, producers, and other creative people. As a supervisor, I must check my personal tastes at the door and do the best to service my client.

Personal History

I fell into this job by happenstance, and think most working music supervisors would say the same. For almost eight years I hosted a radio show in New York City called "Transfigured Night," named after Schoenberg's groundbreaking 12-tone composition. The show aired on WKCR Friday mornings from 1 a.m. to 5 a.m. The station was a jazz station, but jazz was not in my vocabulary, so I focused on "new music" and was thrilled to expose New York City listeners to their own local sounds. Although a seemingly crazy hour of the day, it was the only on-air slot where I could blend my knowledge of Bay Area rock and classical symphonic music.

Ironically, it wasn't such a crazy hour for New Yorkers. I found it easy to entice composers, musicians, conductors, theater people, and DJs to be interviewed at 1 a.m. and play music. Some of the fabulous guests I had on the show included Ravi Shankar, Jah Wobble, Philip Glass, Don Cherry, Fred Frith, John Zorn, Michael Tilson Thomas, Eric Bogosian, and Astor Piazzolla. I can certainly say in retrospect that the show was a fabulous, unforgettable experience that enriched me like nothing else.

One listener, Gary Pollard, contacted me to help him with music for his film *Going Up*, about the demolition and reconstruction of a building on Wall Street shot in time-lapse photography. Because the images where quick and fluid, finding music to accompany those images would be a challenge, but it was a challenge I wanted to undertake. Immediately I thought of using music from many of the composers who had visited the station: David Moss, Christian Marclay, John Zorn, Steve Reich, Ned Rothenberg, Don Cherry, and the like. Both Gary and I agreed that this sort of pairing would be perfect and I made requests to use these artists' compositions in the film for $100 each.

That was then; this is now. Today Gary would be paying $1,000 or more per track in this sort of film. But the key to this particular music supervision job was having the relationships with those artists and knowing that each was a phone call away. Being able to present a new situation and involve music in the appropriate, artistic way that both the musician and the director appreciated was tremendously fulfilling. This job, however, I would later learn was something of an anomaly. Most supervision jobs are not this fluid or fun.

I made another foray into music supervision in the nineties when a lawyer who was handling clearances for a multipart documentary film, Jennifer Fox's *An American Love Story*, asked me to take over the job because of the time needed to complete the work. It was a challenge; there were 96 cues of music in this documentary, which is about an interracial family in which the husband is a musician. I had three months to complete the job and a very limited budget. More difficult was a midstream change of distribution due to the increasing buzz around the film. This necessitated going back and resubmitting requests.

Working on this sort of film was an entirely different experience from the first project. The former was highly creative, and the latter highly administrative. A music supervisor needs to know how to handle both. Although *Going Up* was a film where I could choose any music I wanted within budget, thereby basically creating the score for the film, *An American Love Story* was all about clearing what music was already in the film. For example, the husband, Bill, played a Bob Dylan song sitting on the couch, and we had to obtain permission for the scene to stay in the film. If we had not been able to obtain permission for the scene, the filmmaker would have had to remove it.

The Supervisor at Work

A music supervisor is an individual who assists filmmakers in finding the right music that works for their films—whether it be original-score, music-library, or commercial music—and has the knowledge to properly secure the licenses to that music. Supervisors work in film, television, video gaming and at advertising agencies. Many music supervisors are independent contractors, because most films and television programs these days are produced by independent or quasi-independent production houses. Gaming companies and ad agencies many times have their own in-house creative directors who sometimes act as music supervisors.

Supervisors must be able to communicate to directors every issue that pertains to music prior to picture "lock," or the time when the production has reached its final stage. Some jobs require more clearance ability if the project has designated music, and some require the supervisor to bring other talents to the table. A music supervisor might have to locate public-domain songs, or songs from a certain historical era. Another job may have a music supervisor physically attending recording sessions and making sure the composer's cues are what the director needs, as well as making sure paperwork is prepared and administered accurately. All of these different aspects of a music supervisor's job come into play depending on the scope of the tasks required.

Sue Jacobs, a New York City-based supervisor who came to the field after working on soundtracks at Island Records and managing composers, says, "The job tends to be 30 percent licensing. It's more about business and for the business minded, not just for creative people." She continues, "It is not a good job for you if it is all about cool music. There is so much administration and you are trying to find the best composer and music for the money; you must always be looking outside the box."

Alex Patsavas, music supervisor for a variety of television shows, rarely works with composers. "I work alongside composers. They mostly communicate with editors and producers." Patsavas refined her skills working for legendary producer Roger Corman. *Roswell* was her first television show, and she has loved working in TV ever since. "I've been a fan of TV's ability to get your music quickly on the air. We work with a compressed time frame. There is spotting on Tuesday, mixing on Friday, and the show will air on Sunday."

There is some variation in the job. An on-staff music supervisor at a television network or at a production house is often called a music director. This person will have a different hat to wear. Music directors have a more general job; they tend to oversee music usage for many shows and therefore the rules and regulations of the network take priority over each individual show. A music supervisor for a major sports arena is going to have different work requirements than the music supervisor for a game company or an ad agency. Each position requires subtly different strengths, but there is a great deal of commonality and overlap.

Music Budget for Productions

One general area of concern for the music supervisor is the music budget. Many filmmakers put music in their budgets last; it is generally found in post-production costs. It seems like most content creators would rather pay for a better shot than pay for a piece of music if given the chance. Ironically, music may be better able to create a mood and enhance the directors' intentions than extra money for a crane shot. Still, it is hard to convince the people holding the purse strings to put more money in the music budget.

"Everything starts with the budget of a movie," explains Jacobs. "Everything starts with cost. I have more latitude depending on the budget. If I have a medium-budget film and have a lot of background music in bars, I will want what is the best quality I can get in that price range. There is no point in giving music to directors that they can't afford."

A general rule of thumb is that music should be 10 percent of the overall production budget for a film. That would include composer fee, music supervisor fee, clearance fee, and all licenses of commercial and library music. It would not include the music editor's fee, sound effects, Foley and the like, which would be included in other post-production costs. Productions that want to include more music, or create original recordings, will need a slightly larger budget. It is extremely important to have a contingency line item in the budget in case there are overages.

There are several strategies that a good supervisor can use to save money and still put the best music possible in a production. Essentially, the supervisor can secure whatever initial rights are needed followed by options. For instance, to keep initial costs down when licensing commercial music for an independent or modestly budgeted picture, the music supervisor can secure only film-festival rights to the music in question. The hope is that the movie will get picked up for distribution at the festival, and more money will be available to acquire broader rights later on.

If this is the case, and the supervisor has acquired limited media rights initially, the options for other medias should be listed in the contract with provisions for payment at a later date. Furthermore, a good music supervisor should be able to give the producers a general idea of what the overall fee will eventually reach. A guesstimate figure is good enough, but be careful not to underestimate and get yourself into trouble later.

Another approach to save money is to secure what is called a "step deal," where a number of rights are secured for a low fee, but an additional fee will be given to the licensor when certain "steps" are met. These steps are based on the film's revenue at the box office, such as $1 million or $3 million or higher. This is a good option when you know your film is seeking a distributor for all media formats.

The media format rights I'm discussing—which I will describe in more detail in Chapter 5—include the following: film festival, theatrical, Internet, all television, VOD (video on demand), home video (includes DVD), educational, in-flight, and closed circuit television. Sometimes these rights include promotional use and trailer use, also called "out-of-context" use. Whatever they want to encompass, broad rights tend to be more costly.

Going Over Budget

Keep in mind that music has become increasingly more expensive to license. "Fees have expanded to include the rights for all media," opens up Patsavas. "We clear for perpetuity with home video rights these days. We don't do step deals." The filmmakers' and studios' needs for more rights, along with the downturn in retail sales for the record labels, have led to a tremendous rise in licensing fees. Also, there is more pressure from above to deliver revenues on the corporate side of the record business, which has become more "corporate" due to consolidation.

"I've seen fees double," says Cherry Lane West Coast Creative Director Joie Alvarez. "All TV rights in perpetuity have gone from $7,500 per side to $15,000 per side that includes all new technology. There is Internet, ring tones, VOD (video on demand), etc. The price reflects where the media is reaching. There are so many outlets and there is so much more [technology or media] now being requested. "

Skills and Tasks of a Supervisor

The first and foremost skill for this crazy work is to have a passion for music and a passion for business. All successful supervisors would agree. As I've already said, however, being able to check your personal tastes at the door is equally important; first and foremost comes the client. Knowing what the client's needs are, what will work with the budget constraints, and knowing what creative people want to complete their visions, are all key concerns. If a music supervisor or music director repeatedly suggests songs that can't be cleared, that may be the wrong person to have involved in the project.

Being able to understand the language used in creating music and then understanding the business side of music are also tremendously important. This job is not only about music, but also about solving puzzles and putting the pieces together in a very delicate way. One creative person wants to use another creative person's work; the music supervisor is the mediator between the two. The supervisor must tread lightly, be smart, and know the protocols. Having a terrific contact base and the skills of a good researcher are helpful as well.

Jacobs says, "The hardest thing to deal with is the lack of experience of producers." Trying to explain about how the music business works and explain the rights and why things cost so much is equally trying, she says. "You are constantly trying to explain it to people and some will fight you all the way. Why is it so expensive? So you tell them." It is hard dealing with independents who are green and may not actually care about music rights, but this is part of the job.

GETTING THE GIG

Once you have secured a job as a music supervisor, it is necessary to have a contract drawn up that outlines all the terms of your job. Since this job is so diverse, it is easy to get roped into more work than you've contracted for. Your contract should specify a timeframe, due dates for licenses, duties in securing the music, composer needs, job specifics, etc. Generally a contract might include the following:

▶ Contracting parties

▶ Title of the project

▶ Responsibilities of the supervisor

▶ Soundtrack deal option

▶ Credit and credit placement

▶ Fee and schedule of payment

▶ Additional payment, if deferred payment is involved

▶ Indemnification

▶ State of law

As always, it's a good idea to get an experienced entertainment lawyer to draft or look over your contract. Once this is signed and done, you can begin working.

SPOTTING

Many jobs require you first to read the script, watch the production, and/or attend a spotting session. At a spotting session, the supervisor goes through the script or movie and highlights areas that require music in the scene. This is a skill that comes with practice.

For example, you may see something like this in a script: "Joey waits outside in his car for Jane to come out and join him." Is Joey listening to music in his car or just hanging there? If he is listening to music in his car, how old is he and what would he be listening to? What time period is the film shot in, or what sort of guy is Joey? Is the film set in the 1950s with doo-wop music, or is it set in the present with Radiohead on Joey's iPod? Or, should the song be less familiar and just set the mood? If Joey isn't listening to music, should there be dramatic underscore there? Is Joey nervous about seeing Jane, or is he upset about something else? All these concerns affect what music will be chosen. Also, what is the producer willing to spend on a song for this car scene? Maybe the scene doesn't need a hit pop song, but something that sounds light in the background and can come from a music library? These are all questions to ask at a spotting session with the director.

A spotting session for original dramatic underscore will take place with the nearly finished film and will require the composer's attendance. In that case, the composer and the director generally work out how much score is going into the movie. The supervisor's job is to figure out what music is required outside of the score and how it is going to all fit together.

MUSIC SELECTION

This part of the job appears to be the most fun and alluring for any person wanting to enter this field. This part can be fun, yes, but it can also be very arduous. Remember that no job is easy. When you have clients such as filmmakers, ad agencies, and corporations who want to use a Rolling Stones, Madonna, or Gwen Stefani song in their productions, the supervisor has to inform them that it is probably not going to happen. In most cases the top artists are out of the question unless money is no option or the right project comes along for them. Your job will then be to find appropriate artists who *will* license their music within the timeframe and budget your client can afford.

For the independent film *Audience of One*, which had a very limited music budget of $10,000, we started and ended up with this:

Economical Song Substitutions	
Original List	**Settled/Final List**
TV on the Radio "Dry Drunk Emperor"	16 Horsepower "American Wheeze"
Eagles of Death Metal "Chase the Devil"	Devotchka "Dark Eyes"
Nitin Sawhney "The Preacher"	Jenny Lewis "Run Devil Run"

It isn't impossible to license music from well-known artists at bargain prices, but it generally has to be a project to which the artist feels a connection. Bruce Springsteen gave a free license to "Born in the U.S.A." for an HBO documentary project about 9/11. (Thank you, Bruce.) Coldplay licensed the track "Clocks" for a minimal fee to a drug company working to create a vaccine for HIV. Bob Dylan licensed a song to an NPR series by the Kitchen Sisters, and there are many other examples. So it *is* possible to obtain a license from various high-profile artists. If there is a slight chance it may happen, give it a try. You don't have anything to lose by asking, but you should keep your feet on the ground at all times.

Be prepared for rejection or silence, however. There are many wildcards that figure into securing music licenses. Sometimes, licensing representatives at labels and publishers will not even submit a request to their writers unless they really think it may be of interest to them. We have been surprised when approaching some bands who we thought would be amenable to certain topics and discovering the opposite. When ESPN's X Games were founded and I was Music Director for ESPN, we approached many artists who we thought would parallel the virtuosity and energy of the athletes. The Datsuns did not want to be a part of one of the top-tier ski movies because they are snowboarders. I thought Henry Rollins, former lead singer for the Butthole Surfers, would be into extreme sports, but he's definitively not. Sammy Hagar is a huge dirt biker; will he want his music used in a basketball show?

"Before Beck would license a song to ESPN for a snowboard show, he wanted to know exactly which snowboarders were going to be in the piece," says Kevin Wilson, Senior Music Coordinator and Sound Design for ESPN. "Don Henley never licenses to us because the network hired Rush Limbaugh as a football commentator. On the other hand, Mike Edwards of Jesus Jones was really into the Tour de France and wrote a song for it. You get more out of artists who enjoy the sport and get excited."

At ESPN we included the Red Hot Chili Peppers' version of "Hot Fun in the Summertime," which was written by Sly Stone, on a CD soundtrack for the ESPN X Games with the intention of using the song in the production. We could put the song on CD because of the compulsory mechanical license, but ironically we could not clear the publishing to use on the television coverage of the games themselves. Our producers were not happy and unfortunately there was nothing we could do to get around it. Sometimes this happens and it is out of a supervisor's control.

Another example: We cleared the publishing of the song "Bat Country" by Avenged Sevenfold for a freeride biking DVD release. Although the song was written by members of the band and they approved the use, the master license, which had to be authorized by management, did not clear. The manager felt the song was too big and wanted to charge twenty times the price of all the other tracks, which also included songs by Death Cab for Cutie, Wolfmother, and Marilyn Manson.

RE-RECORDING AND PRODUCTION

If a music supervisor is going to become involved in the recording of a song, production skills come in handy. The musicians have to be contracted, studios booked, engineers secured, union paperwork filled out, and copyists paid. All of these jobs can go through an experienced music supervisor who has had production experience.

The situation where a supervisor needs to hone her producing chops is when a client wants to save money by creating his own master, or wants to update a great song by having a new band or artist re-record it. This works well when there is a juicy catalog of material to pick from and the director, or agency, requesting the material has an open mind. Yes, we like that!

On the documentary *The Guitar Man*, the production re-recorded many hit guitar songs from the seventies and eighties in order to make the songs in the film recognizable but more relevant for today's market. A singer was needed for the song "On Broadway"; the producer was keen to use Norah Jones. We contacted management and they stated she was not only recording her new release, but was now acting in two upcoming films. So that was a "no." But it gave the opportunity for other, upcoming artists to get some exposure.

Having a music supervisor who knows his way around a mixing board is sometimes very helpful.

Mark Alcarez

ADMINISTRATION

The music supervisor is also generally in charge of filing the music cue sheets and the music section of the film's end credits. (Cue sheets are discussed in more detail in Chapter 8.) Cue sheets are extremely important and require a lot of details that most often need to be provided accurately. Timing of each cue and the order in which each piece of music is heard in a film is very important and listed in sequence on this cue sheet. The writer and publisher information is also imperative.

In the end credits is a listing of all the songs heard in the film in the order that they are heard and are found at the end of the film scrawl. The general form is:

"Takin' Care of Business"

Written by Randy Bachman

Performed by Bachman-Turner Overdrive

Courtesy of EMI-Capitol Special Markets

Publishing information is generally not required for the end credits scroll, but is sometimes requested by the publisher. Sometimes the licensor will want specific language attached to the credit, and it is important to respect this.

SOUNDTRACKS

Soundtracks are those lovely CDs that are released in conjunction with a film that includes music from, or inspired by, the film. Many game companies are also now releasing CDs, especially if music is an important aspect of the game. Independent filmmakers with strong soundtracks or films about music release them; almost every Hollywood blockbuster releases one. But truth be told, the majority don't generate much money—they sell less than 5,000 units—and are considered an afterthought. Yet, the music supervisor is often tasked with overseeing the assembling of a soundtrack CD and putting the licensing together.

Because soundtracks are an entirely different medium than a game or film or television show, the contracts for the music will be entirely separate. It is a bad idea to try to include both the mechanical royalty rates and advances in music synchronization licenses. If you must include something, insert a clause that states that this will be discussed, in good faith, at a later time should a soundtrack materialize.

Although landing a soundtrack sounds illustrious and fun, some times it can be a mistake. Jacobs learned a lesson the hard way. She landed a big record deal for the director of *Girl Fight*, who was not excited about it. "I was driving an album out of my marketing ideas," recalls Jacobs. "The director wasn't really interested in the record deal. She was happy to keep her music small, and I was trying to be a mass marketer. That was a tough lesson for me, because I was not keeping my eye on the director's vision. I could have had a 50,000-unit deal, but it wasn't what the director wanted."

CHAPTER 5

Making Your Clearance Request

As I discussed earlier, music clearance is the process of requesting permission to use someone else's music in a client's film, TV show, video game, or other production. Clearance is about thirty to fifty percent of the job of a music supervisor. In this chapter, we're going to learn all of the elements that go into a good clearance request.

Clearance can be an unwieldy, lengthy, and frustrating process, and is heavily administrative. Not too many people enjoy actuating the mechanics of it, but a good music supervisor, music director, or clearance company will have the finesse, experience, and contacts to make the process comprehensive and as smooth as possible. Lawyers also dabble in this line of work, but only a select few really understand the skill involved and have the built-in relationships that make it work.

Ask music supervisors about the job, and you will hear plenty of crazy stories about the clearance process. For instance, we worked with a producer of a documentary about a transgender gospel choir. After sending in the clearance requests for the gospel songs in the film, we received four denials in the first week. One of the publishers said that it did not have a problem with the subject matter, but one of their writers was a conservative Christian and had a problem with it. So we resubmitted the requests under a different title and revised the description of the film (without being completely disingenuous). Sure enough, all four songs cleared.

For Sam Green and Bill Siegel's 2003 Oscar-nominated film *The Weather Underground*, we included a track, "Winter in America," by activist and poet Gil Scott-Heron. I approached the label first to clear the song, and the label representatives said it would not be a problem. We then sent the request in, but heard no response. After a bit of prodding we found out that the artist was doing jail time. We tracked down management, and found out Scott-Heron was soon being released. Management was then anxious to secure a license and get paid.

We quickly resubmitted everything again, but he was back in jail again before we could get him to sign the paperwork. The director then wrote a personal letter to Scott-Heron; soon after, we got our signature and wired the money to secure the license.

These are just two of the many crazy roads I have traveled down to obtain a clearance. Both of these stories illustrate that sometimes the supervisor has to go the extra mile. The client is paying a supervisor for contacts and her ability to access them. Also, the client pays for industry experience and the ability to solve problems creatively. All relevant contacts generally are one or two phone calls away, and should be approached tactfully with the correct presentation.

The Code of Process

Securing rights is a tricky process. Essentially, any content user asking permission to use someone else's creative work is doing so through another person or mediator; there are many more people involved than just two artists. Because licensing fees are subjective, companies to which you make your requests are attuned to every nuance of the potential use. Some artists are themselves sensitive about use; some are indifferent as long as you pay them for their music. Whatever their thoughts, it is ultimately the prerogative of both the artist and the entities that represent the artist, and you must respect their opinions.

Also, bear in mind that there are many levels of protocol that go on behind the approval process. Many times, copyrights are controlled by large businesses that are huge corporate behemoths.

These businesses have agendas of their own, and on top of that are overwhelmed with the amount of requests that come across their licensing departments' desks. Our office has sometimes had to educate licensors about what rights are best for them to grant.

Many times supervisors are also following legal guidelines set by the client's counsel or the employer's general counsel. As Music Director for ESPN, my primary function was to implement legal policy set by the network, which was in turn part of the larger corporate framework of ABC and Disney. As such, I had to make sure all music used on the network strictly adhered to their policies. That was my only job.

Because of this, working to clear a piece of music from an individual or a smaller company—such as an independent label or freelance catalog representative—can be quicker because independents have closer access to the artist, but you must respect the process with independents just as much as you do on the corporate level.

Who to approach?

When you begin to clear any piece of copyrighted work, the first thing you need to find out is who controls the work. Warner Bros. Records is not the same as Warner Chappell Music. Do not assume they are related. They are not owned by the same entities and maintain two very separate goals. Warner Bros. Records recording artists are not all signed to Warner Chappell Music Publishers. A Sony artist, such as Harry Nilsson or Jessica Simpson, is not necessarily contracted to Sony/ATV Music Publishing. Remember that for music clearance, approval must be granted from the two copyright owners: the publisher that represents the songwriter or composer, and the master holder or record company that represents the recording.

If the publishing and ownership information is not clearly stated on the album or CD, you need to do research and find out who the contact is. ASCAP and BMI might be good places to start. If a piece of music says "copyright control," permission must be granted from the writer directly because the song is not yet published. (Many times this is hard to do and ultimately no license is given.)

Another source of copyright information, if you cannot find it through the performing rights organizations, is the Harry Fox

Agency. Harry Fox is the foremost mechanical licensing collection and distribution agency for music publishers in the United States. This basically means that, for publishers signed to Harry Fox, the agency will collect the royalties when people release cover songs of the publishers' works. (Mechanical royalties are described in more detail in Chapter 2.) Songfile is their online song search engine and mechanical licensing tool for labels pressing less than 2,500 units.

Although Harry Fox may be a good place to do research on copyright ownership, you can no longer obtain synchronization licenses from this company. They used to negotiate synch licenses, but stopped doing this in 2002. Their focus today is strictly on mechanical royalties.

When Permission Is Not Needed

There are a few instances that do not require permission or a license for synchronization with an image. If the composition you are using is in public domain, you will not need a synchronization license from the writer/publisher of the work; if you are using a copyrighted recording of that public-domain work, however, you will need clearance from the owner of that recording.

Conversely, if you have re-recorded a copyrighted song for your production, you will own the master and will not need to clear the master with any record company. However, you still must clear the copyright to the song itself through the publisher. For instance, if a friend records a Dave Matthews song and you use this recording instead of Matthews', then you only need permission from the publisher, not the record label.

Sometimes re-recordings are done for budgetary reasons. For *The Guitar Man*, the song "Love in Vain" was re-recorded by Peter Sears of Jefferson Starship. The producer budgeted money to cover the cost of the re-recording, but ultimately it cost less than a license for the original Starship recording. Re-recording is also attractive because the party doing the re-recording now has copyright ownership of a master. As we've learned, when you own a master, you can use it in the film, all other media, as well as on a CD soundtrack. All you need to do is clear the publishing.

The Permissions You Need

Following is a chart of a variety of licenses that need to be acquired when music is used in various media.

Media Permissions		
Media	**License to be secured**	**Source**
Film	Synchronization License Master License	Publisher—writer Record Label Master owner or Artist
Television	Synchronization License Master License	Publisher—writer Record Label Master owner or Artist
Internet (streaming)	Performance License Master License	Performance Rights Societies SoundExchange
Internet (download)	Master License	Master owner
DVD	Synchronization License Master License	Publisher—writer Record Label Master owner or Artist
VOD (Video on Demand)	Synchronization License Master License	Publisher—writer Record Label Master owner or Artist

Generally the clearance process starts with requesting permission from both the master owner and the publishing entities at the same time. Occasionally, when it is doubtful a song will clear and the song is written by the same person or group who is performing the song, it is best to approach the publisher first. Because the publisher generally receives permission from the writer, and the writer tends to be in the band, there is a hope that the band's approval could lead to the master-use license also being granted by the record company.

But a music supervisor should be ready for any response. For instance, we attempted to clear the Red Hot Chili Peppers song "Soul to Squeeze." The master (owned by Warner Bros. Records) and one-half of the publishing cleared, but the second half of the publishing did not. Hence, the song could not be used. Likewise, the song "Siva," written by Billy Corgan, was cleared by the master owner, but we never heard back from the publisher after repeated attempts. The song could not be used.

With the song "Bat Country," written by members of the band Avenged Sevenfold, we attempted and cleared the publishing but were denied the use of the master. In this case, both approval parties were the same, but one cleared and the other didn't. Go figure.

In the case where the publishing/synchronization license clears but the master does not, a client could make a soundalike re-recording of the song to create a new master, as discussed above. One of my clients wanted to use the Joan Baez version of the song "Let Your Love Flow," written by Larry E. Williams and made famous by the Bellamy Brothers. The publishing cleared but the master did not. Ultimately the client made and used a new recording.

With *Maquilapolis*, a documentary film about factory workers in Tijuana, director Vicky Funari was in touch with members of the group Café Tacuba. She told them about the project and was certain they would allow her to use two songs from their Warner album release *Reves/Yosoy*. We proceeded to secure licenses but it took management almost three months to get us a signed letter. A very favorable fee was quoted when we approached Warner, but there is no sense in approaching the licensors unless a document from management is intact.

There is also the occasional reciprocity case. Bruce Conner, known for his experimental films, created two short films based on the David Byrne/Brian Eno songs "America is Waiting" and "Mea Culpa." Conner got to use these songs for a very low price in his films, and Byrne can exhibit the films as he wishes in perpetuity on his websites or in any manner he chooses.

Lastly, and very importantly, do not think that because your friend, or friend of a friend, or the road manager you met at the show, or the girl you slept with who does the hair of the lead singer, can authorize approval! Even when managers say, "Yeah man, that sounds like a great project. We'd love to be involved," this is not an authorized approval. Not until those lovely friends have put it down on paper, sent it to the approving party, and notified them is this legitimate.

Making Your Request

There is a protocol for submitting a request for permission to use a copyright. The more you know about how to submit a request, the faster your request will move through the system and the quicker you will receive an answer. It is all in the finesse of the request.

GENERAL PRINCIPLES

To start, copyright holders do not need a sob story. Trust me, they've heard it all before. If you are an independent filmmaker or working on a small budget, tell them that, but don't go on an on about how you raised the money from your buddies or that you are doing the project on credit cards, or you've mortgaged your home or you have every record this artist has made. They just want to know the facts. If the fact is that you are making this project on a small budget, say it is a small budget, and give them the budget figure. If you can't live without the piece of music, then say how much this piece means to your creative piece. Don't be a doting, gushing fan.

So, cut straight to the chase. Don't waste anyone's time. Give them the facts in one page. This request form should be either faxed or emailed to the copyright holder. Do not call them to talk to them about your project!

Also, keep a paper trail. If you are an emailing, computer sort and hate paperwork, then keep a file on your computer of all the emails and correspondence. Better yet, print each piece of paper and keep it together in a file. When the copyright holders don't respond or say they did not receive the request, tell them exactly when and how you sent it. You will look terrifically professional, they may ask you to resend it, and they may take you more seriously the next time.

Please keep in mind that copyright holders are being inundated with requests. Some companies only have two persons handling all the requests. With the plethora of new media and requirements by various sites, and companies, the clearance departments at the record labels and publishing concerns have not hired enough staff to maintain the level of requests. So you must be patient and courteous, but also firm and persistent. It is important to let them know you are serious about your request without being annoying.

To sum up, here are some points to keep in mind:

▶ Songs and recordings belong to the publishers and labels. These companies are under no obligation to give you permission or even respond to your requests, though most do.

▶ Lack of response does not mean you have been granted permission to use the copyright.

▶ In most cases, you will need separate permission to change the lyrics of a song. You may not need permission if the song is a parody, but you should contact a lawyer before you proceed with that idea.

▶ Permissions take time, anywhere from two weeks to two months or longer. Licenses being sought for free or for very low prices may take much longer. Remember to allow time for this process in advance.

▶ Licensors are very busy people, and it is important to follow up with them, usually by fax or a polite phone call, every two weeks. Create a paper trail of every contact you make.

WHAT TO INCLUDE

If you call the licensing department at a publisher or record label, you will often hear a recorded message that requests all the information below. Some companies have forms to fill out or have the information they request on their website. At the end of this chapter, I have included a BUG Music request form, which will give you one example of a basic template in the industry. There is a Sony/ATV request form in Appendix D.

Song Title

This is, as best you know it, the song's title. Don't mess it up. Try to be as accurate as possible, and make sure all the *the*'s and *and*'s are in the right place. Don't guess. If the spelling is incorrect, they may have problems finding the song, which could result in delay. Remember, there are probably dozens of other requests passing through the office on any given day.

Artist(s) or Songwriter(s)

This is the name of the artist performing the title or songwriter who wrote the title. Once again, this is self-explanatory, but be sure to check spelling and proper names. The sloppier you are, the less accurate your request will be. A publishing clearance may only need the name of the writer, but they may want to know which recording you are using for various reasons, so it may be a good idea to include that information. A master request, on the other hand, only needs the name of the performing artist. Master holders generally do not care who the writer is.

Licensee

The name of the person or production entity wanting to license the content. This will be the name of the film company, such as Mother Lode Productions LLC.

Production Name

The name of the production. Example: "On the Run."

Description of Your Project

The short description of your project is a critical part of your request. It should run about two to three sentences and tell the recipient of your request several important things: what the production is about, the legal name of the production company, the names of any important individuals involved, and what sort of production it is: independent, documentary, video game, website, etc. If you are a non-profit company, it is important to state that.

However, be careful not to make it seem like you are requesting the music completely for free by downplaying your project; licensors are sensitive to this. For instance, one of my clients received the following response: "I represent Oliver's publishing worldwide. I appreciate the fact that you are a non-profit company—but Oliver has worked long and hard at his music career and we do need to charge for the use of his works." They then proceeded to inquire more about where the film was being broadcast, what the budget was, and what other artists were involved.

Here are a few examples of project descriptions to get you started:

▶ Documentary: *Downside Up* is a first-person documentary about America's largest museum of contemporary art, the Massachusetts Museum of Contemporary Art, which opened in the abandoned factory where the filmmaker's family once worked. Mother Lode Productions, which produces modestly budget films for public television, is requesting the following song.

▶ Indie Feature: Liberty Studios in New York City is producing an independent feature about two inner-city brothers, one of whom is developmentally disabled. Their mother (Vanessa Williams), who is dying from tuberculosis, tries to get the brothers adopted together. The story follows the boys to adulthood; they stay close while dealing with life's obstacles.

▶ HDTV Series: This pro-ski series presents footage by the team at Matchstick Productions, who travel the globe filming from helicopters and snowmobiles at world-class resorts. Highlights include Seth Morrison, Jay Quinlin and Shane McConkey skiing off a 600-foot cliff with parachutes. The series features renowned skiers C.R. Johnson, Pep Fujas, Sarah Burke, Wendy Fisher, Mike Douglas, Eric Pollard, Hugo Harrison, and Vincent Dorion.

▶ Corporate: Verizon Wireless is looking to use the listed song in a radio spot to promote the artist's ring-back products. These spots will air on a dozen radio stations in the western region only to drive sales of the featured ring-back tones.

The licensor may ask to see a script, a listing of stations, a list of the cast and crew, storyboards, or a website. Be prepared to send additional materials to them if necessary.

Sometimes, licensors may request to see the entire film. This isn't a good idea, especially if the film isn't completed. Don't send your entire production, only the scene in question.

Description of Use

This refers to the type of use in which the content will be seen or heard, and a description of the scene or use. Music works are used in one of four ways in productions:

1. background or source: this is music heard in the background or from a visual on-screen source;

2. theme: this is an upfront use of the work on the film's soundtrack;

3. visual vocal: this is an onscreen shot of a performer singing the work;

4. visual instrumental: this is an onscreen shot of a performing an instrumental version of a piece of music.

Chose one and follow it with a scene description mentioned in this area. The scene description should be accurate, concise, and detailed. Be aware that this is the crux of the request. How someone uses content is the most decisive factor of a request. If a piece of content is denied, it is generally due to what is stated in this section. Below is an example of two descriptions of the same scene. Example A resulted in a denial; Example B was sent to the same person and was accepted:

▶ Example A: *Transcendence* is the story of the world's first transgender gospel choir—their struggle for social change and fight for recognition in the world of organized religion. Built around intimately told personal stories, the film portrays a group of people who face a profound dilemma—how to reconcile their gender identity with the belief that gender deviation goes against the word of God. This film is being fiscally sponsored by the International Documentary Association. Usage: vv; chorus sings

▶ Example B: *Gospel Speaks* is a grassroots documentary about an urban choir formed as a ministry to serve and give hope to member's own underprivileged and marginalized community. The film documents the choir's formation as an outreach ministry in a small, independent, urban church, highlighting how the personal struggles of the choir members have made them better representatives of their faith. Usage: vv; chorus sings

Duration

This is the amount of the work you are actually going to use in the project. It should be as accurate as possible. If you are looping music, state the entire length of the loop. If you are requesting multiple uses, state the length of each separately. If a song comes up and down in the mix, then you may want to add up all the times it is audible and put the total timing.

Example: 00:15, 01:21.

Territory

This is a list of the countries, states, or regions in which your product will be displayed, distributed, or available to the public. It could be the United States, or it could be all U.S. territories and possessions. It could be North America, worldwide, Europe, Asia, Milwaukee, western region radio, Sacramento convention center, Madison Square Garden, etc. If your project will only screen in a particular city or at a particular festival, explain that here. If there are only certain territories, mention that here too.

Term

This is how long you would like to license the song for your project. It is the length of use of the content in years, months, or days. You can also request a license forever, called "in perpetuity." Film festival licenses are generally one year long, whereas foreign television is generally five to seven years. These days, theatrical licenses may only be six months, because everything—especially indie movies—moves to home video so quickly.

Example: 1 year, 10 years, perpetuity

Media

This is the medium or media you are planning to use to show your project. If you are pressing only home video, which is a broader term than DVD, you should state the number of units you expect to press initially. If you are planning to exhibit at a convention or trade show, mention the amount of attendees if you have that number. Generally, the most important factor in a fee is the amount of people, or eyeballs, the copyright reaches. Hence, if new technology is not reaching the masses, the fee should be low and over time get increasingly higher.

This is the ever-changing category. As long as our world keeps moving forward with technology, this section will move with it. There are so many ways to deliver media these days that the licensing departments can't keep up with them. Many times you may find yourself explaining new technology to them. You shouldn't worry, though, because they will find a way to charge you for it. As I have explained, quotes tend to come in higher for new technologies because the departments don't know what to charge.

Here are examples of various media rights and their definitions:

▶ Film Festival: Exhibition in film festivals around the world.

▶ Theatrical: Exhibition to an audience in theatres and other public places where motion pictures are customarily exhibited

▶ All Television: Television broadcast where transmission is via wires, wireless, cables, satellite, or other communication channels. This right includes Free TV, basic Cable, Pay TV, Subscription TV, pay-per-view, video-on-demand and other on-demand services

▶ Free TV: Exhibition over television or broadcast stations, networks and/or independent stations that furnish the broadcast without a charge to the viewer.

▶ Basic Cable TV: Exhibition or use by means of wires, wireless, cables, satellite or any other communication channels where the public pays for the transmission service provided by cable systems, but does not pay a premium.

▶ Pay/Subscription Cable: Exhibition or use to the public for which subscribing members pay a premium over and above the basic fee for basic tier of programming whether the programming is transmitted over-the-air or by wires, cables, satellites and/or microwave. This tier also includes on-demand.

▶ Home Video: Exhibition in audio-visual home use devices such as DVD, VHS, VCD or any other similar audio-visual device.

▶ Industrial: Exhibition at corporate sales meetings, dealer conventions, trades shows, and to the general public at auto shows, kiosks, sporting events, and at locations where the product is sold.

▶ Video Game: Exhibition into a multimedia disk platform where the music is used in conjunction with computer monitor visual displays for replay on personal computers and protocol platforms.

▶ Internet and Websites: Exhibition on the Internet but does not include any downloading, store, save or manipulation of the composition.

▶ In-Flight: Exhibition on in-flight services.

▶ Educational: Exhibition in non-commercial outlets including but not limited to educational facilities, hospitals, military installations, oil rigs, religious facilities, non-profit institutions on aircraft and ships at sea.

▶ Trailer/Promo: Also called "out-of-context" use.

▶ HDTV: Exhibition for only HDTV Satellite broadcast. This excludes rights for any terrestrial television.

▶ VOD: Exhibition as digital video-on-demand cable systems.

▶ Streaming: Exhibition as streaming media from a website. No download ability is available and no ability to control the stream is available.

▶ Download: Exhibition through the ability to download the production onto your computer or hard drive where the program is stored and able to be played back at a later date and time. This is one of the newest media being requested, due to the ability of iPods to carry films as well as music.

▶ Ring Tone: The ability to download a portion of a song onto your portable phone to be used solely as a messaging and announcing device. There are 'true tones,' which include the original master, or 'ring tones' for those tunes that are re-records.

▸ Podcast: Exhibition of music through a web-based radio show. These are downloadable and can be accessed at a later date and time.

You might also request "broad" or "all media" rights, which includes everything. Some individuals get creative and ask for "all media known and unknown."

Media Options

These are media format rights that you may need down the road. They are not your initial rights requested, which would be in the previous category. But you may want to get an idea of the cost, so you can ask how much they will charge you if you need these rights in the future. These quotes are generally good for 24 months after the start date of the contract. If you decide to secure this right prior to the 24-month term, you simply send in a check for the amount stated in the contract and let the licensor know you are exercising the option for the additional media rights. This saves the licensee the time of having to renegotiate rights in order to continue using the song in a project. Please note that not all licensors will be willing to quote these other medias ahead of time, and some will ask you to return when distribution is secured.

THE WAITING GAME

After your request is submitted via snail mail, fax, or email, you must wait for a response. This can take from a few days to a few months. For this reason, websites and online business—as well as other projects where there is a locked release date—need to assess their needs for music rights clearances well before going "live." For other productions, the waiting game is not fun but it is part of the gig.

Sometimes nudging the copyright holders every two weeks is a good idea. With any luck, you will eventually get a response. As we will learn in the next chapter, if approval is granted and a quote issued, it will be good for 90 days. If permission is denied, you can try to get more information by politely asking why. If the song is approved at a higher price than you expected, give it a good appeal and see what happens. Remember that a quote is simply a quote, not a concrete fee. Now you are ready to negotiate!

BUG MUSIC
SYNCHRONIZATION QUOTE REQUEST FORM

If you are interested in using one or more Bug songs in a commercial, film, video, live dramatic performance, interactive media videogame or television broadcast, you must request a quote for a synchronization license, not a quote for a mechanical license.

PLEASE NOTE

For writer, publisher and master recording/artist information, please check the ASCAP, BMI and All Music Guide websites.

If you are clearing film festival rights for an independent film without commercial distribution, please note that is not Bug's policy to issue quotes for additional rights (such as all linear progression media, theatrical release, television broadcast, etc), until such time as an actual distribution deal is in place.

Please complete the following and fax to (323) 555-5555 or email to info@bugmusic.com.

Your name:

Company name:

Phone number:

Fax number:

E-mail address:

Mailing address:

PROJECT TITLE:

Type of project:
- Film
- TV
- Commercial
- Live Dramatic Performance
- Interactive Media Videogame
- Home Video/DVD

Other (please specify):

Production company (if any):

Distribution company (if any):

Overall budget of project and music budget:

CHAPTER 6

Pricing and Negotiation

If everything were as easy as just waiting for a response and taking it on face value, where would the fun be? Pricing and negotiation are where the tricks of the trade make a difference, where finesse comes in, and where ridiculousness sometimes meets frustration.

The Art of the Deal

The reply to your request is, of course, going to be either a yes or no; occasionally, the copyright holder will ask more questions before giving you an answer.

If you get a no, it is something akin to a date rejection. Is it the color of my hair? Is it the way I dress? Is it that I live across the bridge? Rejections are not pleasant to receive. If your request was professionally written and submitted, however, rejections are generally given only for contextual or budgetary reasons. The copyright holder either does not want to be associated with your project and the particular scene you described, or the fee would be way out of your reach and the copyright owner doesn't want to compromise.

On the other hand, if the date goes well and you get permission, the copyright holder will usually reply with a fee quote written on the original request or attached to an email. Some copyright holders fax back one of their own forms for you to sign.

The quote is generally good for 90 days. It is also important to understand that this is a quote and not necessarily a final fee. The two words are often used interchangeably, but if the quote is too high, you should feel free to make a counteroffer. If you want to give a good reason to reduce the price, you can lessen some of the terms of your request. You can restructure the request so that perhaps the term is not so long, or a few of the media rights listed could be future options, or the territory is more limited. Get your clients, the filmmakers who want to use the content, to be very specific about what rights they really need and when they need them. Do they require rights for all cable television, or could it just be the greater New York City area? Is the territory all of North America, or really just the United States?

Like the world we live in, some licensors are difficult and may not change their initial quotes. Most, however, can be reasonable and if you have a good reason to request a price break, they will listen and possibly reduce the fee. After all, they are trying to sell a product. Here are some examples of counteroffers:

REQUESTER:

The project is Borderline and the songs are "From a Distance" by Julie Gold, "Ring of Fire" by June Carter Cash, "Rock the Casbah" by the Clash and a few others. MFN status was defined by both Painted Desert ("Ring of Fire") and Universal ("Rock the Casbah") and Cherry Lane ("From a Distance").

You quoted $500 for home video/DVD rights for 2,000 units. This comes to a $.25/unit price, which is outrageous. Universal, Painted Desert Music, and Cherry Lane have all come in $.10/unit and $400 for the film festival license, for which you quoted $500. Will you match these prices to go MFN with the other labels/publishers? Also, you wrote that you wanted MFN with masters. There are no masters because the band is performing all songs live, on video.

Thanks, TRW

PUBLISHER:

Okay. I can approve reduction to same—MFN basis all songs & masters used in the production.

REQUESTER:

For the songs "Devil in Disguise" and "I'm Your Toy," the masters have come in at $2,000 per song for all foreign media for 5 years because DVD and film fest are separate quotes which are both worldwide. Can you match the $2,000 per song quote to go MFN with master?

Thanks, TRW

PUBLISHER:

I agree with you that $12,000 is too high. I am coming down to $7,000 per song on this. It's the lowest I'll go.

If this doesn't work and the quote is still ridiculously high, this may be an indication they do not want to be a part of your project. We received once a $30,000 quote from the publisher of a musician who was terminally ill. All the other quotes for the project were in the $1,000 range. It became very obvious that the writer did not want to be a part of the project, and we respected his decision.

There are some licensors whose clients are surprisingly famous—Bruce Springsteen, Bob Dylan, and Jimi Hendrix, for instance—who reliably answer requests with prices right in the industry-standard range. Then there are others, such as the licensors for the Rolling Stones, who never return emails and only look to respond to requests that start at $25,000. That's why we don't hear many Rolling Stone songs in documentaries or independent films.

The Price You Pay

Although pricing is subjective, there are certain fee ranges that are customary for given uses. As you consider the pricing of a license, remember that you are not just requesting a license to use a given song in a movie. Rather, you must get licenses for whatever media formats the movie with that song is going to appear on: theatrical, TV, DVD, or even download. I discussed these uses as part of the request process in Chapter 5.

Many media formats are flat-fee based. Others are unit- or royalty-based. Those that are unit-based sell individual products or individual downloads, where the number of users can be calculated. These would include DVD, VHS, and Internet downloads. If you are pressing a small number of units—say, under 10,000—a per-unit price is sometimes more cost effective. In larger quantities, a flat-fee buyout of rights is best.

Flat-fee based media formats include any theatrical right, any TV rights, Internet streaming, in-flight, and corporate exhibition rights. Video games are somewhere in the middle; game companies pay an advance on units sold, but they are keen to do a flat-fee base because the risk is so high and so few games sell huge numbers.

The following are very rough, ballpark figures for the types of fees we are seeing to place commercial songs in independent, modestly budgeted movies, which is the bread-and-butter of the clearance business:

▶ Film Festival: $200–$1,000/side or $400–$2,000/song; rarely do we see prices higher than a $1,000/side.

▶ Cable Television: $750–$2,000/side depending on the term and what network is airing the show.

▶ Art-House Theatrical: $500–$2,500/side; these days films aren't in the theater long due to home video, so if you keep the term short, like 6 months, the fee will be less costly.

▶ Theatrical: $1,250–$2,500/side per step. (See step deal details below.)

▶ Home Video: $0.08–$0.15/side per unit fee with an advance on anywhere from 1,000 units to 10,000 units; if you are pressing more than 10,000 units we suggest doing a buyout. Buyouts can range from $1,000–$5,000+/side.

▶ Network TV: Generally covered by the networks' performance rights blanket licenses, but if a show is going to re-air somewhere else, then the production company needs to secure a synch and master license.

▶ News Shows: A one-time airing is generally permitted, just as it is with Public Television, but if there are home video or other uses, it will require a license.

Take all these figures with a grain of salt. As I have already explained, quotes are coming in higher than ever before because media formats are expanding so rapidly. Clearance wizard Evan Greenspan says, "Entertainment companies need to make money so they are increasing their fees." He continues, "The biggest issue besides the broadening of media today is where to draw the line on downloading technologies. Fees are increasing due to future medias being built into to the requests and old medias are being renegotiated."

Many of my clients are now requesting downloading rights for music in videos played on iPods, cell phones, in-store kiosks, and VOD. All these medias are being quoted on a flat-fee basis because the accounting is not quite there yet for figuring out just how many downloads have taken place. But the fees are coming in very high.

"The media has changed how we license music," explains Kevin Wilson, ESPN Senior Music Coordinator and Sound Design. "All the deals with the sports leagues are for all media. We have a large part of remote shows for broadcast that tend to see other forms of media. We are looking to strike more deals with bands like when we licensed a whole Red Hot Chili Peppers album for the X Games. We do a deal with a group or two bands to do three baby bands for college basketball. We secure a finite number of games across all media."

"There are massive changes in the area. New medias are being added every day," adds Greg Barron, Director of Licensing for Cherry Lane Music. "There is a redefining of what 'all media' is. There is more digital use and more digital sales, online streaming, and downloadable clips. A lot of past projects are coming back for online rights."

This last area has caused quite a bit of havoc. For instance, director Nancy Kelly received an offer in 2006 to have her 2003 film *Smitten* made available as a download on educational websites. There was one piece of commercial music in the film, a song by the Tindersticks. When she requested this new media right, the master holder wanted $5,000 for download rights. The publisher would probably have wanted the same; ultimately, the song would have cost her $10,000. Her distribution is through an educational company, and she didn't pay more than $1,000 total for the song initially. As you may have guessed, she removed the song.

Most Favored Nations

When a quote comes in from one side, that side may insist on a Most Favored Nations ("MFN") clause. This somewhat tricky term comes from international politics; for one country to grant "most favored nations" status to another means that it will apply a general, favorable set of trade rules to that country and treat it the same way it treats other "most favored" nations.

In the licensing business, the MFN clause means that, regardless of what fee was actually quoted, the copyright holder or holders insisting on the clause get the same fee as either: a) the other "side" of the same song; or b) the other co-publisher; or sometimes c) the other songs in the production. In the case of a or b, it means that all the copyright holders to a particular song will be entitled to the highest fee paid to any one of them, no matter what they all originally quoted. For example, if the publisher quotes $500 for the song and the record company comes back with $1,000 for the master, both companies will get $1,000. If the MFN clause applies to other tracks, the rights holder insisting on the MFN clause gets the highest price that any other song in the movie is getting.

To explain further, say we want to license the song "Who Do You Love." Warner Chappell, the publisher, quotes $500 but includes an MFN clause as to the master holder. Then, the master holder, Sony, quotes $1,000. Because of the MFN clause, we have to pay the higher price to both of them, and the fee for the song will be $2000.

Let's say another song in the same production was quoted at $750 each for synchronization and master-use, but both the publisher and the master owner insert an MFN clause as to the rest of the project. If we pay $2,000 for "Who Do You Love," we would also have to pay $2,000 for the other song.

The only limitation on the MFN clause applying across all songs in a film is that the songs must be of the same use. So if a project has 10 songs in it, and there is one song that is used as theme and the rest are background, the other songs would not be at the same fee as the theme song because they are being used in a different manner.

Remember, the fee for an MFN song always honors the highest fee paid to an entity for that track, or for any other track, depending on what the MFN clause says. Sometimes, if one fee is much higher than the rest, it is possible to bring the high price down through negotiation, but not always. (For instance, some licensors will take mercy on you when you say that other tracks have an MFN clause, and so that particular song's high quote would have a result of making the filmmaker pay much more for other tracks as well.)

Two examples of MFN clauses in contracts follow. The first is an MFN clause for a particular track only, the second applies to all the tracks in the same project:

Example 1: Our consent to the foregoing is given with the proviso/stipulation that no applicable master record company owner or co-publisher shall receive a proportionately more favorable remuneration of any kind including, but not limited to, the Fee. In the event that you pay any master record company owner or co-publisher of the Composition a higher pro-rata fee than the fee paid to us hereunder, you shall pay to us the difference between such higher pro-rata fee and that fee paid to us.

Example 2: If Licensee pays to any third party an initial license fee greater than that paid to _____ hereunder for the right to record a master in synchronism or timed-relationship with the Picture for similar type, duration and use the Initial License Fee and/or Additional License Fee payment payable hereunder shall be increased to such greater amount and Licensee shall immediately pay to _____ the difference between the Initial License Fee and/or Additional License fee payment.

The MFN concept sometimes works to the filmmaker's advantage, and sometimes not. It works well if the project is one that you want all prices to be the same and all the artists involved are about the same level and stature. It can make the licensing process predictable and can bring down prices when some owners find out what the other rights holders are getting.

MFN clauses do not work well when the publishers and master holders vary wildly in terms of price and stature. For example, we worked on a video game, *Stubbs the Zombie*, where the producer got a bunch of hip bands to cover old tunes; the Flaming Lips recorded "Somewhere over the Rainbow." Because if its stature, this song was quoted about three times more than all the other songs. Eventually, we took the song out because the MFN clauses on the other bands' songs would have required us to pay them as much as we paid for "Somewhere over the Rainbow." This would have tripled the cost of licensing music for the game. (The actual moral of this story is: Don't record songs for a production prior to getting them cleared. That way you know which songs are unrealistic and expensive and which ones are possible and affordable.)

Step Deals

A step deal is a license grant, most often for theatrical distribution of films, where the licensee must pay additional fees when it earns certain amounts of box-office revenue. This works well for independent films because the filmmakers don't have to pay so much upfront, and the licensor feels good about participating in the film's financial reward. Cherry Lane Director of Licensing Gregg Barron says that "we see low-budget films doing step deals. It allows for some sort of build-up for box office receipts and an option for home video." (In all of Greg's twelve years in the business, however, he says he has only seen one film that made enough money to make a step payment.)

Here's an example of what the terms of a step deal look like:

Step Deal:

Term/Terr/Media: Perpetuity/World/All Media now known only

"Song title" (writers) Publisher (Society) [percentage]

Use: 1 bck/voc up to 3:00

Step Deal:

$2,500 up front (covers theatrical)

$2,500 for $3 million worldwide Gross Box office receipts and

$2,500 for each $3 million thereafter as reported by Daily Variety

$2,500 upon release of film on all television

$2,500 upon release of film on linear only home video

All fees MFN w/ all songs of similar use and timing

Public Television

"We want most of all to enrich man's spirit," said Lyndon Johnson upon signing the Public Broadcasting Act of 1967. "That is the purpose of this act." He continued, "Public broadcasting will get part of its support from our Government, but it will be carefully guarded from Government or from party control. It will be free and it will be independent—and it will belong to all of our people." Here's to 40 years of public broadcasting in the United States!

This Act is what allows our tax-paying government to allocate federal money to over 1,000 local radio and television stations for programming and marketing purposes. Music licensing is covered in this funding; this means that any show that airs on PBS does not need a music clearance from either publisher or master owner.

Instead, PBS administers its own statutory license, as written in by Congress in the U.S. Copyright Act, which makes statutory payments to publishers. In 1978 the Corporation of Public Broadcasting (CPB) provided the funding to pay the statutory royalty payments for music heard in programs over the PBS system. Composers who are signatories to the collection agency Harry Fox may receive a compulsory rate payment (anywhere from $71–$92 per cue) through this statutory license.

According to United States Code Title 17, Section 114(b), copyrighted masters are exempt from fees for music heard on public TV and radio, hence they do not receive payments. However, most shows aired on PBS end up being released as a DVD or broadcast outside the United States; therefore both licenses still need to be obtained for these uses.

Steve Freidman administers the statutory licenses for PBS. "We distribute programs and offer other services," he says. "We don't create shows. Our shows are delivered by satellite to stations and schools have the right to take off-the-air shows for classroom use." Public broadcasting works by making shows available to its member stations via satellite; affiliate stations can download and broadcast the program during a select period of time. Public broadcasting is a valuable part of America's educational outreach, which I hope will remain supported by our government.

PBS's licensing exemption can lead to some interesting circumstances. Filmmaker Tom Shepard's film *Scout's Honor* won two awards at the 2001 Sundance Film Festival, the Audience Award for Best Documentary and the Freedom of Expression Award. After receiving his accolades and returning home, he received a cease-and-desist letter from EMI, Tracy Chapman's publisher. He used a Chapman song over the end credits of the film without permission. He had tried to clear the song through Harry Fox, who at the time was clearing synchronization rights, but he had received no reply by the time of the festival. Well, someone at EMI Publishing saw it and brought down the hammer. The song had to be taken out.

Ironically, PBS picked up the show for broadcast on their *Point of View* series. Although Tracy Chapman's management was irate about Tom's exhibition at Sundance without permission, they couldn't do anything when Tom put the song back in the film for PBS broadcast. The irony here lies in the fact that he could use the song in a showing on PBS to about 45 million people, but management wanted him to pay $2,000 for a showing to possibly 800 persons. Does that make sense?

More on Valuation

Copyright valuation is a very fickle concept. Unlike a painting, a copyright is not a tangible object. You can't hold it. But like a painting, when for sale, it will get what the market will bare, and sometimes more. Publishing catalogs are always for sale at the right price; some even go up for auction, like a painting.

A copyright's sale and licensing value is based on use, popularity, chart position, and desire. Its value is *not* based on beauty, style, or delicacy of notes or a composer's lyrics. Price is built on popularity and the willingness of the buyer or licensor to pay a fee for what they think it is worth based on how many ears will hear it and what those ears want to hear.

Obviously, if you own copyrights, it is very important that you have an idea of what they are worth. One client of mine gave away three of his songs to a film in exchange for a steak dinner. Well, if you are really that hungry and want only credit, then perhaps that sort of fee is right for you. But ultimately, such arrangements devalue the songwriter's intellectual property.

Upon trying to license "Arc of a Diver," by Steve Winwood, the copyright holder told me that it would be impossible to license the song for use in the film, but a lesser-known Winwood song would be fine. What is the difference? Both songs were written and performed by the same person, and are part of the same publishing catalog. Yet one song holds a higher value than the other.

In order to charge the appropriate price for a song license, the licensor must look at all the factors involved in a song request, which I listed in Chapter 5. The answers to all these questions will help assess the situation and will inform the decision of what to charge.

One final note is that licensors should understand the real number of persons a new media format is reaching. Although the internet can theoretically reach a trillion people, any given piece will only be seen by a limited number. Also, HDTV programming can only be seen by a certain, limited number of homes. Certainly those figures are growing, but why charge large fees now when pricing should go hand-in-hand with viewership?

SELLING A CATALOG

If you own a catalog of songs, the value of the income streams helps you decide what to charge not only for individual songs, but if you are at a point where you want to sell your catalog or sell a portion of it to another entity. This might happen if you are an indie artist and have retained your publishing all along, but then one of the bigger publishers such as Warner Chappell, EMI, Universal, or BMG comes waving a nice fat check in front of your face. How can you resist? Everyone has different needs, but beware when they come waving that check and asking you to sign on the dotted line. Assess a few things and actually read the small print. Get a lawyer, and review that contract thoroughly!

"Copyright owners are savvier about protecting their assets," says Eddie Gomez, VP of Creative Services at BUG Music. "The deal these days is about commitment. The trend is about rights and wanting to own a portion of the pie. BUG is doing more administration deals and the songwriters are retaining as much of the songwriting as possible." An administration deal is when an established publishing house controls the management of the copyright in exchange for a piece of the royalties, but no ownership is involved.

If you want to sell your copyrights, please be careful. There should be no acquisition without a true understanding of how and what the potential publisher is going to do with the copyrights. The buying publisher should provide an advance that is commensurate with the value of the package of copyrights and copyright's income stream. If your music is performed abroad or sold outside your country of origin it is important to also look at sub-publishing revenues (money coming into the local publisher where the music is heard). Please consult an expert in this field should you be contacted by someone who is seriously interested in buying your copyrights.

CHAPTER 7

Music Placement and Representation

In the previous chapters, I talked about the difficulty of securing licenses from the major labels and publishing houses. Acts like Madonna and the Rolling Stones are in the happy and rare position of being able to deny and/or ignore requests based on whatever whim they happen to be indulging that day.

However, there are many artists for whom copyright licenses could provide a much-desired stream of income. Indeed, many independent artists who make records in their home studios think their music would be ideal in a television show or movie. If you are one of these people, what are you waiting for? There are a variety of individuals who can help place your music in into films, trailers, advertisements, video games, and television shows. Those lovely people are called music placement representatives, agents, or "song pluggers." They represent bands, artists, and indie labels. Major record companies have the same type of people in-house, but there are a variety working independently who are open and willing to work with the most undiscovered artist, as long as the quality is good and the music is "placeable."

"Business has gotten stronger," says Michelle Bayer, owner of Shelly Bay Music. "With more independent labels merging with the majors, more supervisors are calling us looking for stuff. They say,

'I need this tomorrow, and you guys can do it. Warner Bros. has too much red tape.' We can deliver to them almost instantly through an FTP site or MP3."

If a music supervisor is trying to locate music for a scene that is not going to kill the director's budget, many times she will go to a music placement rep and find something a little under the radar. Often too it will be a "one-stop shop" deal, in which both the synchronization and master are controlled by one entity.

Being able to work with so many bands is what fulfills Lisa Klein, owner of music placement company OpticNoise. "Unlike a manager, I don't have to answer the phone at three in the morning," she explains. "I work with a band called Sex and Reverb," a one-man recording project scored a hit with the song "Strange But True." "Supervisors pray to get stuff from me by them. They are the most licensed artist I have. I licensed two tracks in two days."

Another independent representative, Danny Benair, is the owner of Natural Energy Lab. Benair formerly worked in-house at Polygram Music Publishing, and he now represents a band called the 88's. They have made more money from licensing than any band he knows.

"Their songs have been used for end titles, open titles, and trailers," he recounts. "They have made over $100,000 from placement and are making their next album in Lake Arrowhead with film and TV money. The band has no publishing or record deal. It is extraordinary. You would have thought they were as big as Coldplay," Benair adds. "Their music can be heard in the films *You, Me and Dupree, Freeride,* and *Failure to Launch.* It just shows that a band can exist without a label."

But getting placement takes a lot of hard work. Music placement representatives are constantly in contact with music supervisors, trailer houses, and in-house creative directors at ad agencies in order to know what projects are percolating and what the immediate needs are. The representative plays a very gentlemanly, salesman-type role, offering selections from her stable of artists and keeping on top of projects. Representatives know that although they represent a bunch of terrific music, there is only room for one song. And that song may not be chosen by the music supervisor or director; cost, lyrical content, or some other factor may come into play.

Creative Directors

On the other hand, major labels and publishers have in-house representatives who plug their catalogs to the outside world. They are called creative directors and help clients look for content, or the right song for a project. (In-house music supervisors at an ad agency and video game companies are also called creative directors. Their roles are related but broader.) At publishing companies, these in-house folks sign writers and do searches when requested. Many times film producers cannot afford a particular song, so they call the creative directors and ask if they have anything that sounds similar. These departments move fast to find the right flavor, style, and rhythm that will coincide with the needs of the client.

When a song is chosen to be licensed, sometimes a lot of money is involved and sometimes not. Many times exposure is the driving force. The current trend in network TV is to place the band and song info at the bottom of the screen when the song is played in hopes of catapulting a young band to some moment of fame and intrigue. In reaction to this, some viewers will do a web search about what music is being used in a production. This exposure is what feeds the fuel of creative directors and is why they do what they do. They love to help the career of an artist and, even more so, to put money in the artist's pocket when least expected.

Eddie Gomez, VP of Creative Services for BUG Music Publishing, says, "Rosie Thomas of Geraldo and Calexico told me how valuable it was to have BUG working her catalog. She was so grateful. She knows she doesn't write mega-hits but she has been able to stop living out of a basement."

"Getting a placement for somebody is really special," says former EMI exec Seth Berg. Now an independent catalog representative, he feels proud when he makes placements. "I did that on my own," he explains. "You're never quite sure when you work at the label. Doing it independently makes me feel good."

Berg represents an artist you may have heard of named Frank Sinatra. Most supervisors would steer clear of Sinatra due to high prices, but Berg is trying to change that image and create win-win situations for both. For one episode of *CSI*, he was able to brand the whole show with Sinatra's music. He basically cut a volume deal with the show because they used a number of songs. "The majors can't do that," says Berg. "Cutting creative deals is what independents do best. We are thinking differently because it is as much work pitching one song as it is five." Because Sinatra did not write any songs, Berg also works very closely with the publishers, the other "side," so they do not price Sinatra-performed songs out of the water for productions with which he has already cut master deals.

Berg also works with a number of attorneys who represent artists, working the master catalogs of Peggy Lee, Sammy David, Nat King Cole, and Rickie Nelson to help facilitate uses. "The labels want someone to shake the branches and work with the estates," Berg explains. "'Luck Be a Lady' is a great song for any lottery advertisement and it was very precious when we did a re-record of it for Pechanga Resort and Casino."

"We approach video game campaigns, trailer houses, music supervisors, film and TV people," says Gomez, a 13-year veteran. "Content—no matter what it is—likes music. There is a hipness factor, the one thing that grabs their audience no matter what the age is."

The Process

So how can you hook up with one of these agents? Independent music placement representatives generally get referrals through colleagues and friends. The reps also check out shows, MySpace, magazines, and other places that they can hear music. Benair started his business when import records were $25 and supervisors would spend a bundle of money getting cutting-edge material. "I would have access to very interesting and up-and-coming music not heard by the average person," says Benair. "I do hunting and pecking on my own. I'm always looking."

Some artists signed to major labels are also able to use outside independent licensing companies, because working with an outside representative can be the best and most efficient way to get songs placed.

Sugaroo works eighteen indie labels and numerous individual artists out of Los Angeles and New York City offices. The company seeks out labels to fill a genre void. "You can't work with too many labels of the same type of music, because they will start cannibalizing each other." Bayer gets approached by labels that have heard of her company and are looking for placement. "We make our decision by the sort of material we need at that particular time."

There are plenty of good companies to choose from, so certainly take the time to check them out. Here are a few:

▶ Natural Energy Lab

▶ Optic Noise

▶ Sugaroo

▶ Shelly Bay Music

▶ Ocean Park Music

▶ Big Sounds International

▶ South Bay Music Group

▶ Media Creature Music

▶ Position Music

▶ The Orchard

▶ Indyhits

▶ Love Cat Music

THE PERCENTAGE DEAL
Once the artist or label and representative decide to work together, they sign an agreement that sets out the terms. Generally these are short-term agreements, such as one year with automatic renewals. There are generally two different financial arrangements to choose from, the percentage deal and the re-titling deal.

The former is fairly self-explanatory; an agent charges a percentage of the revenue from the placements they secure. Klein, who has about 3,000 to 4,000 tracks to plug, says most of her material is unsigned. "Our commission is 20 percent to 50 percent; an unsigned band would be 50 percent." Benair and Berg do the same.

Benair says, "We sign a very loose-term deals. Coming from a band background, I don't need to tie someone up. We give them 30 days' notice to leave. I don't want to have bad relationships with artists. We do the best we can while we represent them. Artists leave because they are signed to big label, but management is happy and come back with other bands. My philosophy is about the here and now. I don't have someone tied up."

Klein adds that her exclusivity is loose. If artists want to shop their music themselves, they can. In general it is not good to have two agents representing the same catalog. It is confusing for the person on the receiving end because they don't have one specific contact if they want to use the piece.

THE RE-TITLING DEAL

Some newer deals include the ability to take a portion of publishing. Some call this "re-titling," where representatives re-title the song in order to collect a portion of publisher share via performance royalties.

"We call it 'alternate title,'" says Tyler Bacon, owner of Position Music. "We create an alternate title of the song so to participate in the performance income. We created this so we don't need to do a publishing deal or transfer a copyright. They keep 100 percent writer share, and we take 100 percent publishing share. Alternately we can do a co-publishing deal where they may get 75 percent of the overall income and we take only 25 percent."

Bacon, who works on a non-exclusive basis, only plugs those songs he registers as an alternate title. "If we get a song in *One Tree Hill*, we collect our portion of income. If the artist placed the song outside of us, we take in nothing. Some artists are making good money; some would like to make less money and retain their ownership."

By taking a portion of public performance, the song plugger can earn significant amounts. Primetime TV can range from $750 all-in on the low end to $3,000. "I just got my biggest deal with *Law & Order: Criminal Intent*," gleams Bacon. "It's for an indie artist we signed seven years ago. The actress in the show starts the episode recording the song, and later in the show they shoot a video for it. The song was put out on a compilation four years ago. So that's a great success story."

With the explosion of cable television channels and performing rights societies paying handsomely for music used on television, the last five years there have brought many changes in the industry and a plethora of placement executives.

"It has become the Wild West," exclaims Benair. "There are a million people doing this. It is not like before. The part that is disturbing about it is that many don't have an idea of what the job is. They do it for the wrong reasons by obtaining half the publishing and fifty percent of the fee. This turns the situation into a co-pub situation, and they are doing it with not much thought."

Klein agrees. "It's a rapidly changing world. Five years ago is was me and a handful of other representatives. To get a license for an indie, the fee would be $750 for both sides."

THINGS TO BEWARE

Ownership rights are the biggest issue when an agent takes on a new client. It is extremely important for artists to know exactly what rights they have. If a manager presents a band to an agent and does not know the ownership history, the agent and band can end up getting screwed and missing opportunities. (If you have a manager, give them this book so this doesn't happen!)

"A manager came to us with a record and asked us to work it," recounts Benair. "The manager said the band owned the master and publishing. A company wanted to use the song in a big car commercial. I later found out the band did not own the master. So when I had to work with the label that did, they low-balled me. What I learned from this experience is that you never listen to what a manager says."

Be cautious. Managers may not clearly understand what rights they have regarding all the music by the artist they represent. Hence, a catalog agent is cautious to enter into contract without knowing exactly what is at stake. "A lot of my friends are managers," reassures Benair. "But when they are not clear to you, you are setting yourself up for big problems. Managers are sometimes just eager to get their stuff used."

Klein recounts one horror story. "I worked with a British band who I met through their publisher. The band owned their masters. I placed some of their tracks in a show. They were great and I wondered, 'Why isn't this band huge?' So I get a call from a clearance person at the network where the song was placed, and this person is freaking out," Klein continues.

"A label in New York City said they owned a portion of the master." Klein soon discovered that management was in breach of their contract with the label, and had taken all of the band's equipment and disappeared. "It took three years to work out all the problems this case brought on. Finally we settled with the network, who gave enough money to walk away." That is why there are indemnification clauses in contracts; they protect the agent from any sort of legal claims of ownership. But a clause won't repair an agent's reputation!

As with everything else, prices are also going all over the map. Some labels have taken note of the placement industry and now want more money because they know the content users, in this case mainly TV, will pay more for the music. Other labels will give music away for free. "Major labels started hiring in-house representatives and indie labels started giving away their music for free, just to be heard and get placement. Bands will go out of their way to create an instrumental track of a song for the show *Road Rules* just to get exposure," says Klein.

PRESENTATION

The most important aspect of the job is the relationships with the content users. "This job so much depends on relationships and trust," urges Klein. "Supervisors are saying if they don't know where the music is coming from they just throw it away. They only work with people they know." It is hard to get in without having a solid relationship. When working with a known supervisor, such as Alex Patsavas, who places music in such shows as *The O.C.* and *Grey's Anatomy*, you must have a strong relationship if you want them to consider your music.

How the music is presented is also important. No demo tapes are accepted. The track listing must be on a separate piece of paper and not on the physical CD itself. A full jewel case is best. No flats. When supervisors get the material, they like to file it and it's difficult to find if it's a flat case.

"I like full albums," recounts Patsavas. "It's useful to get the whole thing. I just listen to the entire CD. I'm a digital person. I put everything on my iTunes." Supervisors maintaining digital libraries is a common trend; this way, if they are looking for material, they can easily find it and know exactly who to contact.

At the end of network television shows, there is often a song played over the final scene and end credits, including a credit that gives the name of the song, artist name, and record label. In this case, the song is usually given as a trade for this prime exposure on a show. No fee is paid but the exposure far exceeds what a record label would be able to generate from an advertisement. Viewers' ears are more alert, attentive, and sympathetic to the song.

CHAPTER 8

Responsibilities of Content Users and Content Creators

Securing a license and having the contract tucked snuggly in your file cabinet is sometimes not enough to comply with all the requirements of certain entities, including the U.S. government. No, the administration and paperwork continue! Licenses need to be secured, signed, sealed, delivered, and, most importantly, paid.

Solid quotes, confirmations, and draft memos are plenty for securing "E and O" (Errors and Omissions) Insurance, an indemnification policy that filmmakers need to take out on their films before a distributor will touch them. However, many distributors of product now insist on countersigned contracts in order to pay the filmmakers; the draft memos we used in the past are not enough. For instance, I have worked with larger distributors, such as Zeitgeist and Sony Pictures Classics, who need all contracts signed and countersigned in order to process the final payments to producers.

Countersigned contracts wouldn't be such a problem except for the fact that copyright holders sometime take months from the time that the deal is struck to actually issue the contracts. They are simply swamped and backlogged.

Copyright Filing

Make sure all of your compositions are filed with the U.S. Copyright Office, as I covered in Chapter 2. Even though this is no longer a requirement, filing the copyright will get you attorney's fees and statutory damages should you have to litigate.

Performance Rights Filing

As I've described, the performance rights organizations—ASCAP, BMI, and SESAC—are the U.S. organizations that collect and distribute performance royalties for publishers, writers, composers and authors. There are many similar organizations around the world; writers and composers of music should join one in the country where most of their material is performed. So, if you are an American whose music is most popular in Germany, you may want to join GEMA.

If you are a content creator, make sure that your membership with your chosen organization is current and that all of your songs are registered with that organization.

Monitoring Requirements

If you are a content distributor, there are numerous other requirements to make sure that your broadcasts, exhibitions, and/or sales to the public are being conducted legally and with the appropriate licenses. Even after these licenses are in place, the exhibitors and broadcasters need to report their music uses to the appropriate rights organizations. There are several industry protocols for doing this, and I encourage you to learn more if these rules apply to you.

CUE SHEETS

This is one of the most important requirements that music supervisors typically handle on a television show or film. A cue sheet is a list of all the music heard in a production in the order that it is heard. It includes the exact timings and all the precise writer and publisher information. Cue sheets are completed near the end of the process, but before the TV show is broadcast or film is released. It is very important that this information be as accurate as possible, because the performing rights organizations use these cue sheets to monitor the use of music in productions and, ultimately, pay their registered writers and publishers.

PBS MUSIC CUE SHEET

PBS Red Book:

L NOLA CODE:

SERIES:

PBS BROADCAST RIGHTS:

ACQUIRED? _____

DB OK?

B   in MURS?

ORIGINAL BROADCAST DATE (PBS):

Producing entity:

PROGRAM LENGTH: (approx. MINS., excluding any internal breaks)

SERIES:

Presenting station or entity:

Program copyright owner:

Contact name & info (phone &/or fax &/or email):

PROGRAM:

#	MUSIC TITLE OR DESCRIPTION (may include, in parentheses, such info as recording artist, album title, label, track #...)	WRITER(S) (i.e., composers, including any lyricists, or arrangers of public domain works)	PUBLISHER(S) or other OWNER(S) of publishing rights	DURATION OF MUSIC CUE (MUST be filled in, even if only approx.) in min/sec	USAGE (indicate EXACTLY ONE per cue): 1-BACKGD; 2-FEATURE; 3-THEME; 4-CONCERT FEATURE	PERFORMING RIGHTS FOR U.S.A. (leave blank if unknown): 1-ASCAP; 2-BMI; 4-SESAC; 5-other; 6-public domain	SOURCE or TYPE, IF APPLICABLE (NO MORE THAN ONE per cue): 1-specially composed; 2-sync cleared (incl. for public TV, by producer-not relying on PBS agreements or 17 USC Sec. 118); 3-unpublished| OR: PBS pays PTV sync to ____; HFA Song ID# or other source of pub. info	X=DRAMATIC ("grand right" use")	X=REPEATS a previous cue
1									
2									
3									
4									
5									
6									
7									
8									
9									
10									
11									
12									
13									

There must be one cue sheet per show, and these should be prepared during or shortly after production when the music information is easier to obtain. Editors, music editors, and supervisors will be the most helpful in putting these together because they will know exact timings to be reported. I have provided a sample PBS cue sheet with this chapter, however you may want to check with your presenters or distributors to see if they have specific cue sheets to use.

The producers' title and contact information as well as series number and name are noted at the top. If you know the original broadcast date, include that. The music title or description will be the title of the piece of music. If your composer is writing an original score for your production, make sure that she titles each cue of her music for the film. Each piece of original score music should also be registered with the composer's performing rights organization.

"I title each song," says composer John Califra. "I generally title them on what the scene pertains to. Like an extended cue for 5 minutes long where the main lead is lecturing his son, I called that 'Life Lessons.' Titles are taken from the scene." Here are some additional notes on cue sheets:

▶ The writer information should be on the sheet as well as publisher.

▶ The "share" field contains what percentage share of ownership each writer of a particular cue controls. The same goes for publishing.

▶ If the writer does not have a publishing concern but is a registered writer with a performing rights organization, include the writer's information and put "copyright control" in the publisher column.

▶ Length of the music cue, reported in minutes and seconds, must be accurate.

▶ The usage, which should be familiar to you from our usage request in Chapter 5, is either: 1) background, 2) feature, 3) theme, or 4) visual vocal/instrumental. The performing rights society can be provided by the publisher or writer.

▶ If you are only producing a show for home-video or video-game distribution, cue sheets are not necessary because there is no public broadcast and no performance rights. For any program that will be transmitted via public broadcast, cue sheets are usually obligatory.

OTHER REPORTING CONCERNS

Entities using vast amounts of content must also comply with delivery requirements, especially for Internet webcasting. When trying to understand what rights are required, it is best to make reference to the two "sides" of the publishing. If you think about what is needed for the writers and then what is needed for the master holders, you will be able to decipher which licenses are necessary for your particular use.

If you are in the business of any of the following, please make sure the following licenses are covered:

Selling Music (includes CD sales, digital downloads, and ringtones):

▶ Publisher (mechanical license through Harry Fox Agency)

▶ Master Owner (negotiated license through record label)

Terrestrial (non-Internet) music public performances (includes TV, radio, venues, and clubs):

▶ Publisher only (blanket performance license through ASCAP, BMI, or SESAC)

▶ Master clearance is not necessary for "terrestrial" performances.

Streaming music digitally (includes webcasting):

▶ Publisher: (blanket public performance license through the ASCAP, BMI, or SESAC and a license though Harry Fox to replicate each song on the providers' service before streaming)

▶ Master (digital master license through SoundExchange)

All these providers must become licensors with U.S. performing rights societies to be authorized to exhibit a public performance of music. A content provider should become a licensee of all three performing rights organizations in the United States. Forms are available on each organization's website or you can contact them to discuss which filing will work best for your entity. Content providers for the web—online radio stations, interactive web-based games, companies who want to stream music—have requirements that are different from other broadcasts.

Some organizations reporting require a monthly music use report. This is a listing of songs that are heard on a given website. These reports are sent to the performing rights organization in spreadsheet form. Information that needs to be included is: 1) title of each song, 2) artist name, 3) writer name, and 4) number of uses of a given work. A webcaster must also report the number of listeners and the number of rotations of each song. These reports apply to jukebox sites, songs-on-demand sites, archival programming sites, cybercasts, and interactive web-based games that use music. Other websites that sign up for blanket licenses will not need to provide music reports; instead, blanket licensees submit annual or quarterly reports that provide general information about the company, such as corporate revenues, site hits, hours of airing, etc.

SoundExchange

A small revolution in performance rights happened in 1998 with the passage of the Digital Millennium Copyright Act (DMCA). Ever since recordings started being copyrighted in the early twentieth century, the owner of a sound recording copyright has by statute not been entitled to performance royalties. So, even though the publishers receive huge income when a song is a radio hit, the record company that owns the sound recording is not entitled to performance royalties. This has always been a bee in the bonnet of the record labels, who have attempted to have it changed by Congress. They have always been unsuccessful because of lobbying from the broadcast industry, however, which doesn't want to have to pay huge new fees to play sound recordings.

However, the recording industry was able to secure a sound recording performance right under the DMCA for digital transmissions only. This means that regular radio stations need only pay for ASCAP, BMI and SESAC licenses, but Internet radio stations and digital satellite-radio stations like XM and Sirius must pay for those licenses *plus* master-use performance licenses. To collect these new royalties, the RIAA set up an organization called SoundExchange. SoundExchange issues licenses and collects monies to distribute to the owners of music recordings heard over the web.

SoundExchange requires a monthly usage report, which includes: 1) title of each song, 2) artist name, 3) record label name, and 4) album title or ISRC number (a unique identifier for each song watermarked on the song during the mastering process). Similar to the requirements for the performance rights organizations, SoundExchange asks for this reporting each month, as well as a quarterly report of financials. I have included some SoundExchange forms in Appendix D.

Because SoundExchange is much newer than the other performing rights organizations, there are a few kinks in the system. For one, SoundExchange has a number of licenses to choose from, and securing a license by going to the website is not the easiest. If you are considering going into digital broadcasting, get a lawyer to interpret their complex legislative language. Their licenses are not cheap, and without knowing exactly how your business is set up and operating, it is hard for their administrators to recommend one license over another. On the other hand, if you are content provider, such as a record label or an artist that owns masters, they can be very helpful and they may have money already waiting for you. However, there have been many complaints from artists who have registered and who know they have performances, but have not yet seen a dime.

Conclusion

As you can see, filmmakers have different requirements than video game publishers, who have different requirements than Internet streaming companies and corporate users. All of these various requirements are important for compliance and delivery reasons. Because of the copyright police—and I cannot stress this enough—it is important to get professional help when securing these rights. This chapter is intended as an overview to get you thinking about the issues involved. Remember that a small mistake can cost lots of money, time, and aggravation.

CHAPTER 9

Resources and Research Tools

I sincerely hope this book has given you the confidence you need to tackle any music licensing situation. Keep in mind that if you need more guidance, there are plenty of resources you can consult for help.

Before reaching out to those resources, however, try to understand exactly what rights are needed for your project. As we've discussed, each situation is slightly different. If you are making a CD of other artists' music, you should know that you don't necessarily need to get permission from publishers but only from the record labels. On the other hand, if you want to synchronize music to images, you will need permission from both. If you are hosting a convention and a band is playing live, you will have to secure a blanket performance license from a performing rights organization. But, if you are taping a band live to use in a television show, direct permission from the publisher of the song is necessary.

At the outset, before you ask for help, try to make sure your information is as accurate as possible. Make sure spelling is correct, and the song title punctuated properly. This will help make the search smoother. Is it Hue Masakela or Hugh Masekela? Is it Jon Legend or John Legend? Is it Prince or the Artist Formerly Known as Prince?

We had a client request two songs from the soundtrack to the recent film *Pride and Prejudice*. She mentioned they were written by Jean-Yves Thibaudet. With no actual CD in hand to confirm this, we checked the recording on the All Music Guide, a great online resource for information of commercial recordings. On the website, the composer of these tracks was listed as Thibaudet. We tried to find the publishing company by looking up the writer on ASCAP, BMI and SESAC websites. This composer is French, however, and wasn't listed on any of the U.S. performing rights organization sites. So we contacted the French performing rights organization, SACEM, via email and they told us the pieces are published Universal Music Publishing. We sent a request, but Universal came back saying they do not have these pieces in their database.

So we were a bit stumped. I asked the director again where she got her information. "I got it from iTunes." So, now concerned that we had been proceeding with bum info, I quickly took a look and discovered that the composer of the tracks was actually the film's composer, Dario Marianelli. Thibaudet was only the soloist. So we went back to ASCAP, found Marianelli, and secured a license.

This is a very typical situation. The client does not necessarily have all the proper information, but that's fine because it is the music supervisor's job to figure this all out.

Research is all the more difficult with foreign artists. For example, I worked on a documentary about apartheid, for which a client wanted to license a Venezuelan version of "Tico Tico." The publisher, Peer Music, said that the writer credit changes if the version we are using is not in English. So we had to confirm which version we were using and make sure we had the appropriate info and license for that version. Likewise, a client will come to us with a song title that is not the original song title because the original title is in another language. This happened once when a client asked to clear the song "L'Amour A Tous Les Droits," by African artist Ismael Lo, for a rerecording. The writers are all French, but the title they used was actually in English: "How I Love my Life."

Content can be secured through clearance houses, music supervisors, or lawyers. Even more recently, some websites have been attempting to price and issue licenses for music directly online. Certainly, anyone can attempt to clear content, but it is a delicate and unwieldy process that can be made much easier if you let a specialist handle it.

Clearance Houses

A clearance house or clearance company is a business that acts as a mediator between content owners and those who want to license content. Some clearance houses perform many additional tasks, like music supervision, while others have a more limited scope of only doing clearance. There are lots of clearance houses in the U.S. music industry that are worth their weight in gold. Below is a list of quality entities, starting off with the one that I run:

▶ The Rights Workshop

▶ EMG

▶ Clearance Quest

▶ Diamond Time

▶ BZ Rights

▶ Signature Sound

Evan Greenspan, who runs EMG, states, "Music clearance problems can cost you time, money and sometimes a few sleepless nights. Let's face it; who needs the headaches?" The key to a good clearance person is that person's ability to get to the bottom of things quickly. Persistence and courteousness are two good traits to have. But remember that only on a rare occasion does it all go smoothly with the best clearance house.

You need to be careful to work with a reputable company. I have heard many a horror story where clients have hired companies that take up to six months to locate a copyright holder. Ask for references and check up on those references. Most clearances should take anywhere from two weeks to two months, except for rare circumstances. For television productions, the turnaround should be much quicker. For foreign artists and writers, it can be much slower. For instance, we waited almost three months before hearing back from Yann

Tiersen, who composed all the music to *Amelie*. He tours quit a bit, but eventually we received a positive response.

Music Supervisor

Well, this is the obvious one. As I discussed in previous chapters, a good music supervisor should be able to understand the clearance process, whether or not this person actually handles the clearance. If they provide clearance for their clients, they have more of a handle on what can and cannot work in a production. If a supervisor is busy booking studio time and overseeing original recordings, then they may want to work with a clearance house to get answers about what clears as they focus on other issues. A lot depends on the budget of the film and the expertise of the music supervisor.

Lawyers

Lawyers who have passed the bar in a particular state can, if necessary, take your issues to court. In general, entertainment lawyers tend to be litigators or transaction-based lawyers. Of course, they are worth your weight in gold when the shit hits the fan. Transactional lawyers, or lawyers who don't necessarily litigate cases for a living, also provide clearance services. They tend to cost more; most charge by the hour instead of per clearance. But then again, when you have a lawyer, there is legal bargaining power behind him that a regular clearance person might not have.

Evan Greenspan says, "When I started doing this I wanted to know if I should go to law school. I asked a lot of people and the consensus was having a degree would never hurt, but would not significantly help because it does not help your relationship building process."

The Web

We all know the web is an amazing tool. There was a time when music supervisors and clearance individuals would have facilitate copyright searches by getting the information off the liner notes and sleeves of CDs and then calling the research divisions at ASCAP or BMI. If their offices were closed, we had to wait until the next day. Now, of course, our information society operates 24 hours a day and it is incredible what you can find on the Internet. Perhaps the most important flow of artist information on the web occurs between artist sites and associated fan sites. A great example of this is wilcoworld. com, Wilco's official site, and viachicago.com, the "semi-official" fan site. The band releases bonus tracks, tour schedules, concert presale opportunities, and other information through its official site, but it's the fan site that builds the buzz and enhances the effect of band info throughout their fan base.

Currently, the most exciting usage of web technology for music research must be the wealth of sites that use various permutations of collaborative filtering to suggest new artists and songs to a user based on music that has been previously identified as a favorite. Pandora, the commercial manifestation of the Music Genome Project, has been the most successful, and in our experience, the most useful so far. Purevolume, Amazon's recommendation engine, and many other options are available to tell you what you might like to listen to, based on what you've already heard.

While BitTorrent-based illegal download services have eclipsed it in popularity, Limewire and other "old school" based file-sharing networks (Gnutella, SoulSeek, etc.) still have many users happily offering the fruits of their collections to the world. The lack of a first-class search engine in front of these networks makes them terrible research tools, while at the same time ensuring their survival.

Below are even more websites that can be very helpful research tools.

ALL MUSIC GUIDE

If you don't have the proper song title or writer you can go to one of my favorite research tools, the All Music Guide, which is located on the web at www.allmusic.com.

This site allows you to search a song by track, album, artist, and/ or genre. The page with songs listed on an album also provides the names of the writers. No publishing information is given, but a thorough list of all recordings is provided. This list can help you pinpoint what record label originally released a given song. There is also juicy band information, reviews, bios, and groovy "sound like" information to help you learn more about various artists, moods, and themes. If you are a musichead, you'll love the additional production credits they divulge including engineers, producers, featured vocalists, and guest musicians. Recently they have ventured into the media recognition area, which you can find on the new Sony Playstations.

The allmusic.com home page.

PERFORMING RIGHTS ORGANIZATION WEBSITES

When researching the publishers of a song or composition, the first place to look is with the performing rights societies. It used to be that researchers would go to Harry Fox, but it no longer provides synchronization licenses and has not done so since 2002. The performing rights organizations are non-profit agencies—as I've said, they collect performance royalties for writers and publishers whose music is heard in a public places—and they provide publishing information for all their registered writers. Their information tends to be about 90 percent accurate, due to the fact that catalogs are bought and sold regularly and ownership tends to change.

You can research the copyright holder by going to one of the three performing rights societies and searching its databases by either song title or writer name. The websites are located at www.ascap.com, www.bmi.com, and www.sesac.com. ASCAP's database also allows you to search by performing artist but it is best to use a song title or writer name. As I've said, most commercial writers of music are, generally, members of one of these three U.S. organizations—ASCAP, BMI, or SESAC.

Many foreign writers have sub-publishing deals with one of the U.S. organizations, so you may be able to find their information on the U.S. websites. However, this is not always the case. If you know a band is from another country, you can directly contact that country's performing rights society, but sometimes you need to speak the language or have a local login to obtain the information.

Here are a few important foreign organizations, whose websites you can easily find via Google:

▶ PRS (United Kingdom)

▶ SACEM (France)

▶ JASRAC (Japan)

▶ SGAE (Spain)

▶ GEMA (Germany)

▶ SOCAN (Canada)

▶ APRA (Australia)

▶ SIAE (Italy)

IMDB (INTERNET MOVIE DATABASE)

This extensive database is filled with an amazing amount of information about movies and individuals involved in films. There is scant editorial information, just credits, but that is enough if you want to find out a director's or composer's filmography. Of course, the lists may not be complete, or they may be too complete, but they are a start. It is a truly entertaining link-to-link-to-link website that answers many questions in your research process.

You can also go one step further and get IMDbPro, which costs money. It has thousands of contacts in the movie industry—addresses, telephone numbers, etc.—which are not available in IMDb. The pro site also blocks popup ads and generally runs a bit more quickly.

POLLSTAR

PollStar is a terrific subscription service if you want management and touring information on almost any band. The cost is currently $295 a year, but it is a great professional resource when you want to get directly to an artist or that artist's management. It will also tell you when a band is in your neck of the woods, which can be helpful if you want to decipher where they are on your radar. Go to www. pollstaronline.com to check it out.

Public Domain Searching

To search to find out if a song or other piece of content is in the public domain, one place to look is www.pdinfo.com. Here there is a list many songs currently in public domain. Of course if you need more certainty, there are resources in Washington, D.C., who can do a search at the Copyright office and find out for you, for a fee of course. As I discussed earlier, though, don't hold your breath for a particular piece of work to enter the public domain if it already has not.

Keep in mind that if a song is in public domain in the United States, it may not be in other countries, so it is essential to do a thorough search. If the work is in the public domain here, and your production only needs rights domestically, you will of course not need to secure foreign rights. Conversely, many works are unprotected in other countries but still under protection in the United States. As always, please check prior to assuming and moving forward.

CHAPTER 10

Thoughts and Conclusions

The process of securing music rights is an ever-changing road filled with pitfalls, protocols, and personalities. The reach of media has expanded to such an extent that neither clients nor licensors are ever fully aware of the market saturation in order to charge a fee. This aspect, compounded by the reality that licensing entities cannot keep up with the volume of requests, has bogged down the system to a point where content users are frustrated with the clearance process and licensors are fraught with inefficiencies.

We need to engage in conversations that will help create a balance between content users and owners. Demand is increasing, and administration must increase to ensure that the system will not screech to a halt or leave out smaller players. If the corporate copyright owners could turn over licenses and negotiate deals like a bar serves drinks, coupled with a contract administration system that issued licenses quickly, copyright users would find the process more user friendly and access it more often. Ultimately, copyright owners would generate more income and users would decrease their liability.

Many of the large entertainment conglomerates such as Warner Bros., Universal, EMI and Sony/BMG have purchased competing independents to enhance their ever-growing catalogs. When they do so, it is hard for them to provide the service and attention that the independents formerly offered. The larger entities consolidate duties but do not field enough manpower to handle requests and contracts in order to generate more income. The lack of resources hinders the conglomerates' ability to turn over licenses in a timely manner. Content users become frustrated and ultimately move forward by incorporating the requested copyright into their work, only to get their hand slapped later by a nasty cease-and-desist letter. Each time this happens, the "offenders" spread the word about how malicious the recording industry has been. If the content user had been able to secure a reasonably priced license through a comprehensible system, both parties, I believe, would have found themselves in a better position.

In a perfect world, any request for a license under $10,000 would be approved or declined within 24 to 48 hours. Now, licenses for educational purposes often take over six weeks for an approval. For example, one publisher issued a statement 30 days after the request issued saying, "I received your request; unfortunately, I have not been able to get to it." Ironically the songwriter was deceased; hence the approval was being generated from the estate.

A request like this should be answered within 48 hours. Although copyright holders many times must go to a third party for approval, they may want to consider taking a bigger decision-making role so there is no need to go to this third party for a request within a certain fee or usage range.

Catalog representatives familiar with their artists' personal concerns regarding the use of their music—they may not want to license to "negative" subject matters or something they find objectionable—may want to speak on behalf of their clients and reduce the approval waiting time. A two-page contract could be issued and out the door with terms for payment within 30 to 60 days. Companies could hire college graduates to handle the administration, respond to communications, and move the approvals forward.

We have also seen requests issued for more substantial sums of money take less time to clear initially, but then we wait six months to a year for a formal contract to be generated. If you are the songwriter or artist benefiting from this license, that means you will not see any income for six months. This sort of delay and control is something a songwriter may want to consider when a large publishing concern is knocking at his door. He may want to hold on to his publishing and have a lawyer, accountant, or administrator handle his licensing. This way, payment is more immediate.

At the Rights Workshop, we see licensing fees running the full spectrum. Nothing surprises us, except when the occasional ridiculous fee rolls in from a small company; when that happens, we immediately know the licensor is unfamiliar with the particular request and even industry-standard rates for the rights requested. Amazingly, we are also beginning to see this with established companies on a regular basis. As we sit on the opposite side of the fence and witness what all licensors charge, we have heard questionable substantiations from many a licensor for the exorbitant fees they are demanding.

For instance, a quote for broad rights to the Edgar Winter song "Frankenstein" in an indie film came in at $25,000. This fee was for one side, which means the master holder would probably get the same fee, bringing the song to a grand total of $50,000. To put this in perspective, the Doors and Metallica came in at $8,500 per side in the same film.

The math shows us how impossible this song would be for a filmmaker to license. If there are 17 artists in the project, with an overall budget of $1.5 million, then there are 34 sides to clear. If each side is going to charge $25,000, the total for all 17 songs would be $850,000. Does the publisher really think the filmmaker is going to spend this kind of money? It doesn't make any sense for the copyright holders to price themselves out of a market where they can make substantial amounts of money.

Most other businesses in the world that sell, license, or rent goods and services want to have good relationships with their clients. Licensing deal-makers, on the other hand, often take an adversarial stance and don't seem to care if they have created a nice working relationship that the user will honor in the future by returning to this licensor. If you don't succumb to their fees, and try to find another solution, they will turn around and sue you. It is a litigious business that has brought on many unhappy returns.

Another issue that rears its ugly head more and more is the gouging of independent filmmakers, in particular documentarians, in the context of securing rights for film-festival exhibitions. Filmmakers are not paid to exhibit their films in worldwide festivals, yet many times the copyright holders charge enormous fees for this use. There is no real standard fee for this; it can be anywhere from free to $2,500 per song. Understandably, copyright holders want independent film makers to secure rights prior to lock so they can identify which songs will clear and which ones will not. But once a song is approved, the fees attached are often beyond what a filmmaker can pay, especially when there is no solid distribution deal yet in place.

For film-festival licenses, Warner Special Products charges $200 per license for the master only. On the other end of the spectrum, EMI Music Publishers charges anywhere from $350–$1,200 per license for the publishing only. If the filmmakers want to expand the rights into other media formats, these fees will balloon. The practical effect of all of this, coupled with the possibility of a song denial, can force documentary filmmakers to cut pivotal scenes out of their stories. In my view, especially in the documentary context, these restrictions on usage should not be in the hands of the copyright holders.

For instance, in a documentary about schizophrenia, the director captured the protagonist singing a Pink Floyd song. Clearance for the song was denied and the scene cut. Had she included the scene she would most likely have been infringing. So at what point is a copyright holder able to dictate what filmmakers want to say in their films?

Fair Use Revisited

The answer is fair use. Fair use is a legal doctrine that allows, under Section 102 of the Copyright Act, anyone to copy, publish, or distribute parts of a copyrighted work without permission in limited circumstances: as commentary, news reporting, parody, or as scholarly work. Fair use does exist, but unfortunately any given fair use is not a fair use until a court says it is. This has the practical effect of forcing many content users to get licenses in order to avoid unpleasant legal consequences, even if they would win the fair-use court case in the end. Hence, it is important to seek legal counsel to get an opinion if a certain situation would be considered fair use. A lawyer must be able to go to bat for you if litigation is threatened.

There are a few rules of thumb to follow to evaluate fair use. They are: 1) the nature of the work, 2) the purpose and character of the use (educational or commercial), 3) the amount and quality of the work the user uses, and 4) if the use affects the value of or market for the original work. First, see if what you want to use falls into any of the criteria, ask a music supervisor, and then ask your lawyer before deciding that you don't need to clear the music.

For instance, in a documentary project about a young preacher there are a few seconds of a secular song heard which in passing. It should have been fair use, but we cleared it anyway. I've cleared four notes of a Herb Alpert song for a use in a film. If you can't identify the song in the film, then there is a chance it could fall under fair use in a documentary piece, but once again please seek legal advice to get a second opinion. If it is four distinguishable notes, then it is a good idea to clear it.

Some industry observers believe that content users' fair-use rights are being unfairly abridged by copyright owners, who attempt to extract licensing fees by using threats of litigation even in situations that should qualify as fair uses. Because the copyright holders have resources to take cases to court, most smaller content users are forced to give up their fair-use notions and make the licensing deal. The Center for Social Media conducted a report funded by the Rockefeller Foundation about fair use and called it the "Creative Consequences of the Rights Clearance Culture." In their report they note that the ever-increasing fees attached to copyright permissions. The 1987 documentary film *Eyes on the Prize*, about the American Civil Rights Movement, has yet to be released to the public because of rights issues that would cost over $500,000.

There have been reports issued by various arts organizations that speak about these issues; one entitled "Will Fair Use Survive? Free Expression in the Age of Copyright Control" argues that increasingly heavy assertions of control by copyright and trademark owners are smothering fair use and free expression. With background on copyright, trademark, cease and desist letters, and dozens of firsthand stories from artists, scholars, bloggers, and others, this document paints a striking picture of an intellectual-property system out of balance.

One alternative, the Creative Commons license, offers an alternative to a full copyright and puts licensing rules into the hands of the creative owners. Creative Commons is an organization that helps individuals publish their work online "while letting others know exactly what they can and can't do with their work." An individual ultimately licenses their music and songs under their own terms for sampling, synchronization, and file sharing. One can protect their own music from commercial use or remixing of any kind, while designating exactly what a content user *can* do with the music, i.e. put in a not-for-profit film as long as appropriate credit is given. For example: A user can ask a price for sampling but not for licensing. An artist can request a fee for licensing and advertising, but not for theatrical use. Its functionality is based on a theory that larger labels and publishers may want to consider adopting.

New Uses

The Internet has introduced new forms of usage. Fees attached to these new uses and media formats are inexplicably high. Similar to an emerging piece of technology, the prices start high and may go down in the future. Currently, copyright holders substantiate these high fees by saying the medias have the potential to reach millions of people, but in reality they rarely do. One company charged a non-profit $10,000 for Internet download rights on a 47-second use of a song in a one-hour documentary about a Massachusetts museum. This fee does not parallel the exposure, which is what fees are generally based on. A major network show like *CSI* reaches 40 million people and can afford such a fee, but a documentary cannot.

Recently a PBS television station issued new rights requirements for their content providers. They requested non-exclusive internet rights, including podcasting and download for two years, as well as for all third-party material included in the content. This is the direction of the future and copyright holders have yet to price accordingly, and I suspect shortly after this book's publication they will.

Striking the Balance

The entire point of the copyright system is to reward creative people for their efforts. There is no question that artists must be paid or they would not continue creating valuable works, and there is no question that they have the privilege of saying "yes" or "no" to requests to use their property. When their decisions are in the hands of huge corporations that do not understand the creative world, however, a rift forms that upsets the beauty of the system.

Having been surrounded by artists most of my life and having witnessed the struggle surrounding the artistic process, it is my intent to protect artists' rights and, at the same time, provide a moving platform where the incorporation of these works by content users can be a painless, beneficial affair. Placing artists on pedestals and protecting copyrights like hungry hawks does society no good. There is a middle ground; each side will must make a true effort to see how the other side works. Once achieved, licensors and content users will be able to work together in greater, fluid harmony—a key component to a truly rich society.

Brad Bird and Michael Giacchino

From left to right: Brooke Wentz, Brad Bird, and Michael Giacchino.

The following is the transcript of a 2005 discussion the author conducted with Pixar animator Brad Bird and film composer Michael Giacchino. The broad conversation covers numerous film and music topics, and specifically the interplay between the two art forms.

Brooke Wentz: All right guys, come on in. I want to open up with a film; it's my impression that this is something that brought you two together and that you bonded over.

(Ms. Wentz shows a clip from the classic 1960s animated adventure *Jonny Quest*.)

Brad Bird: Yeah, give it up for *Jonny Quest*.

BW: So is that true? Did I read right?

BB: I love the show. You'd see that opening title sequence, which has everything a ten-year-old boy could want—I mean, you have mummies and pterodactyls and flying saucers and jet packs and karate and automatic weapons and lizards. It's a greatest hits list of everything you would want to see when you're ten.

Michael Giacchino: Yeah, my daughter is now five, and the mummy episode is her favorite thing in the world. She loves the mummy; she and my son walk around the house going "bomp bomp bomp," and they just do this thing with the music. It's just funny to see.

BB: Another thing I liked about the show was that it displayed genuine jeopardy. If somebody died in an episode, they didn't come back the next week.

MG: You must have hated *The A-Team*.

BB: Yeah, can't say I'm a fan.

BW: So did you bring this up?

MG: Sure, it came up the first time we met.

BW: And where did you first meet?

BB: I had heard Michael's music already; Teddy Newton, one of the character designers on *The Incredibles*, had worked with him way back. Where did you work with him?

MG: Well we met at Disney, and then I started my own company, Mission Control, and Teddy was the first guy I hired. We were producing video games for DreamWorks at the time.

BB: So Teddy knew Michael's stuff and mentioned that he was really good, and also that he does the music for *Alias*. At this point we had already hired another composer, and it didn't work out. Once word got out that we weren't going to move forward with this composer, word got out and CDs were just avalanching through the doors from every composer known to man. But when Michael's disc came in I paid attention.

The thing I liked about it is that it had a lot of different styles on it. It wasn't just this one little cell approach to music. There were a variety of different sounds—very eclectic, very musical—and it seemed to consistently suggest the kind of things you look for in movies, straight emotional lines that grab you. I kept eliminating discs and Michael's was always there. I wound up meeting with Michael at Pixar; we just talked about what we were looking for from the project, and it just went from there.

BW: Do you want to add anything to that?

MG: I think that what was funny about our first meeting is that we talked about music, but we ended up talking a lot about animation in general—old stuff that we grew up with, like *Jonny Quest* and *The Flintstones*. I love animation; I'm a closet wannabe animator who was never quite good enough to be that guy for real.

BW: Did you think that scoring to animation was going to be a challenge, after having scored video games, or did you already know it like the back of your hand?

MG: It's all very similar to me—it's always about going for the emotion in whatever it is you're doing, video games—whether or not it's readily apparent—have stories to tell. When I was in video games, it was always about sitting down with the designers and mapping out the storylines—at what point should the character feel heroic, at what point should the character feel sad? What emotion are we going for? So moving to TV was similar, and the same for the movies: you're always looking for that story or that subtext.

BB: What separates great movie composers from other great musicians is that they understand the emotional aspect of moviemaking. You may or may not like the music of John Williams, but the fact remains that he's very successful at understanding the strategy of movies and soundtracks, how they're supposed to get under your skin and make things emotional.

One of the things we kept coming back to during the creation of *The Incredibles* is that there's logic and then there's movie logic. And movie music to me is keyed into movie logic. There are great, really effective soundtracks that aren't necessarily great scores. I think my favorite are both: you're not aware of the music while you're watching the movie, you're just engaged and then later you play the score and go, "wow, that's great music." On the flip side, there are soundtracks that don't work well with the film they're married to, even though as music they can be just fine.

BW: You've probably aware of the fact that many soundtracks have a theme that resurfaces throughout the film.

BB: Yes, not every score is like that, of course, but the broad majority is. I find that that kind of style—the Wagnerian thing with leitmotifs and stuff—is not appropriate for every film, but for a lot of films it is. It's similar to the way you remember a particular person when you smell a certain perfume. The way leitmotifs work is that these short musical passages create connections with certain parts of the film, which can then be recalled by playing the passages again. You're often trying to do that visually as well, to make connections between other things in the film and set up little ways of making statements, and leitmotifs play into that kind of thinking.

BW: Can we talk a little bit about your work with Michael Kamen on *The Iron Giant*? Which was very different, obviously, from your score. I'd love to hear how you felt about working with him. The soundtrack's very different; not more orchestral, but it's more lush. Your score is more jazzy—and sort of funny because of the nature of what it is and the quirkiness of *The Incredibles*, there's more humor in *The Incredibles* than in the *Iron Giant*.

BB: *Iron Giant* was meant to be smaller scale, more heartfelt; *The Incredibles* was more razzle dazzle. What I wanted Michael Kamen to do is what we ended up with: a really jazzy leaner, not being afraid to overstate things at certain points, remember that jet shot? A shot where I was kind of echoing *Jonny Quest,* there's this point where the mom decides to put on the outfit and fly the jet and this music builds up. Michael [Kamen] was like "are you sure you want it like that?" and I'm all "come on!!!" The first jet shot is [mimics music loudly] then it goes quiet again. He was there thinking there's really only one way you can mix this, and I said, I know, and I'm going to do it that way so he happened to be on the stage

MG: I'm like, I know there's a jet in this scene, and they're going to want you to hear the jet sound...

BB: Yeah, so in the mix I'm like *turn it up* to the mixer, it was meant to be that kind of the movie. Another thing I want to mention about Michael Kamen—while he was wonderful to work with—I began to become aware of a kind of "music school" thing going on. I sometimes felt that he had a lot of people that he had studied with at Juilliard, and that he sometimes decorated things a little bit to impress the music school guys. I would try to say, "Be more straight-out emotional with it."

It was interesting, at first I was a bit worried that I couldn't communicate because I was not a musician and I was frustrated because I don't know the musical lingo. But the thing I learned through working with Michael is that you don't *need* to know the musical stuff if you know the emotional.

Michael Kamen had a very interesting way of working that was different than Michael Giacchino: he [Kamen] was sort of famous for being able to play the scene, and he'd improv and switch things around right on the spot, and sometimes what came out the very first time was just amazing. We did this scene where the Giant gets electrocuted, and the kid [the character Hogarth Hughes, voiced in the film by Eli Marienthal] is kind of crawling over his body and looking at him. The way Michael had scored it was depressing and down, and he said, "Well, the Giant's dead." And I said, "No, this is like an outer space thing that has landed in this kid's backyard. You have to do it from the kid's point of view; this is amazing, it's the most fascinating thing ever and he gets to crawl over it." So the very next take he had a different frame of mind and did this wonderfully light, innocent music (because the Giant wasn't a personality to the kid yet). That just taught me that it's all about projecting what is going on emotionally in a given scene, and if you can talk on those terms, they can translate it into music. You can't fail taking that approach.

BW: OK, I have a clip from *The Incredibles*. We have the one of Dash [one of the characters] running, can we cue that up?

MG: The thing that was cool about working on the movie is that we did it over months—so we did a version of that scene in February—it was one of those things—"should we do it? It's almost ready, I don't know, should we do it?" Then kind of late in the game we decided to just go for it, and it was great. It's was the most difficult scene in the whole movie. But it came out great because we were able to go there, record a version of it, figure out what was working, what was not working. Then, in May, we went back and did it again. This time, we felt like we were 80 percent there. It was such a complicated scene, and we really wanted to balance the music and sound effects. Finally, in June, we were able to get to the final little things that we wanted to touch up on.

This was mainly a jazz score, but it also needed support from the orchestra—it's kind of one of those traditional film scores mixed with jazz elements of certain '60s scores.

BW: Let's talk a little about the obviousness of the 007 theme.

BB: Well, I used *On Her Majesty's Secret Service* in the teaser. The original recording didn't do what I needed it to do for the trailers, so I actually bought the rights to the music and then I had it rescored before Michael got involved. I needed something that was a very simple signature, and the thing I liked about *On Her Majesty's Secret Service* was that it sounded like a hero thing gone bad. The original never quite got there, though, so I explained that to Michael, how I liked that it sounds *almost* like a hero thing. He started with that one little bit of direction, but then he took it in a million different directions. If you take into account the entire score, you barely hear that version of it, because it only comes in a couple of times in the whole movie. But because it's in the opening, that's what imprints on everybody's brain.

I wanted a very simple signature to suggest Mr. Incredible in his prime. I wanted to then fill it out and break it down and build it up in a way that is more interesting, so that when Mr. Incredible gets a family, the theme grows and develops and becomes a lot more interesting.

MG: The standard superhero thing, the most basic superhero thing you can do—a fifth, C to G—becomes the basis of Mr. Incredible in his prime: young, narrow minded, his whole life ahead of him, everything going great. Then, as he grows older and starts a family, his life gets complicated. He becomes more of a guy juggling a bunch of tasks instead of a superhero; he wants to be out there saving people, but he has to raise his family, make money, and work at an insurance company. And the music makes the same big shift, following the arc of his life story.

The goal from the very beginning was to have the music start at this simple place, and then it's like a roller coaster. I think where a lot of films go wrong is when they present a roller coaster ride that goes up and down but doesn't really build as it hurtles toward the end. So the biggest key was Brad's initial design of a slow takeoff and a big ending.

BW: There are so many musical references in *The Incredibles*, so many subtle nods to other film scores.

BB: We're definitely paying homage to Hoyt Curtin, who did the themes to *The Flintstones*, *The Jetsons*, and *Jonny Quest*, as well as to Lalo Schifrin and Les Baxter. Those sounds were in my head; I mentioned "oceans of brass" to Michael, and the horn guys were thrilled. They're used to being just one color in the background, but they were front and center for this film. Sure, they were *tired* at the end of it, but they were happy.

MG: They were upset the last day, they wanted to do more!

BW: How many days did you work with them?

MG: Eight days total, with a 100-piece orchestra.

BB: All in the room at the same time; it wasn't one of those things where we recorded the drums two weeks later.

MG: I was really committed to doing it the best way possible, with all the musicians there at the same time. We recorded to analog tape—it was even mixed on tape—and it didn't go to Pro Tools until we were at Skywalker Ranch for the final dub.

BB: People were emotional when we brought the old analog deck into the room—it was like "Bessie, she's back"—because they really love that sound and it's a warmer sound than the digital.

MG: It's a little more time consuming, but I don't think there's any comparison in the sound, I just love the sound.

BW: And where did you find the musicians?

MG: These are guys I've worked with quite often in town—especially on *Alias* and *Lost*—for the past four to five years. In a manner of speaking, they're part of the team; you know, working the same guys all the time, I can rely on them, I know what they can do, and I know what they can't do.

BB: That was another thing, that even though all my first teachers in animation were Disney masters, I ended up not being fulfilled. I wound up going to TV and doing really fast-paced work, stuff you couldn't spend any time buffing. Given the choice of doing really good animation of not-so-great ideas, or doing really quick animation of great ideas, I chose that the latter. What I wanted to do was elaborate animation of good ideas, so I worked on *The Simpsons* and other shows. I didn't have an attitude about TV.

Michael, on the other hand, would go up for films, and the producers would ask what other films he'd done. And when he'd say he hadn't really done any, they would come back with, "Well, once you've done a film then you can do a film for us." I was like, "huh?" I figured that if you had experience with TV, you're more than ready for film.

With TV, you have to be on your toes, you have to act quickly. You can't sit there and fuss over an idea forever, and the orchestra and Tim Simonec—who conducted for Michael and orchestrated the music—worked very quickly. If something didn't quite sound right, it got better fast because Michael and Tim were both used to doing sessions for *Lost* and getting a great sound, one that I think is much better than most stuff on TV. You could even manage relatively sophisticated changes, if necessary, because these guys were so accustomed to working fast.

MG: For example, on the TV shows, we have three hours to do 30 minutes of music.

BW: Do you do that every week for *Alias*?

MG: Every week for *Alias*, every week for *Lost*. I usually have about two days to write those shows and orchestrate them, but the sessions they just fly by, and we've never gone overtime. You just can't get caught up every little imperfection that might occur—good enough is our gold standard.

BB: On movies, what was cool was that, if you worked on the soundtrack in two parts (which we did), if something didn't quite hit, Michael could rework that spot, go back, and redo it at the next session. The orchestra was very efficient, so it didn't have any impact on the schedule.

MG: It gave us time to go back and try things, even on a whim, because we had the time to do it.

BW: Did you go to any of the sessions, Brad?

BB: Oh, I was at all of them.

MG: He sat right next to me every step of the way.

BW: On a different topic, I really like the presence of the vibraphone in the score.

MG: That is an instrument that's not used near enough, if you ask me. Emil Richards, this famous percussionist, came in. He's like 75 years old, but he can play the vibraphone like no one you've ever seen. He's also got an amazing collection of percussion stuff—a truck full—and there's stuff where you're like, "What is this thing?" He's got the most bizarre instruments; it was just amazing, like going through a museum.

BB: Some of his stuff was 100 years old, like his gamelan percussion pieces from Bali.

MG: So we got to take advantage of his huge truck full of stuff, and we did all this exotic music.

BW: Did you end up using a lot of it?

MG: Oh yeah, we did all this stuff that's in the final soundtrack. A lot of times, we'd just wander back there through his pile of instruments, and he'd let us know what they were capable of. Then we'd run back and go through the score and figure out where we could use these things. It was a great creative atmosphere.

BW: Brad, not only did you do the voice for one of the characters [Edna Mode], but you seem to have a really good sense of sound and a deep appreciation for it. How involved were you with the sound of *The Incredibles,* and did you do lots of voice-over to get it right, or do you just have a good ear and a knack for getting what you hear in your head?

BB: I'm very specific about what I want on the screen. With the case of Edna, it's common practice for us to do temporary soundtracks with a work in progress, using people within Pixar to do the voices with the idea that, in the end, we're going to replace everybody. But people seemed to like that voice, so it stayed in.

One of the reasons I love film as a medium is that I love all of the arts, and it's the only medium I know of that has all of the arts in it: you have architecture, music, color, acting, sound. It's like a big salad bar of the arts, and I love the whole process: staging all the shots, being involved in the sound, the whole thing.

Just in terms of the sound of a film, you can get into voice characterizations and acoustics and sound design, all sorts of things. You can affect the emotional feeling of a movie so much by how you manipulate the sound. You know, I have friends who come to the mix at the end; they just give a day's worth of attention and make a few notes. I don't know how they can do that, because to me it's just so cool, how could you not want to be there for the whole process?

BW: Let's talk about sound design for a moment.

BB: Well, Randy Thom was the sound designer for *The Incredibles*. I had worked with him on *The Iron Giant* as well. He's a fellow [San Francisco] Bay Area sound guy, he's been around for a long time and has worked on a lot of great films, but he's a real wizard and we had a great time.

BW: Had you heard any of the voices before beginning work on the film?

MG: I would get rough versions of the film, with most of the parts voiced by the producer's assistant, Laurie. So I had heard many versions throughout the process. I didn't get to *do* any of the voices.

BB: Maybe someday…

BW: Are there big differences between working on *The Iron Giant* and *The Simpsons*, compared to a project like *The Incredibles*?

MG: Not so much between *The Iron Giant* and *The Incredibles*. The big difference is that they weren't closing down the studio while we were making it, which was nice. That's what was going on while we were finishing up *The Iron Giant*. They also have this thing at Pixar called "marketing." That is incredibly helpful, because people already know what the film is by the time it comes out. That is a switch from *The Iron Giant* strategy.

BB: Pixar is a wonderful studio, and they support the artist and challenge everybody to do their best. It's a very enlightened company.

BW: Are you going to be doing more things with them here in the Bay Area?

BB: I hope so, I like it up here and I want to stay here. I hope I can get another film there, but you know, it just depends whether they want to do what I want to do next. I hope they do.

BW: Michael, what projects are you working on? Film? TV? Games?

BB: He's a film guy now; the curse has been taken off, now he's very popular.

MG: I'm doing a film for Disney called *Sky High.* I'm doing a film for Michael London, *The Family Stone,* and Albert Brooks's next movie [*Looking for Comedy in the Muslim World;* all three films were released in 2005]. I'm doing that right now, which is really cool; that's the one I'm really excited about because Albert Brooks is just a neat guy.

BB: You're doing *Mission Impossible III.*

MG: Yeah, there's a few things happening.

BB: Film's gain is going to be TV's loss.

BW: Are you going to continue with *Alias?*

MG: It just got picked up again—it's going to be on next year. It's at a point now where I might be more overseeing what's going on; there's four years' worth of themes and music that can be used at this point. I love working on *Lost.* I'm fascinated by the show and I have a great time doing it, so I'll keep my hands in that as best I can because it's fun and it's still a great playground for me.

BW: I wanted to ask about how you compose to picture for those TV shows. I worked at ESPN for a long time and we were always using music libraries there. Is composing for TV shows now becoming more popular? Or are they saving money that way?

MG: When you talk about network TV shows, in the heyday of it, live orchestras were always used, the technology to create the synthesized sounds just didn't exist then. But then budgets shrank and synths came of age, and they began to be able to replicate orchestra sounds. By the '80s and especially into the '90s, a lot of shows went to that.

When I met with JJ [Abrams, the executive producer of *Lost* and *Alias,* as well as the director of *Mission Impossible III* and a host of others], I was coming off of working with friends on the *Medal of Honor* video-game series, where I was using 100-piece orchestras for these games. I said to JJ, "If we really want to work together, this is how I want to do it." The way the used to do it, that is, where they score every show every week with the orchestra. He agreed; he went to the network and fought for that money. You have to have someone like JJ or Brad who is firm and can say, "No, this is how we should do it." And you've got to kick and scream and make a lot of noise, and maybe at times you won't be everybody's favorite guy in the room, but sometimes that's only way it will get done.

ABC is actually doing more and more shows with live orchestra. There's three pilots that I'm going to be involved with this summer because of JJ. We'll be doing all three the same way, so the potential exists that there could be five new shows on ABC alone that have live orchestras every week. [Two of these, ABC's *Six Degrees* and *What About Brian,* have since been broadcast.]

BB: The more shows that take that approach and succeed—and it's still pretty unusual—the more the approach becomes the new template that other people imitate.

MG: I'm not against electronic music, except when you use it to sound like something that is live.

BB: It's kind of like a laugh track; you hear the same people laughing for 40 years and you think, these people are all dead now, why are they still laughing?

BW: Do you ever get tired of big orchestras and wish you could just work with a jazz band?

MG: Well, you know, it's different, on *Lost* we have 35 players, about the same on *Alias.* It doesn't have to be a giant orchestra, it just has to be live. My personal preference is for live players. I love live music, that's what I grew up listening to, that's why I'm doing what I'm doing, because that's what I love.

BB: Things happen in the room that you can't anticipate. It's like not a bunch of people making love alone and then later you put them all together electronically—ha ha—draw your own mental picture.

MG: Filmmaking is all about all these different elements coming to life, from the script to the screen, taking the words from the page to the actor's mouth, all of these things. It's the same with the music, it starts on the page but then it comes to life. Every aspect of filmmaking has a moment like that that helps bring the final work to life.

BB: And people feed off that, there's an energy in the room that develops when you play something live. When we were recording, we would finish a cue and people would storm into the booth wanting to hear it. It's almost like the rush from a big wasabi hit.

MG: We would be like, "That is the greatest thing ever," and the orchestra would go, "Let's do it again, I can hit that one note better."

BW: Do you play live in LA?

MG: When I was in the East Coast I was in a band, but I've kind of lost interest in that. I have three kids, I can't even find time to watch *The Daily Show* when I get home.

Hal Willner and Steven Bernstein

From left to right, Hal Willner, Brooke Wentz, and Steven Bernstein.

The following is the transcript of a June 2005 discussion the author conducted with music producer and supervisor Hal Willner and film composer Steven Bernstein.

Brooke Wentz: Let's start with how you guys met.

Hal Willner: It was either on *Night Music* [the short-lived but semi-legendary late 1980s NBC series] or [Bernstein's band] Spanish Fly. I met you with Karen Mantler, and we had a show that night…Bootsy Collins…Karen…and [San Francisco R&B duo] Two Tons o' Fun.

Steven Bernstein: I think you actually knew me from Spanish Fly when I played Night Music with Carla Bley, Alan Toussaint, and Bootsy Collins.

HW: That's right. We were doing two shows a week of *Night Music* back then we had a mix of acts on each episode, based on the old Fillmore shows from the '60s and '70s. Al Green and the Pixies and Syd Straw and Leonard Cohen and Sonny Rollins and Was (Not Was).

BW: On *Night Music,* each artist did their own song and then jammed together at the end.

HW: I wouldn't call it a jam.

BW: A chosen song?

HW: Yeah, it came from the opinion that whenever you live music on a mainstream TV show, everybody gets together and does some uptempo thing like "Rock Around the Clock." Not everyone can relate to that. But the way I figured, everybody really loves depressing ballads. So, for that one we chose Leonard Cohen's "Who by Fire." We knew everybody could relate to that.

BW: And who chose the song? Was that a big ordeal every week to choose the song?

HW: No, it was a dream, except that we had two a week, and that's what made things completely crazy. Two a week and I was doing *Saturday Night Live* at the time. I was also doing records with William Burroughs. I think the best episode we had was Aster Aweke, Kronos Quartet, the Residents, and Conway Twitty. We had the Residents back up Conway Twitty. I thought that, if I ever met a woman who recognized these two artists together, I'd marry her.

But NBC and Michelob, the show's sponsor, called us in afterward, and it wasn't pretty.

BW: So they tried to stop the show after that?

HW: Well, they let us finish the season. You know, it was a hit with the critics and was getting a lot of press. Actually, it would be great to do something like that again. I was just happy to get to do the two seasons it existed for.

BW: And what about your job on *SNL*? Do you book the musical acts?

HW: No, I don't book the groups on that show. Actually, if I suggest a group it's a guarantee they won't get on! I did book two acts, the first was Captain Beefheart in 1981—disaster—and Miles Davis, a year later—also a disaster. He had walking pneumonia.

SB: He went to the hospital right afterward, did you know that?

HW: He locked himself in the dressing room and they had to break in to get him out.

BW: Did he play in his signature style with his back to the audience?

HW: Yeah. And Captain Beefheart, I don't really know what was going on with him back then. He was nervous, hadn't done much live TV, if any, and he wanted to use cue cards. And if you've ever heard his songs, you know, they have these very surreal lyrics. But the cue card guys are like 60 to 70 years old and they couldn't follow the lyrics. They were all going to the wrong cue cards. It's the only time I've ever seen someone finish a song and *nobody* cheered, all you heard was crickets out there. Anyway, as far as my main job at *SNL*, I just score the sketches, the Hans and Franz music, that kind of thing.

BW: Both of you have put together groups of musicians for films. Filmmakers often don't want to venture down that path; most filmmakers have trouble even using jazz music in their films. Have you ever come across any reticence, Steve?

SB: What's happened with the majority of film music now is that it's basically become aural wallpaper that's written to match what's happening in the scenes. So with a lot of films now, it's just a series of textures: if it's action there's drums, if it's sad there's chords of acoustic piano, and then there are songs placed here and there. My philosophy is that the soundtrack is as important as any other component of a film, whether it's the actor or the cinematographer or anything else. I also feel the soundtrack should have a particular sound, so any time I've done a film it's always been with one ensemble. It helps the soundtrack become part of the subtext of the film. And when we do them in New York, we always use musicians that we've done a lot of gigs with already. We can always rely on these years of playing together. It's a much different thing than the L.A. style.

HW: An interesting aspect of working at *SNL* for so long is that a lot of the last two generations of writers and actors grew up with movies that were scored with back-to-back rock or rap songs; they don't have opening themes or other musical themes.

SB: The classic way of writing a soundtrack is to have one theme, maybe two, and to use that throughout the whole film. Then came people like Bernard Herrmann, who never repeated an orchestration. Every single film he worked on used different orchestration, so it gave every film its own character. And that's almost been lost.

BW: Hal, tell us about your Nino Rota compilation [the 1981 album *Amarcord Nino Rota*].

HW: Honestly, it was just a record that I wanted to hear. I was obsessed with movie soundtracks at the time. It seemed to me that the older soundtracks were a product of a very different kind of relationship between composers and directors than we have today. I mean, these composers were often involved in the movie from day one, instead of a director hiring somebody when they were almost finished. When I came across the Fellini soundtracks by Nino Rota, they became some of my favorite records. They were great escape records. I just thought it would be wonderful to hear that music recreated in New York at that time. Carla Bley was very active, Jaki Byard was playing all the time, David Amram; I just thought it would be interesting to have all these people doing these songs.

BW: Sort of New York loft style.

SB: I remember hearing that record the summer it came out and going "Oh man, check out this far-out record." I thought, *that* is the guy I want to work with. When that record came out it was a real revelation for a lot of people.

HW: Similar things had been done, but not quite in that way.

SB: I've also got to point that that record had Debbie Harry and Chris Stein on it, and that kind of broke down, opened a door for a lot of us to say it's now beyond OK to love Jaki Byard *and* Debbie Harry.

BW: Hal, you also worked on Robert Altman's *Kansas City*. This film goes back and forth between story and music, with a heavy emphasis on performance. I want to know how you got all those musicians together, the list is incredible.

HW: I'm often called into these projects because the first idea didn't work.

BW: Who had the initial idea?

HW: Initially it was Johnny Mandel, who wrote "I Want to Live" and a lot of great jazz scores. He also wrote the music to the theme song "Suicide Is Painless" for Altman's *MASH*. He's an amazing musician, but for some reason it wasn't happening with him. So they moved on without him and I got the phone call about six weeks before shooting. Initially, I called a few people together, one was Steve, then there was Don Byron and Butch Morris. We all got together and threw around ideas. I like to look at a project and think about how to do it a little different than one might normally go about it. It may or may not work, but at least it'll be interesting. With Altman, I can do that. Like on *Short Cuts*, he wanted to have this mediocre jazz group, so we brought in people who had never written jazz before. Whereas with *Kansas City*, the idea was to bring in people from different scenes, like the Lincoln Center/Wynton Marsalis scene, the more adventurous avant-garde scene. There were all these different schools in New York who didn't really communicate a lot. So we thought we would bring all these disparate people together. I had Steve as music director, I think that was right after he did *Get Shorty*. So we had this insane scene in Kansas City, we'd brought all these people together and put together about 30 arrangements over the course of two weeks.

SB: Having worked across so many different idioms, I just kind of knew how to talk to people. I don't know if you've heard the stories about Ron Carter, but he's the kind of person who will walk out of a recording session if he feels things aren't the way they should be. So I just had to go up and introduce myself to him and say, "Listen, this is how it's going to be: we don't know what we're doing until 24 hours before, 10 hours, 2 hours. If you're not comfortable with that, you probably shouldn't be here (out of respect)." He was like, no, that's cool. It's interesting; the older guys were cooler with the looseness of it than the younger guys.

HW: The first day, we had no sheet music for them, which was fine with me. Butch Morris was there, he was fine with it too—he improvises most of his big band stuff anyway.

SB: We just worked with barebones arrangements, you know, "Here's a song, here's a scenario." The original idea was to have it be a jam session; these guys are all great and they can just jam. But the reality is that the musicians didn't know all these songs from 1936, so you had to create the illusion that they did.

HW: To do this we got the sheet music and hid it. Also, you couldn't see a microphone anywhere. The engineer, Eric Liljestrand, who was incredible, had them hidden in shoes, hats, wherever.

BW: I would think, too, that if you only had them improvise, it would be difficult for the editors to cut. It has to be condensed enough that it becomes clean enough for editing, so you wrote a score.

SB: We wrote it but we wrote it with a lot of room for improv. The whole idea is that it was supposed to be a jam session.

HW: Unfortunately, while they initially said that they were going to let these songs play out, at the end of it a lot of the songs got cut pretty conventionally. There is, however, a companion film called *Jazz '34,* which is just the music. It's all the performances in their entirety, and it's really wonderful to watch, seeing Fathead Newman and all these guys. What happened was that, with very few exceptions, everyone started getting along. I have to hand it to Altman because he saw what was happening and he arranged for a screening for everyone to see themselves. Most directors don't let people see the dailies.

BW: So it's rare to be able to have all the musicians there, and so intertwined with the film?

SB: Oh yeah, but believe me, there was definite weirdness between people. Olu Dara's son is the rapper Nas, so a lot of the young guys were impressed by *that*.

HW: A beautiful thing in *Jazz '34* was the song "Queer Notions." David Murray is playing, and Nicholas Payton is staring at him, right there on film, wanting to kill him. That's one great moment.

BW: Steve, let's talk about your theme from *Get Shorty*.

SB: This is actually indicative of what you see now for a lot of composers. Nowadays, during the production of a film, it's common to temp a score from a library of source material. The composer is basically allowed to rewrite a score that is similar to what they have temped. My theme for *Get Shorty* is basically a ripoff of "My Boyfriend's Back." John Lurie wrote the music, and Billy Martin and John Medeski—from Medeski Martin and Wood—were both in the Lounge Lizards at that time, and they were both in the band. This band is basically the Lounge Lizards. But yeah, the music is basically "My Boyfriend's Back" mixed with a bit of inspiration from the band US3 and some other things.

HW: I remember when I was working on *Amarcord Nino Rota*, I got some liner notes from Fellini on that. Weirdly enough, he told me that they stole all their themes from Charlie Chaplin films.

SB: *Really?*

HW: Yeah, so I think the temp score thing has been around for a while, at least since *8 1/2*.

SB: On the other hand, on *8 1/2,* you have that theme over and over, and I think you find that less in today's films. You know, where you have one theme that, when the film is over, it's stuck in you head.

HW: Did you see *Punch-Drunk Love?* That was a classic soundtrack by Jon Brion, but yeah, as a rule, the one-theme idea is not done much.

SB: And Jon Brion's an exception anyway.

BW: Steve, you were telling me earlier how the theme from *Get Shorty* was used in another film, do you want to mention something about that?

SB: It was kind of funny, last summer I was sitting in some huge multiplex watching some crappy film with my kids, you know, before the crappy film there are trailers for a bunch of other crappy films and there's a trailer for the new *Car Wash* film, and I hear Ornette Coleman's drummer Calvin Weston and, there's MMW, and all these totally downtown people and it made you feel that you've won a slight battle. That music we made nine years ago is in malls all over America. Those conservative Christians, you know, we're slowly infiltrating their brains. They use that particular track all the time, because what happens is that the studio owns the tracks so they can use them all they want. Nowadays, the last thing that happens on a film is that they write the soundtrack, and sometimes it's not even finished a week before the film opens. So when they put out the trailers, they use that *all* the time—big, big trailers, Eddie Murphy movies and such.

BW: I hope you're seeing some royalties.

SB: Some…

BW: Has that ever happened with any of your stuff, Hal?

HW: No.

BW: Do people ever license your songs from your eclectic tribute records for film?

HW: Only once: *Arthur 2* used a track from the Monk record [1984's *That's the Way I Feel Now: A Tribute to Thelonious Monk*].

SB: With movies it's really funny; Hal and I just worked with Rufus Wainright, and you know, Rufus is this amazing, beautiful, incredible guy and musician. And the funny thing is, kids all over the world love him because he's on the *Shrek* soundtrack. Same with Nick Cave, who's on the *Shrek 2* soundtrack!

BW: It's funny because I hear my daughter singing David Bowie's "Changes," and I realized it's [Butterfly Boucher's version] from the *Shrek 2* soundtrack. Hal, could you talk a bit about your first film work?

HW: Yeah, the first one I did was *Candy Mountain* for Robert Frank and Rudy Wurlitzer. Frank, as some of you know, is a great photographer. There was that, I did a bunch of Daffy Duck cartoons.

BW: Did that all come from your tribute records? You're from Philly, how did you get involved in making these tribute records, are you a musician?

HW: No. You know, it's funny; I've been actually credited as composer on some films. Certain things I've sampled and cut up and put together, and that sometimes now is categorized under the name "composer."

But as far as the tribute albums, that got its start in 1974. I had moved to New York to go to school, and I was really into the surreal jazz artists who were still alive and playing at that time. I managed to become a gofer for Rahsaan Roland Kirk's producer. It was an incredible time that was going to end really soon, but I didn't realize it. So I basically set out to make records that I wanted to hear, they weren't supposed to be "tribute" records.

Growing up it was the variety show, *The Hollywood Palace, Laugh-In, The Smothers Brothers, The Jimmy Durante Show.* Also in the late '60s records like the Beatles' *White Album* took record making to a whole new level; they were like movies for your head. I really loved that type of record making and that was going away with punk and the new rise of the three-minute song and all of that. I wanted to get to that escape thing I talked about earlier. I just started making records that I wanted to hear.

BW: So you just asked friends? Is that how it started?

HW: No, I had to raise money for them so I used to lie to the record companies or backers about who was going to be on the record. That was for the Thelonious Monk record, which had a fairly sizable budget and had all these people on it.

BW: Was it your idea to do the Disney tunes?

HW: Yeah.

BW: Anything that prompted that?

HW: No, I was just supposed to do a Charles Mingus one, and I wasn't in the mood. I wanted to do something kind of fun. So I saw this Walt Disney record on my shelf and thought, "Hmm, this could be interesting." It got a little sidetracked when Disney found out about it. They wanted to do a 50th birthday treatment for Mickey Mouse that year, and they found out I was doing it because I had gotten permission from the music publishers, so I got called into this meeting with lawyers and I'm playing them Sun Ra's version of "Pink Elephants on Parade" and Tom Waits's version of "Heigh-Ho." [*Laughs.*] It was a little rough.

BW: And then you kept doing tribute records—you've done so much—but I also want to talk about how you moved from producing records to doing films.

HW: It seemed like the natural thing. Somehow I got hired as a coordinator at *SNL*. As a kid I was obsessed with old radio, and how the music was done for those kind of things. Shows like *Inner Sanctum* and *The Shadow,* and even on some TV shows like *Andy Griffith,* the way some of those things were scored, it was really basic in concept: follow the mood of the protagonist. *Saturday Night Live* involved putting music to live sketches, and this obsession I had as a kid paid off.

There was as sketch called "The Accordion Killers" on the first show I worked on, and, you know, I just did the radio thing with it.

I've had that job for 25 years. So just through that, you know, it all kind of sprang from that job.

BW: How about the band from *Short Cuts*. I have to admit, the jazz group is kind of wild.

HW: It's not really a jazz group.

BW: Is that woman a jazz singer?

HW: That was Annie Ross, one of the greatest ever, but Bob [Altman] didn't want it to be that good. But it's hard to do bad, you know, "Let's go do a bad job." So I just thought it was a group you would never see together, we had really weird instrumentation based on Miles Davis's version of "Bag's Groove," which was, you know, one trombone, vibes, drums. We had the vibe player Gene Estes, and one of the great keyboardists ever, Terry Adams, on piano. There's one point in the film that he just goes, "What the hell is that chord?"

BW: And the cast in that is just amazing, done in 1993.

HW: Yeah, that song, "Prisoner of Love," Dr. John wrote that with Doc Pomus. Not a great song, but perfect for this—that kind of song that's just weird and you can't get out of your head.

BW: Had you met Tom Waits before that?

HW: Yeah, he'd been on SNL. But he wouldn't write any new songs for us; he has this thing where he's either acting *or* doing music, not both.

BW: So did you go on set and see him there?

HW: No no, that club was built in Los Angeles at Colorado and Cloverfield. They built this club on a back lot and we broke it in one night. We threw a party, had people come in get stinking drunk, and the band played all the songs. It's a shame the club's not there anymore. It was an amazing project. Altman, the way he works—and the reason actors come back time after time—he knows who he's hiring, he provides a strong framework, and then he says, "OK, you show me, do what you do." And everyone on the job goes all out for him.

For this, he just gave us the framework, so from that point, he didn't want to hear anything until we were on set. It was a great experience.

BW: How long was that, was it two weeks?

HW: I got called late. We were in the Loews Hotel in Santa Monica for about three months. It's another example of the difference that can be made when the music people are involved from the beginning. It allows for a whole other experience and association and relationship with the film. So we ended up scoring; there's about 20 minutes of our work in the midst of a three-hour Mark Isham score. We scored our parts of the film with these tracks, and then brought in horns, guitars, and added overdubs on top of the tracks.

SB: We'd take a performance that they had already recorded, and we'd play along with the song. When it ended we'd keep playing, so then there was this body of work they could cut to the film later. Hal and I have different processes, but what each of us does is still a lot different than the way most people score films.

That *Get Shorty* stuff for instance, I mean, this was a huge Hollywood film. It's directed by Barry Sonnenfeld—you know, Mr. Big Hollywood Guy—and John [Lurie] and I are trying to explain to him what the score's going to sound like. But we don't have any computers with mockups, we don't have any tapes, and neither John Lurie nor I can really play keyboards. And we're trying to explain to him what it's going to sound like. Barry Sonnenfeld looked at us like we were crazy.

Some people, like Hans Zimmer, the score they make when they're just temping the film with synthesizers, a lot of that stuff is so complete that it can actually be used. They don't need to rerecord with live musicians, that's the way big Hollywood films do it now.

BW: That's why it was exciting to have you guys here. When we had Michael Giacchino here with Brad Bird, all of a sudden that was the respected composer, and I wondered if that was because he was more tactile and more real.

SB: In *Sideways*, you can actually hear the musicians playing, as opposed to just hearing background, and again, I think that just adds one more dimension to the film, it adds humanity to the film.

BW: Steve, you recently did a documentary film called *Keep the River on Your Right*. You scored that, did you do that whole score in two weeks or did you have more time?

SB: Neither. I wanted to score it, but they took this music from my album *Diaspora Soul*. I told them I loved the film and that I really wanted to score it, but then they showed me this record collection of what they wanted to use and it turned out that it was all this stuff I had listened to before I wrote that record. I had to admit they were on the right track, so they just took that record and used it as if it were a film score; they just cut it into the film.

It was the perfect music—that record's all this crazy Jewish-themed music, Jewish prayers with Afro-Cuban percussion—and it worked nicely.

BW: The opening music is very nice too, a little more avant-garde.

SB: That's the one new thing we did for that movie. We did some remixes; David Shapiro, who co-directed the film [with sister Laurie Shapiro], was really into Lee Perry and the Upsetters, so we did a couple remixes in that style—a little more disturbing sounding. I never did get paid.

BW: Are you working on anything coming up that we should keep our eyes and ears open for?

SB: The new TV show *Stella*, on Comedy Central [which aired in 2005]. I'm writing some of the music for that, that's a really different process. I'm experimenting with a whole new way of writing with this friend of mine, Craig Wedren, who used to be in a band called Shudder to Think. He has been scoring a lot of films lately; for instance, he did *Laurel Canyon*. His name's on there for *School of Rock*, too, but it was one of those things where he has 25 seconds of score music that he wrote. He writes using samples and loops, and then I go in there and do my thing. I overdub my parts over what he does, adding flavor to loops and prerecorded computer stuff.

BW: Do you ever have to quickly put groups together for TV work?

HW: Not for TV, but for film sometimes. Just last week we did a last-minute track for the upcoming *Everything Is Illuminated*, directed by the actor Liev Schreiber. He wanted an authentic Gypsy band.

BW: Hal, do you still have a "wish list" of people you'd like to work with?

HW: No, it's weird, you know, with all these records I got through all my fantasies with it. Leonard Cohen to Yma Sumac, to, you know, they've all sort of been on these.

BW: He's worked a lot with Marianne Faithfull.

HW: Another record next year, based on Sinatra's "In the Wee Small Hours" [resulting in Faithfull's 2005 album *Before the Poison*].

BW: And she came here recently with the Robert Wilson piece [*The Black Rider*], and I understand you just worked with Robert Wilson.

HW: Yeah, we just did. Anyone hear of the Expo 2005 in Nagoya, Japan? They still have these world's fair expos, and Robert Wilson received a commission to do this thing that takes place in a carp pond, where every night at 8 p.m. this water screen comes up. An animated monkey is projected onto the water screen and conducts an orchestra. A huge snow monkey's head then comes up out of the water. It was different; with Wilson, it's always crazy. We had to wear hard hats, but we still had to take our shoes off. Japan is so insane.

BW: You've also worked a lot with Bill Frisell, and last year won a Grammy [for Frisell's 2004 album *Unspeakable*].

SB: Yeah, we kicked Bob James's ass.

BW: The category was what, Contemporary Jazz?

HW: Like the Rippingtons and the Yellowjackets and Bob James.

BW: It's a very different record for Frisell.

HW: It was an idea, it was accident. Bill pretty much made his recording debut on the Nino Rota record, *Amarcord Nino Rota*. He's been on most of my pop projects since then, he makes *everything* sound good. We finally got to make a Bill Frisell record together, so I just thought it would be incredible to try. Initially it was going to be Bill's homage to George Clinton, but we ended up getting into doing these turntable/guitar duets.

BW: You got turntable credits.

HW: Yeah! So then eventually we had these tracks with Bill and he really caught on to it and started to really make it his own thing. He got rid of the samples, put his band on, wrote strings. Steve wrote some horns. It was a great record; it didn't sell much, but we won a Grammy!

Reinhold Heil and Johnny Klimek

From left to right, Brooke Wentz, Johnny Klimek, and Reinhold Heil.

The following is the transcript from a 2005 discussion the author conducted with film and TV composers Reinhold Heil and Johnny Klimek.

Brooke Wentz: Let's talk about working on the music from one of your signature projects, *Run Lola Run*.

Reinhold Heil: Well, we started in the fall of 1997 in Berlin and continued in 1998 in Santa Barbara, and most of the music was done in Santa Barbara. It was a low-budget film, about $1.5 million, so we had to do everything ourselves; we wrote the lyrics and did all the vocals because we couldn't afford a singer. Then we found out that Franka, the lead actress, had taken singing lessons. We thought, "Well, she'll do." That turned it into a really unique piece. We didn't have any input from any other people or other musicians. It was the first time we tried to merge a film score with electronic beats and the whole groove thing that was happening then.

BW: It works perfectly because of the way the whole film moves forward—the lead character runs throughout most of the movie. What I love about this film is that it goes from this hard-driving music and these songs to silence.

RH: The interesting thing is that you see the same basic movie three times. There's an introduction, then it's the same story played out repeatedly in three 20-minute episodes, with very few differences between each episode. Just little possibilities change, encounters with different people affect the outcome differently.

This is a good way of making a cheap movie: taking the same footage and using the majority of it three times. The trick is to do it intelligently and make it entertaining, while at the same time make it digestible for people and enable some sort of appreciation for seeing the same thing over and over again. To that end, we used three totally different pieces of music.

Johnny Klimek: And three different destinies as well…

RH: Also there's a distinct character to each episode and the music is more or less aggressive—the music is what really indicates that everything is going to be fine this time. It's a wonderful little study in how to score things differently.

BW: Depending at what point you are in the film, the music could be "go go go" or it could cut out completely, creating a sort of aural patchwork throughout the film.

RH: There have been other movies that used this style of music, but I think that, in past films, the music was never made specifically for the movie. It was always techno stuff licensed and applied to the film after the fact. I'm not sure if we were the first people to actually score this type of music to the film, but we really sat down and scored to the film, so you see the curves of intensity going up and down. You will hardly find a licensed piece of music that has these subtleties.

JK: Unless you license *Run Lola Run*.

BW: Have people done that?

JK: Yeah, we've made money out of that film from licensing the music. And guess who buys it? Hollywood, of course. There was an episode of *The Simpsons* that used it, and something for the NFL. We don't know much about football.

BW: When the director, Tom Tykwer, came to you to write the music, did he specifically say that he wanted a techno thing throughout the whole film?

JK: Yeah, he had a clear concept of the energy and the pacing, and we actually sat down months before the work on the music—unlike the film he's doing now, where it's *years* before.

RH: I think this was actually in the fall of '97, when we were working in Johnny's bedroom. We worked out the introduction of the movie, and then we paced the rest of the scenes without really knowing them, you know, what kind of beats per minute, et cetera. That way, Tom had something to edit to and—this is a key reason why it worked so well—the timing of the edits worked perfectly with the music.

BW: Tom is also very much into music, and he apparently wrote some of the lyrics, so he has come off being a writer, which I think is kind of unusual. Very few directors are into writing their own music.

I would love to know from your perspective how you feel when the director comes in and says he wants to write some music too.

JK: If we like the director it's great, it can be wonderful. In the case of Tom, he's a great guy to work with. We actually sit down and write pieces exactly for what we're doing, a process we started years and years ago. I recently listened to some choral music we wrote and recorded last year. It's amazing to listen to it after so long and realize it's so on point. We're about to go score a film in two weeks in Germany. Tom hasn't finished shooting it yet, but we have the kind of relationship where we've been involved since the beginning stages of writing the script. We talk to him and get enough information that we can work on a piece, and some of what we've completed is perfect for the film already. It's telling the story just within the music. I don't know if you know the book *Perfume,* but it's going to be a challenge because the main character just sort of smells things. He doesn't talk much.

RH: He doesn't have a body odor, no pheromones, and that's why he's not a very social person. But he has the keenest sense of smell, so he becomes renowned for creating the world's finest perfumes. [The film, *Perfume: The Story of a Murderer,* was released in late 2006, with Ben Whishaw in the lead role.]

BW: Let's talk a bit about *Winter Sleepers,* the first film you did with Tom. How did you meet him originally?

JK: Well, my brother used to be the singer in his band…

BW: This was in Nina Hagen's band in the late '70s, correct? You were a keyboardist, and you wrote and produced?

RH: Yes, then the band broke up and we started a kind of anti–rock star project. We, as "the bosses," hired the front people. The poor person who suffered the most was Alf, Johnnie's older brother. He's still recovering. [Laughs.]

BW: But then you guys met up with Tom in Berlin and played in various groups there?

RH: Yeah, there was that band, and then we went to Australia and got another band together.

JK: We were the first act that Virgin Records America signed, and we even had hits.

RH: Then Johnny decided to go into the underground techno scene.

JK: I didn't decide, it just sort of happened. The whole techno movement happened, the wall came down in '89. In East Germany, there were huge spaces opening up, and this whole underground club scene blossomed. It produced a whole network of underground DJs producing records at home and getting them played in the clubs.

I just happened to click with certain people, and I had this little studio at home where I could do these little DJ records. That brought me into the whole techno scene. It was a very innovative place to be, and we happened to be there at the right time. Once the wall came down, it was complete madness for a couple years. Suddenly there were two million people partying in the streets.

BW: Was there a lot of creativity in music and art at that time?

JK: I think there always was, but when the wall was up, it was like "Jesus there's the bloody wall." I couldn't understand the concept of a wall being around Berlin, but that's how it was. Most important, you could get out of being drafted by going to Berlin, so all of the freaks kind of went there.

BW: You skirt the army by going to a city?

RH: Yes, West Berlin. West Berlin was politically independent, not part of Germany. It was still under post World War II law, and split into four sectors. Theoretically, if the military police found you without an ID, they could shoot you on the spot. But the draft didn't exist in West Berlin—in a way reality didn't exist in West Berlin—which was perfect for the politically left-wing or creative person.

BW: And Tom was coming to your shows?

RH: Yes, Nina Hagen shows in the late '70s. He was 15 and drawn to her. Tom was also a pianist. Seventeen years later, when he asked Johnny to produce music for a trailer for *Winter Sleepers*, Johnny played him a tape of stuff he and I had done at the time. Tom said, "No way, that's not the same guy, is it?" So I happened to find an old fan.

JK: Working with Tom is a dream for us. We started from nowhere together. He was a struggling filmmaker and we were making these DJ records. I really miss that working relationship, especially when you compare that to working in Hollywood now. All of it is exciting, but in Hollywood, the creative side seems to be dwindling. We just had that experience working on *Aeon Flux* recently. It was horrible.

BW: Maybe you can talk about some differences...

JK: With *Aeon Flux*, they'd fired the previous composer, and it was like "Let's get the guys from *Run Lola Run* because it's sort of a hip MTV-style blah blah blah." so we took the job. We were supposed to do an edgy electronic score for it. But the production of the film was aimless; I remember one situation walking into the editing room and seeing all these new editors because the old ones had been fired. We'd give our opinion, Charlize [Theron, who played the title character] gave her opinion, and after a while we were like "What the fuck is going on here?" There was no leadership, it was just a bunch of us clowns in the editing room, and that was a problem. *And* it was the most expensive film I'd ever worked on.

RH: Not to bash it too badly, but I think part of the problem was in the material that was shot. There's not really a filmmaker's vision, and part of the problem lies with the studio. With big studios, the filmmaker has to have proven himself to be given free rein; if it's a small filmmaker who has only done one feature [as was the case here with director Karyn Kusama], they still don't trust them.

JK: And if a film starts out compromised, it can usually only end up that way. On the other hand, we're so lucky we have *Perfume* to go into, where everybody is so happy to come together. Otherwise, I would really be questioning how long I could stand to play this game. Anyway, it's rare that you get this gem of a relationship that has lasted ten years.

BW: Did Tom edit to your music in *Perfume*, the way he did with *Run Lola Run?*

JK: On *Perfume*, the film was cut first. This is very "John Carpenter–esque" if you think about it. I think he was a very big influence on Tom in terms of filmmaking and music. This sequenced, repetitive stuff is hardcore Carpenter-type scoring.

BW: Also, that kind of whirling sound, which you use in very tense situations; that, and the little voices in the sound. I was wondering where you're getting those—who does sound design?

JK: Tom. He sits with us to get it started, then we get some space and put the puzzle together. He's there with the editors, driving them insane. He's in everything, very controlling, but in a pleasant way.

RH: He can't really delegate. He has to be there for every process. It's going to be a big challenge for him on *Perfume* because he's shooting a $70 million film. There's an incredible amount of footage being shot, and there's assembly being done on all this film already, Hollywood style. Tom will get into the process at the end of this month, but he'll want to see every inch that has been shot. He will sit through every bit of the footage.

JK: This is also part of the magic. You see something like *Run Lola Run* and it just works: music, editing, dramatically, everything. We know that, this time out, it's going to be a longer process than usual. It's the biggest film ever made in Germany. We hope something special is going to come out of that, unlike some of these huge Hollywood blockbusters that turn out to be just crap. Sorry!

BW: You also worked on *The Matrix Revolutions*, I'm really curious to know if you guys enjoyed working on that.

RH: We only did one piece—a source piece. Although they let us score it to picture, they only gave us a one-minute scene; we didn't see any other picture and we could work to it but it's actually used as a source piece playing in a club. The interesting part of it is that it is still supposed to enhance the story a little bit even though it's just "scorsing," as they call it.

JK: In the case of *The Matrix* as well, the story of how we got the gig is interesting. It was a little scheme that I devised because I knew the [Wachowski] brothers would be interested in Tom, and I also knew one of the producers. So I thought, "Okay, let's get Tom to write an email to the Wachowski brothers saying we'd do a song for it. When they heard it was Tom, they were all about it. Tom flew in from Berlin, I came in from Australia, Reinhold came a day later, and we met the Wachowskis and spent three hours just talking about philosophies of film. It wasn't really about music until the next day. I think that's important when you have these possibilities of putting a connection together. It's also exciting, it was actually pleasurable. Larry and Tom are still in contact; sending scripts to each other and whatnot. They've developed a friendship.

BW: That's exciting and you didn't have to do much work.

JK: And you get paid *really* well to just do a piece.

RH: We loved the first *Matrix* and were kind of disappointed with the second one and Johnny was saying "we should get the gig, we should get the gig." But that wasn't happening, so we tried going to the producer. And when *that* didn't work, he concocted his little scheme of getting Tom to email the Wachowskis. Now we're faced with music from *The Matrix Reloaded* as temp music in *Aeon Flux*—karmic.

JK: In the case of *Aeon Flux*, we didn't have a budget for an orchestra. We thought the creatives wanted something really special, so we sat down for three weeks and really created a sound for the film, something new and different. But then it slowly started changing, to the point where it was temped with huge orchestras and choirs and just becoming unrealistic…bastards [laughter].

BW: How about *One Hour Photo?*

RH: They were in the very late stages of production and already had music, but they tested it and the reaction was abysmal. The director, Mark Romanek, is a wonderful filmmaker whose background is in music videos, and he's done some of the most groundbreaking videos ever. But he's also an amazing and intelligent filmmaker, and didn't want to do a music video–inspired movie. He wanted to more firmly establish himself as a good filmmaker. But he was drawing talent from movies that were hip, that he liked, and he used the composer from *Traffic* [Cliff Martinez]. He's a wonderful composer who does these amazing soundscapes—very simple, slow, hovering atmospheres—and in *Traffic* it just works. But that is a movie where there's a lot of stuff happening. In *One Hour Photo*, there's not a lot happening for the first 45 minutes, so having those minimal soundscapes was kind of sleep inducing. It didn't test well despite the fact that it was gorgeous music. It just wasn't right for the film. So they scrambled to find a composer who would do a new soundtrack for very little money. [*Waves hand.*]

JK: We had the challenge of propelling this film without making it obvious or bringing beats, but it really needed to be pushed forward, so we decided to create a score that would turn it into a psycho thriller. This turned out to be a big point of contention with Mark Romanek, who didn't want it to be one. He spoke to Francis Coppola looking for advice, and Coppola said, "Make your mind up, either make it a thriller or an art piece." We got the go-ahead to make it a thriller, and we were off.

BW: So, the music, is it usually just the two of you creating, or do you bring in others?

JK: Just the two of us, when we work with Tom it's the three of us.

BW: Would you like to go back?

RH: I'm not going back.

JK: I'm not going back. We've done four or five films this year, a lot of which was for a German movie.

BW: What film was that?

RH: It's called *Sophie Scholl: The Final Days*. It's very artsy.

BW: You're doing so much work in Hollywood now you can't leave it?

JK: Well, I think that it's really important to get out of there sometimes. Even though I'm from Australia, I spent 17 years in Berlin and I grew up creatively with the experimental side of art, music, and film. I made my way through that. I miss being in that environment. It's rare that you get that in Hollywood. It's just a gig. Creativity is for hire out there, and it probably scares those at the top because they want control. So I'm happy to get up and out and do something, and then come back to Hollywood.

BW: You're also writing the music for *Deadwood* on HBO, and is that a regular sort of job?

RH: They had two other composers on it and were scrambling for a sound. There isn't really much music in it, actually. It's a really subtle kind of thing, as with many HBO series. There's not a whole lot of music in *Six Feet Under*, but music that's there is really quite nice. We came in about halfway through the first season of *Deadwood* and sort of found a sound they were really happy with.

BW: It's really interesting that you're involved in that project because it's set in 1876 in South Dakota, yet all the music you've been doing before it has been very contemporary.

RH: It's actually our agent we have to thank for getting this gig because when she got the call from the producers to find a new sound on *Deadwood*, she said, "I have just the guys for you," and referred them to us. So we just kind of dabbled and put five or six pieces on an episode for them, wherever we thought it was suitable to have music.

JK: We actually experimented with a lot of acoustic elements. We'd record acoustic elements from that period, and process them to create a very weird, irritated atmosphere that's hard to pin down. You don't know if it's electronic or organic because it's taken from organic materials but then treated electronically. It's the same with any project we work on, creating a base sound that helps define the story.

For instance, it was the same for *Perfume*. What's the base sound? How do we create an atmosphere of smell? The book is all about scent and smell. So we go to these weirdos in New York who are totally into experimenting with classical instruments because it's a period piece. Tom came out and gave a speech about needing the instruments to have air, that sort of thing. We spent time building solid ground for the score, and experimenting a lot on top of that. But the conventional stuff will still come in at the very top, with choirs and string arrangements.

BW: Are you scoring in L.A.?

RH: No, for this one we'll be scoring in Europe. We'll not only be sitting in Munich while Tom is editing the movie, but we'll also be scoring with an orchestra there.

BW: How do you like doing TV as opposed to film?

JK: We actually haven't done much. *Deadwood* is great, we have relative freedom on that show. If you get that situation in TV it's rare. In *Deadwood* it's three minutes an episode. We once did a *big* episode that had seven minutes, but that's rare. That was great. Before *Deadwood,* we did the CBS series *Without a Trace.* That was the opposite: five producers with different ideas, and you'd get all these different votes so in the end you had to do the job three times, even though you only have a week per episode to prepare. There was really no rhyme or reason because everybody was just saying whatever they felt at the moment. HBO is different though, working with them has been brilliant.

RH: Any other TV stuff we've done has been made-for-TV movies, which are very similar, just lower budget. The process is very simi-lar. But we've been very lucky to have gigs where the filmmaker was allowed to make the movie the way they wanted.

Forms

I have referenced numerous application forms and registrations through the book. The following collection of forms, although not nearly complete, is intended to give you an idea of some of the processes involved in making official filings with the government and with organizations like Harry Fox, BMI, and SoundExchange.

Ⓟ Form SR

Detach and read these instructions before completing this form.
Make sure all applicable spaces have been filled in before you return this form.

When to Use This Form: Use Form SR for registration of published or unpublished sound recordings. It should be used when the copyright claim is limited to the sound recording itself, and it may also be used where the same copyright claimant is seeking simultaneous registration of the underlying musical, dramatic, or literary work embodied in the phonorecord.

With one exception, "sound recordings" are works that result from the fixation of a series of musical, spoken, or other sounds. The exception is for the audio portions of audiovisual works, such as a motion picture soundtrack or an audio cassette accompanying a filmstrip. These are considered a part of the audiovisual work as a whole.

Deposit to Accompany Application: An application for copyright registration must be accompanied by a deposit consisting of phonorecords representing the entire work for which registration is to be made.

Unpublished Work: Deposit one complete phonorecord.

Published Work: Deposit two complete phonorecords of the best edition, together with "any printed or other visually perceptible material" published with the phonorecords.

Work First Published Outside the United States: Deposit one complete phonorecord of the first foreign edition.

Contribution to a Collective Work: Deposit one complete phonorecord of the best edition of the collective work.

The Copyright Notice: Before March 1, 1989, the use of copyright notice was mandatory on all published works, and any work first published before that date should have carried a notice. For works first published on and after March 1, 1989, use of the copyright notice is optional. For more information about copyright notice, see Circular 3, *Copyright Notices*.

For Further Information: To speak to a Copyright Office staff member, call (202) 707-3000 (TTY: (202) 707-6737). Recorded information is available 24 hours a day. Order forms and other publications from Library of Congress, Copyright Office, 101 Independence Avenue SE, Washington, DC 20559-6000 or call the Forms and Publications Hotline at (202) 707-9100. Access and download circulars, forms, and other information from the Copyright Office website at *www.copyright.gov*.

Please type or print neatly using black ink. The form is used to produce the certificate.

1 SPACE 1: Title

Title of This Work: Every work submitted for copyright registration must be given a title to identify that particular work. If the phonorecords or any accompanying printed material bears a title (or an identifying phrase that could serve as a title), transcribe that wording completely and exactly on the application. Indexing of the registration and future identification of the work may depend on the information you give here.

Previous, Alternative, or Contents Titles: Complete this space if there are any previous or alternative titles for the work under which someone searching for the registration might be likely to look, or under which a document pertaining to the work might be recorded. You may also give the individual contents titles, if any, in this space or you may use a Continuation Sheet. Circle the term that describes the titles given.

2 SPACE 2: Author(s)

General Instructions: After reading these instructions, decide who are the "authors" of this work for copyright purposes. Then, unless the work is a "collective work," give the requested information about every "author" who contributed any appreciable amount of copyrightable matter to this version of the work. If you need further space, request additional Continuation Sheets. In the case of a collective work such as a collection of previously published or registered sound recordings, give information about the author of the collective work as a whole. If you are submitting this Form SR to cover the recorded musical, dramatic, or literary work as well as the sound recording itself, it is important for space 2 to include full information about the various authors of all of the material covered by the copyright claim, making clear the nature of each author's contribution.

Name of Author: The fullest form of the author's name should be given. Unless the work was "made for hire," the individual who actually created the work is its "author." In the case of a work made for hire, the statute provides that "the employer or other person for whom the work was prepared is considered the author."

What Is a "Work Made for Hire"? A "work made for hire" is defined as: (1) "a work prepared by an employee within the scope of his or her employment"; or (2) "a work specially ordered or commissioned for use as a contribution to a collective work, as a part of a motion picture or other audiovisual work, as a translation, as a supplementary work, as a compilation, as an instructional text, as a test, as answer material for a test, or as an atlas, if the parties expressly agree in a written instrument signed by them that the work shall be considered a work made for hire." If you have checked "Yes" to indicate that the work was "made for hire," you must give the full legal name of the employer (or other person for whom the work was prepared). You may also include the name of the employee along with the name of the employer (for example: "Elster Record Co., employer for hire of John Ferguson").

"Anonymous" or "Pseudonymous" Work: An author's contribution to a work is "anonymous" if that author is not identified on the copies or phonorecords of the work. An author's contribution to a work is "pseudonymous" if that author is identified on the copies or phonorecords under a fictitious name. If the work is "anonymous" you may: (1) leave the line blank; or (2) state "anonymous" on the line; or (3) reveal the author's identity. If the work is "pseudonymous" you may: (1) leave the line blank; or (2) give the pseudonym and identify it as such (for example: "Huntley Haverstock, pseudonym"); or (3) reveal the author's name, making clear which is the real name and which is the pseudonym (for example: "Judith Barton, whose pseudonym is Madeline Elster"). However, the citizenship or domicile of the author *must* be given in all cases.

Dates of Birth and Death: If the author is dead, the statute requires that the year of death be included in the application unless the work is anonymous or pseudonymous. The author's birth date is optional, but is useful as a form of identification. Leave this space blank if the author's contribution was a "work made for hire."

Author's Nationality or Domicile: Give the country in which the author is a citizen, or the country in which the author is domiciled. Nationality or domicile *must* be given in all cases.

Nature of Authorship: Sound recording authorship is the performance, sound production, or both, that is fixed in the recording deposited for registration. Describe this authorship in space 2 as "sound recording." If the claim also covers the underlying work(s), include the appropriate authorship terms for each author, for example, "words," "music," "arrangement of music," or "text."

Generally, for the claim to cover both the sound recording and the underlying work(s), every author should have contributed to both the sound recording *and* the underlying work(s). If the claim includes artwork or photographs, include the appropriate term in the statement of authorship.

SPACE 3: Creation and Publication

General Instructions: Do not confuse "creation" with "publication." Every application for copyright registration must state "the year in which creation of the work was completed." Give the date and nation of first publication only if the work has been published.

Creation: Under the statute, a work is "created" when it is fixed in a copy or phonorecord for the first time. Where a work has been prepared over a period of time, the part of the work existing in fixed form on a particular date constitutes the created work on that date. The date you give here should be the year in which the author completed the particular version for which registration is now being sought, even if other versions exist or if further changes or additions are planned.

Publication: The statute defines "publication" as "the distribution of copies or phonorecords of a work to the public by sale or other transfer of ownership, or by rental, lease, or lending"; a work is also "published" if there has been an "offering to distribute copies or phonorecords to a group of persons for purposes of further distribution, public performance, or public display." Give the full date (month, date, year) when, and the country where, publication first occurred. If first publication took place simultaneously in the United States and other countries, it is sufficient to state "U.S.A."

SPACE 4: Claimant(s)

Name(s) and Address(es) of Copyright Claimant(s): Give the name(s) and address(es) of the copyright claimant(s) in the work even if the claimant is the same as the author. Copyright in a work belongs initially to the author of the work (including, in the case of a work made for hire, the employer or other person for whom the work was prepared). The copyright claimant is either the author of the work or a person or organization to whom the copyright initially belonging to the author has been transferred.

Transfer: The statute provides that, if the copyright claimant is not the author, the application for registration must contain "a brief statement of how the claimant obtained ownership of the copyright." If any copyright claimant named in space 4a is not an author named in space 2, give a brief statement explaining how the claimant(s) obtained ownership of the copyright. Examples: "By written contract"; "Transfer of all rights by author"; "Assignment"; "By will." Do not attach transfer documents or other attachments or riders.

SPACE 5: Previous Registration

General Instructions: The questions in space 5 are intended to show whether an earlier registration has been made for this work and, if so, whether there is any basis for a new registration. As a rule, only one basic copyright registration can be made for the same version of a particular work.

Same Version: If this version is substantially the same as the work covered by a previous registration, a second registration is not generally possible unless: (1) the work has been registered in unpublished form and a second registration is now being sought to cover this first published edition; or (2) someone other than the author is identified as copyright claimant in the earlier registration and the author is now seeking registration in his or her own name. If either of these two exceptions applies, check the appropriate box and give the earlier registration number and date. Otherwise, do not submit Form SR. Instead, write the Copyright Office for information about supplementary registration or recordation of transfers of copyright ownership.

Changed Version: If the work has been changed and you are now seeking reg-

istration to cover the additions or revisions, check the last box in space 5, give the earlier registration number and date, and complete both parts of space 6 in accordance with the instructions below.

Previous Registration Number and Date: If more than one previous registration has been made for the work, give the number and date of the latest registration.

SPACE 6: Derivative Work or Compilation

General Instructions: Complete space 6 if this work is a "changed version," "compilation," or "derivative work," and if it incorporates one or more earlier works that have already been published or registered for copyright, or that have fallen into the public domain, or sound recordings that were fixed before February 15, 1972. A "compilation" is defined as "a work formed by the collection and assembling of preexisting materials or of data that are selected, coordinated, or arranged in such a way that the resulting work as a whole constitutes an original work of authorship." A "derivative work" is "a work based on one or more preexisting works." Examples of derivative works include recordings reissued with substantial editorial revisions or abridgments of the recorded sounds, and recordings republished with new recorded material, or "any other form in which a work may be recast, transformed, or adapted." Derivative works also include works "consisting of editorial revisions, annotations, or other modifications" if these changes, as a whole, represent an original work of authorship.

Preexisting Material (space 6a): Complete this space *and* space 6b for derivative works. In this space identify the preexisting work that has been recast, transformed, or adapted. The preexisting work may be material that has been previously published, previously registered, or that is in the public domain. For example, the preexisting material might be: "1970 recording by Sperryville Symphony of Bach Double Concerto."

Material Added to This Work (space 6b): Give a brief, general statement of the **additional** new material covered by the copyright claim for which registration is sought. In the case of a derivative work, identify this new material. Examples: "Recorded performances on bands 1 and 3"; "Remixed sounds from original multitrack sound sources"; "New words, arrangement, and additional sounds." If the work is a compilation, give a brief, general statement describing both the material that has been compiled *and* the compilation itself. Example: "Compilation of 1938 Recordings by various swing bands."

SPACE 7, 8, 9: Fee, Correspondence, Certification, Return Address

Deposit Account: If you maintain a Deposit Account in the Copyright Office, identify it in space 7a. Otherwise, leave the space blank and send the filing fee with your application and deposit. (See space 8 on form.) (**Note:** Copyright Office fees are subject to change. For current fees, check the Copyright Office website at *www.copyright.gov*, write the Copyright Office, or call (202) 707-3000.)

Correspondence (space 7b): Give the name, address, area code, telephone number, fax number, and email address (if available) of the person to be consulted if correspondence about this application becomes necessary.

Certification (space 8): This application cannot be accepted unless it bears the date and the *handwritten signature* of the author or other copyright claimant, or of the owner of exclusive right(s), or of the duly authorized agent of the author, claimant, or owner of exclusive right(s).

Address for Return of Certificate (space 9): The address box must be completed legibly since the certificate will be returned in a window envelope.

MORE INFORMATION

"Works": "Works" are the basic subject matter of copyright; they are what authors create and copyright protects. The statute draws a sharp distinction between the "work" and "any material object in which the work is embodied."

"Copies" and "Phonorecords": These are the two types of material objects in which "works" are embodied. In general, "copies" are objects from which a work can be read or visually perceived, directly or with the aid of a machine or device, such as manuscripts, books, sheet music, film, and videotape. "Phonorecords" are objects embodying fixations of sounds, such as audio tapes and phonograph disks. For example, a song (the "work") can be reproduced in sheet music ("copies") or phonograph disks ("phonorecords"), or both.

"Sound Recordings": These are "works," not "copies" or "phonorecords." "Sound recordings" are "works that result from the fixation of a series of musical, spoken, or other sounds, but not including the sounds accompanying a motion picture or other audiovisual work." Example: When a record company issues a new release, the release will typically involve two distinct "works": the "musical work" that has been recorded, and the "sound recording" as a separate work in itself. The material objects that the record company sends out are "phonorecords": physical reproductions of both the "musical work" and the "sound recording."

Should You File More Than One Application? If your work consists of a recorded musical, dramatic, or literary work and if both that "work" and the sound recording as a separate "work" are eligible for registration, the application form you should file depends on the following:

File Only Form SR if: The copyright claimant is the same for both the musical, dramatic, or literary work and for the sound recording, and you are seeking a single registration to cover both of these "works."

File Only Form PA (or Form TX) if: You are seeking to register only the musical, dramatic, or literary work, not the sound recording. Form PA is appropriate for works of the performing arts; Form TX is for nondramatic literary works.

Separate Applications Should Be Filed on Form PA (or Form TX) and on Form SR if: (1) The copyright claimant for the musical, dramatic, or literary work is different from the copyright claimant for the sound recording; or (2) You prefer to have separate registrations for the musical, dramatic, or literary work and for the sound recording.

Form SR
For a Sound Recording
UNITED STATES COPYRIGHT OFFICE

REGISTRATION NUMBER

SR   SRU

EFFECTIVE DATE OF REGISTRATION

Month   Day   Year

DO NOT WRITE ABOVE THIS LINE. IF YOU NEED MORE SPACE, USE A SEPARATE CONTINUATION SHEET.

1   TITLE OF THIS WORK ▼

PREVIOUS, ALTERNATIVE, OR CONTENTS TITLES (CIRCLE ONE) ▼

2   **a**   NAME OF AUTHOR ▼

DATES OF BIRTH AND DEATH
Year Born ▼   Year Died ▼

Was this contribution to the work a "work made for hire"?
☐ Yes
☐ No

AUTHOR'S NATIONALITY OR DOMICILE
Name of Country
OR { Citizen of ▶
Domiciled in ▶

WAS THIS AUTHOR'S CONTRIBUTION TO THE WORK
Anonymous?   ☐ Yes   ☐ No
Pseudonymous?   ☐ Yes   ☐ No

If the answer to either of these questions is "Yes," see detailed instructions.

NATURE OF AUTHORSHIP   Briefly describe nature of material created by this author in which copyright is claimed. ▼

NOTE

Under the law, the "author" of a "work made for hire" is generally the employer, not the employee (see instructions). For any part of this work that was "made for hire," check "Yes" in the space provided, give the employer (or other person for whom the work was prepared) as "Author" of that part, and leave the space for dates of birth and death blank.

b   NAME OF AUTHOR ▼

DATES OF BIRTH AND DEATH
Year Born ▼   Year Died ▼

Was this contribution to the work a "work made for hire"?
☐ Yes
☐ No

AUTHOR'S NATIONALITY OR DOMICILE
Name of Country
OR { Citizen of ▶
Domiciled in ▶

WAS THIS AUTHOR'S CONTRIBUTION TO THE WORK
Anonymous?   ☐ Yes   ☐ No
Pseudonymous?   ☐ Yes   ☐ No

If the answer to either of these questions is "Yes," see detailed instructions.

NATURE OF AUTHORSHIP   Briefly describe nature of material created by this author in which copyright is claimed. ▼

c   NAME OF AUTHOR ▼

DATES OF BIRTH AND DEATH
Year Born ▼   Year Died ▼

Was this contribution to the work a "work made for hire"?
☐ Yes
☐ No

AUTHOR'S NATIONALITY OR DOMICILE
Name of Country
OR { Citizen of ▶
Domiciled in ▶

WAS THIS AUTHOR'S CONTRIBUTION TO THE WORK
Anonymous?   ☐ Yes   ☐ No
Pseudonymous?   ☐ Yes   ☐ No

If the answer to either of these questions is "Yes," see detailed instructions.

NATURE OF AUTHORSHIP   Briefly describe nature of material created by this author in which copyright is claimed. ▼

3   **a**   YEAR IN WHICH CREATION OF THIS WORK WAS COMPLETED
This information must be given in all cases.
◀ Year

b   DATE AND NATION OF FIRST PUBLICATION OF THIS PARTICULAR WORK
Complete this information ONLY if this work has been published.
Month ▶   Day ▶   Year ▶
◀ Nation

4   **a**   COPYRIGHT CLAIMANT(S) Name and address must be given even if the claimant is the same as the author given in space 2. ▼

See instructions before completing this space.

b   TRANSFER If the claimant(s) named here in space 4 is (are) different from the author(s) named in space 2, give a brief statement of how the claimant(s) obtained ownership of the copyright. ▼

DO NOT WRITE HERE   OFFICE USE ONLY

APPLICATION RECEIVED

ONE DEPOSIT RECEIVED

TWO DEPOSITS RECEIVED

FUNDS RECEIVED

MORE ON BACK ▶   • Complete all applicable spaces (numbers 5-9) on the reverse side of this page.
• See detailed instructions.   • Sign the form at line 8.

DO NOT WRITE HERE

Page 1 of _____ pages

EXAMINED BY

CHECKED BY

CORRESPONDENCE
❏ Yes

FORM SR

FOR
COPYRIGHT
OFFICE
USE
ONLY

DO NOT WRITE ABOVE THIS LINE. IF YOU NEED MORE SPACE, USE A SEPARATE CONTINUATION SHEET.

PREVIOUS REGISTRATION Has registration for this work, or for an earlier version of this work, already been made in the Copyright Office?

❏ **Yes** ❏ **No** If your answer is "Yes," why is another registration being sought? (Check appropriate box) ▼

a. ❏ This work was previously registered in unpublished form and now has been published for the first time.

b. ❏ This is the first application submitted by this author as copyright claimant.

c. ❏ This is a changed version of the work, as shown by space 6 on this application.

If your answer is "Yes," give: **Previous Registration Number** ▼   **Year of Registration** ▼

5

DERIVATIVE WORK OR COMPILATION

Preexisting Material Identify any preexisting work or works that this work is based on or incorporates. ▼

a

Material Added to This Work Give a brief, general statement of the material that has been added to this work and in which copyright is claimed. ▼

b

6

See instructions
before completing
this space.

DEPOSIT ACCOUNT If the registration fee is to be charged to a deposit account established in the Copyright Office, give name and number of Account.

   Name ▼   **Account Number** ▼

a

CORRESPONDENCE Give name and address to which correspondence about this application should be sent. Name/Address/Apt/City/State/Zip ▼

b

Area code and daytime telephone number   Fax number
Email

7

CERTIFICATION* I, the undersigned, hereby certify that I am the

Check only one ▼

❏ author   ❏ owner of exclusive right(s)

❏ other copyright claimant   ❏ authorized agent of _____
                              Name of author or other copyright claimant, or owner of exclusive right(s) ▲

of the work identified in this application and that the statements made by me in this application are correct to the best of my knowledge.

Typed or printed name and date ▼ If this application gives a date of publication in space 3, do not sign and submit it before that date.

                                                              Date _____

Handwritten signature ▼

_____

8

Certificate
will be
mailed in
window
envelope
to this
address

Name ▼

Number/Street/Apt ▼

City/State/Zip ▼

YOU MUST:
· Complete all necessary spaces
· Sign your application in space 8
**SEND ALL 3 ELEMENTS
IN THE SAME PACKAGE:**
1. Application form
2. Nonrefundable filing fee in check or money
   order payable to *Register of Copyrights*
3. Deposit material
MAIL TO:
Library of Congress
Copyright Office
101 Independence Avenue SE
Washington, DC 20559-6000

9

*17 USC §506(e): Any person who knowingly makes a false representation of a material fact in the application for copyright registration provided for by section 409, or in any written statement filed in connection with the application, shall be fined not more than $2,500.

Form SR-Full   Rev: 11/2006   Print: 11/2006—60,000   Printed on recycled paper   U.S. Government Printing Office: 2007-330-945/60,138

Form PA

Detach and read these instructions before completing this form.
Make sure all applicable spaces have been filled in before you return this form.

BASIC INFORMATION

When to Use This Form: Use Form PA for registration of published or unpublished works of the performing arts. This class includes works prepared for the purpose of being "performed" directly before an audience or indirectly "by means of any device or process." Works of the performing arts include: (1) musical works, including any accompanying words; (2) dramatic works, including any accompanying music; (3) pantomimes and choreographic works; and (4) motion pictures and other audiovisual works.

Deposit to Accompany Application: An application for copyright registration must be accompanied by a deposit consisting of copies or phonorecords representing the entire work for which registration is made. The following are the general deposit requirements as set forth in the statute:

Unpublished Work: Deposit one complete copy (or phonorecord).

Published Work: Deposit two complete copies (or one phonorecord) of the best edition.

Work First Published Outside the United States: Deposit one complete copy (or phonorecord) of the first foreign edition.

Contribution to a Collective Work: Deposit one complete copy (or phonorecord) of the best edition of the collective work.

Motion Pictures: Deposit *both* of the following: (1) a separate written description of the contents of the motion picture; and (2) for a published work, one complete copy of the best edition of the motion picture; or, for an unpublished work, one complete copy of the motion picture or identifying material. Identifying material may be either an audiorecording of

the entire soundtrack or one frame enlargement or similar visual print from each 10-minute segment.

The Copyright Notice: Before March 1, 1989, the use of copyright notice was mandatory on all published works, and any work first published before that date should have carried a notice. For works first published on and after March 1, 1989, use of the copyright notice is optional. For more information about copyright notice, see Circular 3, *Copyright Notice.*

For Further Information: To speak to a Copyright Office staff member, call (202) 707-3000 (TTY: (202) 707-6737). Recorded information is available 24 hours a day. Order forms and other publications from the address in space 9 or call the Forms and Publications Hotline at (202) 707-9100. Access and download circulars, forms, and other information from the Copyright Office website at *www.copyright.gov.*

LINE-BY-LINE INSTRUCTIONS

Please type or print using black ink. The form is used to produce the certificate.

1 SPACE 1: Title

Title of This Work: Every work submitted for copyright registration must be given a title to identify that particular work. If the copies or phonorecords of the work bear a title (or an identifying phrase that could serve as a title), transcribe that wording *completely* and *exactly* on the application. Indexing of the registration and future identification of the work will depend on the information you give here. If the work you are registering is an entire "collective work" (such as a collection of plays or songs), give the overall title of the collection. If you are registering one or more individual contributions to a collective work, give the title of each contribution, followed by the title of the collection. For an unpublished collection, you may give the titles of the individual works after the collection title.

Previous or Alternative Titles: Complete this space if there are any additional titles for the work under which someone searching for the registration might be likely to look, or under which a document pertaining to the work might be recorded.

Nature of This Work: Briefly describe the general nature or character of the work being registered for copyright. Examples: "Music"; "Song Lyrics"; "Words and Music"; "Drama"; "Musical Play"; "Choreography"; "Pantomime"; "Motion Picture"; "Audiovisual Work."

2 SPACE 2: Author(s)

General Instructions: After reading these instructions, decide who are the "authors" of this work for copyright purposes. Then, unless the work is a "collective work," give the requested information about every "author" who contributed any appreciable amount of copyrightable matter to this version of the work. If you need further space, request additional Continuation Sheets. In the case of a collective work such as a songbook or a collection of plays, give information about the author of the collective work as a whole.

Name of Author: The fullest form of the author's name should be given. Unless the work was "made for hire," the individual who actually created the work is its "author." In the case of a work made for hire, the statute provides that "the employer or other person for whom the work was prepared is considered the author."

What Is a "Work Made for Hire"? A "work made for hire" is defined as: (1) "a work prepared by an employee within the scope of his or her employment"; or (2) "a work specially ordered or commissioned for use as a contribution to a collective work, as a part of a motion picture or other audiovisual work, as a translation, as a supplementary work, as a compilation, as an instructional text, as a test, as answer material for a test, or as an atlas, if the parties expressly agree in a written instrument signed by them that the work shall be considered a work made for hire." If you have checked "Yes" to indicate that the work was "made for hire," you must give the full legal name of the employer (or other person for whom the work was prepared). You may also include the name of the employee along with the name of the employer (for example: "Elster Music Co., employer for hire of John Ferguson").

"Anonymous" or "Pseudonymous" Work: An author's contribution to a work is "anonymous" if that author is not identified on the copies or phonorecords of the work. An author's contribution to a work is "pseudonymous" if that author is identified on the copies or phonorecords under a fictitious name. If the work is "anonymous" you may: (1) leave the line blank; or (2) state "anonymous" on the line; or (3) reveal the author's identity. If the work is "pseudonymous" you may: (1) leave the line blank; or (2) give the pseudonym and identify it as such (example: "Huntley Haverstock, pseudonym"); or (3) reveal the author's name, making clear which is the real name and which is the pseudonym (for example: "Judith Barton, whose pseudonym is Madeline Elster"). However, the citizenship or domicile of the author *must* be given in all cases.

Dates of Birth and Death: If the author is dead, the statute requires that the year of death be included in the application unless the work is anonymous or pseudonymous. The author's birth date is optional, but is useful as a form of identification. Leave this space blank if the author's contribution was a "work made for hire."

Author's Nationality or Domicile: Give the country of which the author is a citizen, or the country in which the author is domiciled. Nationality or domicile *must* be given in all cases.

Nature of Authorship: Give a brief general statement of the nature of this particular author's contribution to the work. Examples: "Words"; "Coauthor of Music"; "Words and Music"; "Arrangement"; "Coauthor of Book and Lyrics"; "Dramatization"; "Screen Play"; "Compilation and English Translation"; "Editorial Revisions."

SPACE 3: Creation and Publication

General Instructions: Do not confuse "creation" with "publication." Every application for copyright registration must state "the year in which creation of the work was completed." Give the date and nation of first publication only if the work has been published.

Creation: Under the statute, a work is "created" when it is fixed in a copy or phonorecord for the first time. Where a work has been prepared over a period of time, the part of the work existing in fixed form on a particular date constitutes the created work on that date. The date you give here should be the year in which the author completed the particular version for which registration is now being sought, even if other versions exist or if further changes or additions are planned.

Publication: The statute defines "publication" as "the distribution of copies or phonorecords of a work to the public by sale or other transfer of ownership, or by rental, lease, or lending"; a work is also "published" if there has been an "offering to distribute copies or phonorecords to a group of persons for purposes of further distribution, public performance, or public display." Give the full date (month, day, year) when, and the country where, publication first occurred. If first publication took place simultaneously in the United States and other countries, it is sufficient to state "U.S.A."

SPACE 4: Claimant(s)

Name(s) and Address(es) of Copyright Claimant(s): Give the name(s) and address(es) of the copyright claimant(s) in this work even if the claimant is the same as the author. Copyright in a work belongs initially to the author of the work (including, in the case of a work made for hire, the employer or other person for whom the work was prepared). The copyright claimant is either the author of the work or a person or organization to whom the copyright initially belonging to the author has been transferred.

Transfer: The statute provides that, if the copyright claimant is not the author, the application for registration must contain "a brief statement of how the claimant obtained ownership of the copyright." If any copyright claimant named in space 4 is not an author named in space 2, give a brief statement explaining how the claimant(s) obtained ownership of the copyright. Examples: "By written contract"; "Transfer of all rights by author"; "Assignment"; "By will." Do not attach transfer documents or other attachments or riders.

SPACE 5: Previous Registration

General Instructions: The questions in space 5 are intended to show whether an earlier registration has been made for this work and, if so, whether there is any basis for a new registration. As a general rule, only one basic copyright registration can be made for the same version of a particular work.

Same Version: If this version is substantially the same as the work covered by a previous registration, a second registration is not generally possible unless: (1) the work has been registered in unpublished form and a second registration is now being sought to cover this first published edition; or (2) someone other than the author is identified as copyright claimant in the earlier registration, and the author is now seeking registration in his or her own name. If either of these two exceptions applies, check the appropriate box and give the earlier registration number and date. Otherwise, do not submit Form PA; instead, write the Copyright Office

for information about supplementary registration or recordation of transfers of copyright ownership.

Changed Version: If the work has been changed and you are now seeking registration to cover the additions or revisions, check the last box in space 5, give the earlier registration number and date, and complete both parts of space 6 in accordance with the instructions below.

Previous Registration Number and Date: If more than one previous registration has been made for the work, give the number and date of the latest registration.

SPACE 6: Derivative Work or Compilation

General Instructions: Complete space 6 if this work is a "changed version," "compilation," or "derivative work," and if it incorporates one or more earlier works that have already been published or registered for copyright or that have fallen into the public domain. A "compilation" is defined as "a work formed by the collection and assembling of preexisting materials or of data that are selected, coordinated, or arranged in such a way that the resulting work as a whole constitutes an original work of authorship." A "derivative work" is "a work based on one or more preexisting works." Examples of derivative works include musical arrangements, dramatizations, translations, abridgments, condensations, motion picture versions, or "any other form in which a work may be recast, transformed, or adapted." Derivative works also include works "consisting of editorial revisions, annotations, or other modifications" if these changes, as a whole, represent an original work of authorship.

Preexisting Material (space 6a): Complete this space *and* space 6b for derivative works. In this space identify the preexisting work that has been recast, transformed, or adapted. For example, the preexisting material might be: "French version of Hugo's 'Le Roi s'amuse'." Do not complete this space for compilations.

Material Added to This Work (space 6b): Give a brief, general statement of the *additional* new material covered by the copyright claim for which registration is sought. In the case of a derivative work, identify this new material. Examples: "Arrangement for piano and orchestra"; "Dramatization for television"; "New film version"; "Revisions throughout; Act III completely new." If the work is a compilation, give a brief, general statement describing both the material that has been compiled *and* the compilation itself. Example: "Compilation of 19th Century Military Songs."

SPACE 7, 8, 9: Fee, Correspondence, Certification, Return Address

Deposit Account: If you maintain a Deposit Account in the Copyright Office, identify it in space 7a. Otherwise, leave the space blank and send the fee with your application and deposit.

Correspondence (space 7b): Give the name, address, area code, telephone number, fax number, and email address (if available) of the person to be consulted if correspondence about this application becomes necessary.

Certification (space 8): The application cannot be accepted unless it bears the date and the **handwritten signature** of the author or other copyright claimant, or of the owner of exclusive right(s), or of the duly authorized agent of the author, claimant, or owner of exclusive right(s).

Address for Return of Certificate (space 9): The address box must be completed legibly since the certificate will be returned in a window envelope.

MORE INFORMATION

How to Register a Recorded Work: If the musical or dramatic work that you are registering has been recorded (as a tape, disk, or cassette), you may choose either copyright application Form PA (Performing Arts) or Form SR (Sound Recordings), depending on the purpose of the registration.

Use Form PA to register the underlying musical composition or dramatic work. Form SR has been developed specifically to register a "sound recording" as defined by the Copyright Act—a work resulting from the "fixation of a series of sounds," separate and distinct from the underlying musical or dramatic work. Form SR should be used when the copyright claim is limited to the sound recording itself. (In one instance, Form SR may also be used to file for a copyright registration for both kinds of works—see (4) below.) Therefore:

(1) File Form PA if you are seeking to register the musical or dramatic work, not the "sound recording," even though what you deposit for copyright purposes may be in the form of a phonorecord.

(2) File Form PA if you are seeking to register the audio portion of an audiovisual work, such as a motion picture soundtrack; these are considered integral parts of the audiovisual work.

(3) File Form SR if you are seeking to register the "sound recording" itself, that is, the work that results from the fixation of a series of musical, spoken, or other sounds, but not the underlying musical or dramatic work.

(4) File Form SR if you are the copyright claimant for both the underlying musical or dramatic work and the sound recording, *and* you prefer to register both on the same form.

(5) File both forms PA and SR if the copyright claimant for the underlying work and sound recording differ, or you prefer to have separate registration for them.

"Copies" and "Phonorecords": To register for copyright, you are required to deposit "copies" or "phonorecords." These are defined as follows:

Musical compositions may be embodied (fixed) in "copies," objects from which a work can be read or visually perceived, directly or with the aid of a machine or device, such as manuscripts, books, sheet music, film, and videotape. They may also be fixed in "phonorecords," objects embodying fixations of sounds, such as tapes and phonograph disks, commonly known as phonograph records. For example, a song (the work to be registered) can be reproduced in sheet music ("copies") or phonograph records ("phonorecords"), or both.

Form PA
For a Work of Performing Arts
UNITED STATES COPYRIGHT OFFICE

REGISTRATION NUMBER

PA   PAU
EFFECTIVE DATE OF REGISTRATION

_____
Month   Day   Year

DO NOT WRITE ABOVE THIS LINE. IF YOU NEED MORE SPACE, USE A SEPARATE CONTINUATION SHEET.

1

TITLE OF THIS WORK ▼

PREVIOUS OR ALTERNATIVE TITLES ▼

NATURE OF THIS WORK ▼ See instructions

2

a

NAME OF AUTHOR ▼

DATES OF BIRTH AND DEATH
Year Born ▼   Year Died ▼

Was this contribution to the work a "work made for hire"?
☐ Yes
☐ No

AUTHOR'S NATIONALITY OR DOMICILE
Name of Country
OR { Citizen of _____
     Domiciled in _____

WAS THIS AUTHOR'S CONTRIBUTION TO THE WORK
Anonymous?   ☐ Yes ☐ No
Pseudonymous?   ☐ Yes ☐ No

If the answer to either of these questions is "Yes," see detailed instructions.

NATURE OF AUTHORSHIP   Briefly describe nature of material created by this author in which copyright is claimed. ▼

NOTE

Under the law, the "author" of a "work made for hire" is generally the employer, not the employee (see instructions). For any part of this work that was "made for hire" check "Yes" in the space provided, give the employer (or other person for whom the work was prepared) as "Author" of that part, and leave the space for dates of birth and death blank.

b

NAME OF AUTHOR ▼

DATES OF BIRTH AND DEATH
Year Born ▼   Year Died ▼

Was this contribution to the work a "work made for hire"?
☐ Yes
☐ No

AUTHOR'S NATIONALITY OR DOMICILE
Name of Country
OR { Citizen of _____
     Domiciled in _____

WAS THIS AUTHOR'S CONTRIBUTION TO THE WORK
Anonymous?   ☐ Yes ☐ No
Pseudonymous?   ☐ Yes ☐ No

If the answer to either of these questions is "Yes," see detailed instructions.

NATURE OF AUTHORSHIP   Briefly describe nature of material created by this author in which copyright is claimed. ▼

c

NAME OF AUTHOR ▼

DATES OF BIRTH AND DEATH
Year Born ▼   Year Died ▼

Was this contribution to the work a "work made for hire"?
☐ Yes
☐ No

AUTHOR'S NATIONALITY OR DOMICILE
Name of Country
OR { Citizen of _____
     Domiciled in _____

WAS THIS AUTHOR'S CONTRIBUTION TO THE WORK
Anonymous?   ☐ Yes ☐ No
Pseudonymous?   ☐ Yes ☐ No

If the answer to either of these questions is "Yes," see detailed instructions.

NATURE OF AUTHORSHIP   Briefly describe nature of material created by this author in which copyright is claimed. ▼

3

a

YEAR IN WHICH CREATION OF THIS WORK WAS COMPLETED   This information must be given
_____ Year   in all cases.

b

DATE AND NATION OF FIRST PUBLICATION OF THIS PARTICULAR WORK
Complete this information ONLY if this work has been published.
Month _____ Day _____ Year _____
_____ Nation

4

See instructions before completing this space.

COPYRIGHT CLAIMANT(S) Name and address must be given even if the claimant is the same as the author given in space 2. ▼

TRANSFER If the claimant(s) named here in space 4 is (are) different from the author(s) named in space 2, give a brief statement of how the claimant(s) obtained ownership of the copyright. ▼

APPLICATION RECEIVED

ONE DEPOSIT RECEIVED

TWO DEPOSITS RECEIVED

FUNDS RECEIVED

DO NOT WRITE HERE
OFFICE USE ONLY

MORE ON BACK ▶   • Complete all applicable spaces (numbers 5-9) on the reverse side of this page.
• See detailed instructions.   • Sign the form at line 8.

DO NOT WRITE HERE
Page 1 of _____ pages

EXAMINED BY _____

CHECKED BY _____

☐ CORRESPONDENCE
   Yes

FORM PA

FOR
COPYRIGHT
OFFICE
USE
ONLY

DO NOT WRITE ABOVE THIS LINE. IF YOU NEED MORE SPACE, USE A SEPARATE CONTINUATION SHEET.

PREVIOUS REGISTRATION Has registration for this work, or for an earlier version of this work, already been made in the Copyright Office?

☐ **Yes** ☐ **No** If your answer is "Yes," why is another registration being sought? (Check appropriate box.) ▼ If your answer is No, do **not** check box A, B, or C.

a. ☐ This is the first published edition of a work previously registered in unpublished form.

b. ☐ This is the first application submitted by this author as copyright claimant.

c. ☐ This is a changed version of the work, as shown by space 6 on this application.

If your answer is "Yes," give: **Previous Registration Number** ▼   **Year of Registration** ▼

5

DERIVATIVE WORK OR COMPILATION Complete both space 6a and 6b for a derivative work; complete only 6b for a compilation.
Preexisting Material Identify any preexisting work or works that this work is based on or incorporates. ▼

a **6**

Material Added to This Work Give a brief, general statement of the material that has been added to this work and in which copyright is claimed. ▼

b

See instructions
before completing
this space.

DEPOSIT ACCOUNT If the registration fee is to be charged to a Deposit Account established in the Copyright Office, give name and number of Account.
Name ▼   **Account Number** ▼

a **7**

CORRESPONDENCE Give name and address to which correspondence about this application should be sent. Name/Address/Apt/City/State/Zip▼

b

Area code and daytime telephone number   (   )   Fax number   (   )
Email

CERTIFICATION* I, the undersigned, hereby certify that I am the

Check only one ▶ {

☐ author
☐ other copyright claimant
☐ owner of exclusive right(s)
☐ authorized agent of _____

Name of author or other copyright claimant, or owner of exclusive right(s) ▲

of the work identified in this application and that the statements made by me in this application are correct to the best of my knowledge.

8

Typed or printed name and date ▼ If this application gives a date of publication in space 3, do not sign and submit it before that date.

                                       Date _____

Handwritten signature (X) ▼

☞   x _____

**Certificate
will be
mailed in
window
envelope
to this
address:**

Name ▼

Number/Street/Apt ▼

City/State/Zip ▼

YOU MUST:
• Complete all necessary spaces
• Sign your application in space 8

**SEND ALL 3 ELEMENTS
IN THE SAME PACKAGE:**
1. Application form
2. Nonrefundable filing fee in check or money
order payable to *Register of Copyrights*
3. Deposit material

MAIL TO:
Library of Congress
Copyright Office
101 Independence Avenue SE
Washington, DC 20559-6000

9

*17 *USC* §506(e): Any person who knowingly makes a false representation of a material fact in the application for copyright registration provided for by section 409, or in any written statement filed in connection with the application, shall be fined not more than $2,500.

Form PA – Full Rev: 07/2006 Print: 07/2006 — xx,000 Printed on recycled paper   U.S. Government Printing Office: 2006-xxx-xxx/60,xxx

BMI-03	
Account #	_____
License Type	_____

Radio Station
Blanket/Per Program License Agreement

AGREEMENT, made between BROADCAST MUSIC, INC., a corporation organized under the laws of the State of New York with principal offices at 320 West 57th Street, New York, N.Y. 10019 ("BMI") and

Call Letters   FCC Community
and Band _____ Freq. _____ of License _____
                                                              (city)   (state)

_____
                              (Legal Name of LICENSEE)

Please Check Appropriate Box and Complete

☐ A corporation organized under the laws of the State of _____

☐ A limited liability company organized under the laws of the State of _____

☐ A partnership consisting of _____

☐ An individual residing at _____

_____

(hereinafter "You" or "LICENSEE") licensing the radio broadcasting station ("Station") presently receiving mail at:

_____
                              (Street Address or P.O. Box)
                                                                        (   )
_____
(City)   (State)   (Zip Code)   (Telephone Number)

Location of Station: ☐ *Check box if same as above.*

_____
                              (Street Address)

_____
(City)   (State)   (Zip Code)

email address: _____

with the Radio Station Web Site URL: http:// _____

1.   Term.

The term of this Agreement commences as of January 1, 2001, and ends on December 31, 2006, unless earlier terminated as hereinafter provided.

2. Definitions.

A. **"Background for an announcement"** shall mean mood, atmosphere or thematic music performed as background to an otherwise non-musical commercial, public service, or station promotional announcement not exceeding sixty (60) seconds in length.

B. **"BMI Repertoire"** shall mean musical works for which BMI may own or control the right to grant public performing right licenses at the time of Station's performance.

C. **"Incidental Use"** shall mean music used as themes or signatures; bridges, cue or background music aggregating less than two and one-half minutes in duration in any fifteen minute programming period; public domain music in arrangements controlled by BMI on which BMI pays no royalties; and music which is used only incidentally to the broadcast of a news event or sports event.

D. **"Interim Radio Station Licenses"** shall mean the 1992 BMI Single Station Radio Blanket License and the 1992 BMI Single Station Radio Per Program License.

E. **"Jingle"** shall mean an advertising, promotional or public service announcement containing musical material (with or without lyrics) where the musical material was originally written for advertising, promotional or public service announcement purposes, or a musical work originally written for other purposes, with the lyrics changed for advertising, promotional or public service announcement purposes, not exceeding sixty (60) seconds in length and used with the permission of the interested writer or publisher affiliated with BMI.

F. **"Local Management Agreement"** shall mean any agreement under which any other entity becomes a Local Manager in regard to Station.

G. **"Local Manager"** shall mean any entity not under common ownership or control of LICENSEE which is authorized to resell 10% or more of Station's air time and (1) simulcasts or sells announcements on Station in combination with a radio station owned or operated by the entity, which station has entered into a BMI Radio Station License Agreement; or (2) has assumed, contractually or otherwise, responsibility for the management of Station.

H. **"Programming period"** shall mean a fifteen (15) minute period of broadcasting commencing on the hour and at fifteen (15), thirty (30), and forty-five (45) minutes past the hour without regard to whether such period contains one or more programs or announcements.

I. **"Radio broadcasting"** shall mean audio "over-the-air" broadcasting in all of its forms, excluding: (1) transmission or retransmission of an over-the-air broadcast signal on the Internet and (2) FCC-licensed commercial low power audio broadcasting, with similar technical characteristics and requirements as currently defined in 47 C.F.R. Section 73.801 et seq. Radio Broadcasting shall include, on an experimental basis, simultaneous transmission of an FCC-licensed digital broadcast signal identical in content to the Radio Station Signal licensed hereunder.

J. **"Radio Station Signal"** shall mean Station's FCC-licensed over-the-air radio broadcast transmission.

K. **"Radio Station Web Site"** shall mean LICENSEE's Internet computer service comprising a series of interrelated web pages which is registered with a domain name registration service and which LICENSEE makes available to consumers over the Internet.

L. **"Territory"** shall mean the U.S. Territory and the territories represented by non-U.S. performing right licensing organizations as posted in the licensing section of the BMI web site located at http://www.bmi.com (as may be amended by BMI at any time and without notice).

M. **"U.S. Territory"** shall mean the United States, its Commonwealth, territories and possessions.

2

3.   BMI Grant.

A.   <u>Over-the-Air-Signal</u>. BMI grants to LICENSEE for the Term a non-exclusive license to publicly perform in the U.S. Territory, by radio broadcasting on Station, non-dramatic performances of all musical works in the BMI Repertoire during the Term.

B.   <u>Internet Streaming</u>. BMI grants to LICENSEE for the Term a non-exclusive license to publicly perform all musical works in the BMI Repertoire during the Term by simultaneously streaming the Radio Station Signal over the Internet in the Territory from the Radio Station Web Site without alteration (except for advertising); provided, however, that the territorial scope of the grant of rights is limited to public performances within the U.S. Territory with respect to any musical works that are affiliated with BMI through a non-U.S. performing right licensing organization which is not one of the organizations listed on BMI's web site as Exhibit C to BMI's web site license as such list may be changed from time to time. The organizations listed on BMI's web site are available through a link on www.bmi.com/rmlclicense.asp. LICENSEE shall promptly notify BMI in writing upon making its Radio Station Signal available on its Radio Station Web Site, and upon discontinuing such service.

C.   The rights granted in this Agreement shall not include the right to perform more than thirty (30) minutes of a full-length dramatic or dramatico-musical work (or a substantial part of a short dramatic or dramatico-musical work) such as an opera, operetta, musical show or ballet, but this exclusion shall not apply to such performances from (1) a score originally written for and performed as part of a radio program, or (2) the original cast, soundtrack or similar album of a dramatic or dramatico-musical work other than an opera.

D.   The performances licensed hereunder may originate at any place, whether or not such place is licensed to publicly perform the musical works licensed hereunder, and regardless of the manner, means or methods of such origination. Nothing in this Agreement shall be deemed to grant a license to anyone authorizing any public performance in such other place of any such composition.

E.   Nothing herein shall be construed as authorizing LICENSEE to grant to others, including but not limited to, any cable system, satellite carrier (including MMDS or similar wireless services), online services or ISP the right to retransmit to the public or publicly perform by any means, method or process whatsoever, any of the musical compositions licensed hereunder, or as authorizing any receiver of any radio broadcast to publicly perform or reproduce the same by any means, method or process whatsoever.

F.   This Agreement licenses the transmission of the Radio Station Signal by streaming over the Internet *only* where consumers access such transmission from a page on the Radio Station Web Site and receive such transmission by means of a personal computer or other device capable of receiving such transmissions. This Agreement does not cover the transmission of the Radio Station Signal by streaming over the Internet where consumers access such transmission directly (as opposed to through a hyperlink to the Station's Web Site) from a page on a third party web site, or any uses of music on the Radio Station Web Site other than as part of the Radio Station Signal; such other uses shall be subject to appropriate separate licensing.

G.   This Agreement does not cover transmissions of the Radio Station Signal where consumers are charged a fee for the right to access such transmissions, or extend to uses of the Radio Station Signal where the Radio Station Web Site is packaged or included on a tier of services for additional consideration, or where Radio Station Signal is offered for resale as a pay or premium audio service either independently or with other web sites or otherwise used by any third party as background audio. Such uses are subject to appropriate separate licensing.

4.   License Fee; Minimum Fee; Taxes.

A.   LICENSEE agrees that Station will pay fees annually to BMI hereunder in accordance with the agreement between BMI and the Radio Music License Committee ("COMMITTEE") that is attached as Exhibit A to this Agreement, the terms of which are incorporated herein by reference (the "BMI/COMMITTEE Agreement"). LICENSEE specifically agrees that Station will pay its share of the industry-wide fees for each year from 2003 through 2006 allocated to Station by the COMMITTEE under that agreement and in accordance with Exhibits B and C attached hereto.

3

BMI-03

B.   For each month during the Term hereof commencing January 1, 2003, LICENSEE shall, on or before the first day of the following month, pay to BMI a sum equal to one twelfth of the annual fee payable by Station to BMI hereunder for that year as determined by the COMMITTEE pursuant to the allocation formula in the BMI/COMMITTEE Agreement.

C.   For all periods through December 31, 2002, if Station was licensed under an interim BMI Single Station Radio Blanket or Per Program License, the license fees due and payable and all the additional terms and conditions therein shall be applicable hereunder for such periods, as provided in the BMI/COMMITTEE Agreement, and Station shall submit its Annual Statement (or Annual Financial Report) for 2002 and all other periods. The Interim Radio Station Licenses are incorporated by reference for all licensees whose licenses commenced prior to December 31, 2002. The Interim Radio Station Licenses will be available at BMI.com at www.bmi.com/rmlclicense.asp.

D.   For the period commencing January 1, 2004, if Station elects a per program license, then Station must provide the music use reports required by paragraph 12 below.

E.   In the event that the payment of any license fee to BMI by LICENSEE pursuant to this Agreement causes BMI to become liable to pay any state or local tax which is based upon the license fees received by BMI from licensees, the LICENSEE agrees to pay BMI the full amount of such tax together with LICENSEE's fee payment(s) as invoiced by BMI, within normal payment terms; provided, however, that BMI is permitted by law to pass through such tax to LICENSEE; and provided further that LICENSEE and BMI will cooperate in making reasonable efforts to seek to be exempt from the tax.

F.   BMI may impose a late payment charge of 1% per month from the date the payment was due on any monthly payment that is received by BMI after the date payment was due.

5.   Annual Statements of Gross Revenue.

A.   For each calendar year, starting with 2003, if Station is required to submit an annual financial statement to ASCAP, Station shall submit a copy of said annual financial statement to BMI. If Station is not required to submit an annual financial statement to ASCAP, then for each calendar year of the term of this Agreement, Station shall submit, on or before April 1st, a statement of Station's annual gross revenues for broadcasting for the preceding calendar year on a form to be provided by BMI similar to the revenue range table attached hereto as Exhibit D. Station's annual gross revenues shall include Station's top line gross revenue charged to or on behalf of sponsors and donors, including net promotional revenues as defined in paragraph 1(b) of the BMI/COMMITTEE Agreement. Station's statement of annual gross revenues shall be signed by an employee of Station with financial responsibilities who is authorized by LICENSEE to submit such statement to BMI hereunder.

B.   For each calendar year, starting with 2003, LICENSEE shall submit on or before April 1st of the subsequent calendar year, a statement of Station's Annual Gross Revenues for streaming on a form to be provided by BMI similar to the revenue range table in Exhibit E;

C.   In the event that LICENSEE owns or controls one or more stations that are licensed by BMI under separate BMI license agreements, and LICENSEE's Annual Gross Revenues are derived from any source, either in whole or in part, as the result of offerings of the stations' broadcast facilities in combination, LICENSEE shall make an allocation on a reasonable basis of the *combined* Gross Revenues when filing Annual Gross Revenue Statements for each station as required by the BMI-03 Radio Station Blanket/Per Program License Agreement.

D.   In the event that LICENSEE shall fail to submit the revenue statement required in subparagraph A, BMI may bill, commencing with May billing, and LICENSEE shall pay, in addition to any fees otherwise owed, a late fee equal to 24% of Station's monthly blanket or per program license fee (the "Late Report Fee"). This Late Report Fee shall be fully refundable to Station, but only if BMI receives the Annual Financial Reports on or before December 31st of the calendar year in which report was due. Any late report fees retained by BMI shall be in addition to Station's otherwise allocated annual license fees.

4

6.   Licensee Breach.

In the event that LICENSEE shall fail to make payment or render any report under this Agreement, when and as due, BMI may give LICENSEE thirty (30) days notice in writing to cure such breach or default. In the event that such breach or default has not been cured within thirty (30) days of said notice, BMI may cancel this Agreement. The right to cancel shall be in addition to any and all other remedies which BMI may have in law or equity.

7.   Blanket/Per Program License Changes.

A.   If LICENSEE is operating under a blanket license as set forth in this Agreement, LICENSEE may, as of the first day of January or July during any calendar year commencing January 1, 2004, upon not less than sixty (60) days prior written notice to BMI using a form supplied by BMI, a copy of which is to be forwarded to the COMMITTEE by Station, elect to be licensed under a per program license as set forth in this Agreement; provided that Station has changed formats from a music to a non-music format and LICENSEE is current in all blanket license payments and reports required hereunder as of the effective date of LICENSEE's election.

B.   If LICENSEE is operating under a per program license as set forth in this Agreement, LICENSEE must provide BMI with not less than sixty (60) days prior written notice to BMI of the event that Station has changed formats from a non-music to a music format and LICENSEE shall be deemed to have elected a blanket license hereunder as of the next ensuing January 1 or July 1 following the proper notice.

C.   If LICENSEE is operating under a per program license as set forth in this Agreement, LICENSEE may, as of the first day of January or July, during any calendar year commencing January 1, 2004, upon not less than sixty (60) days prior written notice to BMI using a form to be supplied by BMI, a copy of which is to be forwarded to the COMMITTEE by Station, elect to be licensed under a blanket license as set forth in this Agreement, provided that LICENSEE is current in all per program license fees and reports due hereunder.

8.   Indemnification.

BMI agrees to indemnify, save and hold harmless and defend LICENSEE, its advertisers and their advertising agencies, and its and their officers, employees and artists, from and against all claims, demands and suits that may be made or brought against them or any of them with respect to the performance under this Agreement of any material licensed hereunder; provided that this indemnity shall not apply to broadcasts of any musical work performed by LICENSEE after written request from BMI to LICENSEE that LICENSEE refrain from performance thereof. LICENSEE agrees to give BMI immediate notice of any such claim, demand or suit, and agrees immediately to deliver to BMI all papers pertaining thereto. BMI shall have full charge of the defense of any such claim, demand or suit, and LICENSEE shall cooperate fully with BMI therein. Notwithstanding the territorial scope of the license granted herein, BMI's obligation to indemnify LICENSEE for Internet streaming transmissions shall be limited to those claims, demands or suits that are made or brought within the U.S. Territory.

9.   Local Management Agreement.

A.   In the event LICENSEE enters into a Local Management Agreement as defined in Paragraph 2.F. hereof, within thirty (30) days of such agreement (1) LICENSEE shall provide BMI with a copy of such agreement and (2) Local Manager shall execute this Agreement in the signature space provided below. By signing this Agreement Local Manager becomes a party to this License Agreement and shall assume, with LICENSEE, all of the rights and obligations set forth in this Agreement for the full period the Local Management Agreement is in effect.

B.   In the event LICENSEE becomes a Local Manager by entering into a Local Management Agreement with another station, LICENSEE shall notify BMI within thirty (30) days of entering into the agreement.

C.   In the event that LICENSEE and/or Local Manager do not provide to BMI, on a timely basis, the documentation required by Paragraph 9.A., this License Agreement may be terminated by BMI on ten (10) days written notice.

5

BMI-03

D.   In the event that the Local Management Agreement provided to BMI terminates prior to its stated termination date, LICENSEE and Local Manager shall immediately notify BMI of such termination.

10.   Assignment.

This Agreement shall be non-assignable except to the person, firm or corporation acquiring the Federal Communications Commission license of Station, and upon assignment to such person, firm, or corporation and upon acceptance in form approved by BMI of the application of LICENSEE hereunder, LICENSEE shall be relieved of future liability under this Agreement as long as all Annual Statements have been filed by LICENSEE and all fees due BMI under this Agreement have been paid to BMI. Any assignment contrary to this Paragraph shall be void. This Agreement shall enure to the benefit of and shall be binding upon the parties and their respective successors and assigns, but no assignment shall relieve the parties of their respective obligations under this Agreement.

11.   Arbitration.

A.   All disputes of any kind, nature or description arising in connection with the terms and conditions of this Agreement (except for those within the jurisdiction of the BMI rate court) shall be submitted to arbitration in the City, County and State of New York for arbitration under the then prevailing Commercial Arbitration Rules of the American Arbitration Association. The award made in the arbitration shall be binding and conclusive on the parties and judgment may be, but need not be, entered in any court having jurisdiction, including but not limited to the courts of New York State. Such award shall include the fixing of the costs, expenses and reasonable attorney's fees of arbitration, which shall be borne by the unsuccessful party.

B.   If, during the term of this Agreement, any dispute arises between BMI and LICENSEE concerning the interpretation of any of the provisions of this Agreement, the resolution of which, in the judgment of BMI or the COMMITTEE, either jointly or severally, has or may have industry-wide impact, BMI and the COMMITTEE shall first endeavor to resolve such dispute, failing which either party may refer the matter to arbitration (unless BMI and the COMMITTEE agree on some alternative mechanism for dispute resolution); and LICENSEE agrees to be bound by the resolution of all such arbitrations involving BMI and the COMMITTEE. In the event of such a reference, each party shall bear its own costs, expenses and attorney's fees. In the event of such a reference, either party, as a preliminary matter, shall be entitled to assert that the dispute between them is not properly dealt with under the terms of this subparagraph.

12.   Music Use Reports.

A.   **All Stations**. LICENSEE, upon written request from BMI made on not less than one (1) week's notice specifying the period to be covered, agrees to furnish to BMI (at BMI's request electronically via a secure web site) a report of LICENSEE's performances by Station of all musical works, indicating the compositions performed by title, writer/composer and artist, or by such other convenient method as may be designated by BMI, but such report need not be furnished for more than one (1) week of each year of the Term. If reasonably feasible for Station, in lieu of the one week report required above, BMI may require that LICENSEE transmit to BMI for each day that Station broadcasts/streams its signal, a complete report of its feature performances of musical works by electronic means. If Station simultaneously streams its broadcast signal, Station shall advise BMI on the aforesaid reports of those hours Station's broadcast signal was streamed.

B.   **Per Program License Stations**.

(1) For the calendar years 2004 though 2006, LICENSEE agrees to furnish to BMI and the COMMITTEE on thirty (30) days written notice a full, true, complete and accurate report, on forms furnished by BMI (at BMI's request electronically), for one week per calendar quarter (Quarterly Music Reports), which shall indicate, with respect to all programming during the week, regardless of origin, which have any musical content, the following: (a) the full title of each feature performance of a musical work; (b) the date and time of performance; and (c) the name(s) of the writer(s)/composer(s) and/or recording artist(s). BMI, or a representative of BMI, shall advise LICENSEE which week per quarter this will be done. A feature performance is defined as a performance of music other than music used as incidental use, "background for an announcement" or a "jingle" as defined in Paragraph 2 herein. The Quarterly Music Report shall be submitted with respect to all programming periods, even if no music was used (in which case only the requested identifying information need be completed along with the statement "No Music Used"), but shall not be

6

BMI-03

required to include the information set forth in this subparagraph for music in programming from a radio network licensed as a network by BMI, music in political programming and music in programming periods which LICENSEE concedes contain BMI music. Every programming period which contains music (other than a programming period in which the only music is Incidental Use or part of commercials) shall be listed on the report, even if the music falls into one of the exempt categories enumerated herein. In those cases, however, the category of exemption shall be indicated on the report form, listing the name of the network in the case of a network program.

(2)   Said report shall be due to BMI and the COMMITTEE on or before 30 days after the week to which the report pertains. For the calendar years 2004 though 2006, in the event that LICENSEE shall fail to submit any Quarterly Music Report or fail to report performances of musical compositions as required by Paragraph 12.B(1), the following shall apply:

(a)   *First Instance:* BMI shall advise LICENSEE in writing of same and will issue LICENSEE a warning.

(b)   *Second and all Subsequent Instances:* BMI shall advise LICENSEE in writing of same and LICENSEE shall pay BMI $500 + 5.75 times the per program fee for each of the prospective three months.

(c)   LICENSEE's failure to report timely or correctly may not be cured by LICENSEE's submission of a late report for said period.

(3)   For any quarter in which LICENSEE furnishes to BMI a complete electronic report of its feature performances of musical works for 24 hours a day, for each day, pursuant to paragraph 12.A., LICENSEE will not be required to submit Quarterly Music Reports.

13.   CONFIDENTIALITY

(a)   BMI shall treat as confidential, and shall not disclose to any third party (other than its employees, directors and officers and agents, in their capacity as such, on a need-to-know basis, and other than that as set forth in subparagraph (b) below), any financial or other proprietary documents or information provided to BMI by LICENSEE in connection with this Agreement; provided, however, that if BMI is served with a subpoena or other legal notice compelling the production of any such proprietary documents or information, BMI shall be obligated to give prompt written notice to LICENSEE of such subpoena or other notice. LICENSEE shall inform BMI in writing within seven (7) days of receiving written notification of a subpoena or other legal notice of its intention to object to such production, in which event LICENSEE shall bear the burden of opposing such production. If the subpoena requires a response or compliance in fewer than fourteen (14) days, BMI will inform LICENSEE in writing within three (3) days of receiving the subpoena and LICENSEE must inform BMI of its intention to oppose the production no later than five (5) days before compliance is called for.

(b)   BMI is hereby authorized to provide to COMMITTEE such of LICENSEE's financial information, provided to BMI pursuant to this Agreement, as COMMITTEE may request in connection with its representation of the local radio industry, unless LICENSEE notifies BMI in writing to the contrary. COMMITTEE has agreed to treat as confidential any financial information provided to it by BMI pursuant to this Paragraph.

MISCELLANEOUS

14.   In the event that the Federal Communications Commission revokes or fails to renew the broadcasting license of LICENSEE, or in the event that the governmental rules and regulations applicable to Station are suspended or amended so as to forbid the broadcasting of commercial programs by LICENSEE, LICENSEE may notify BMI thereof, and BMI within ten (10) days of the receipt of such notice shall, by written notice to LICENSEE, at BMI's option, either terminate or suspend this Agreement and all payments and services hereunder for the period that such condition continues. In the event that BMI elects to suspend this Agreement, such suspension shall not continue for longer than six (6) months, and this Agreement shall automatically terminate at the end of six (6) months' suspension. In the event that the condition giving rise to the suspension shall continue for less than six (6) months, BMI at its option, and on written notice to LICENSEE, may reinstate this Agreement at any time within thirty (30) days after the cessation of such condition.

7

15.   In the event that any law now or hereafter enacted of the state, or political subdivision thereof in which Station and/or LICENSEE is located shall result in major interference with BMI's operations or in the refusal of a substantial number of radio stations therein to enter into license agreements with BMI or to make payments to BMI, BMI shall have the right at any time to terminate this Agreement on no less than sixty (60) days written notice to LICENSEE.

16.   Any notice required or permitted to be given under this Agreement shall be in writing and shall be deemed duly given when sent by ordinary first-class U.S. mail to the party for whom it is intended, at its mailing address hereinabove stated, or any other address which either party hereto may from time to time designate for such purpose, and when such notice is so mailed, it shall be deemed given upon the mailing thereof. Any such notice sent to BMI shall be to the attention of the Media Licensing Department – Radio Licensing. Any such notice sent to LICENSEE shall be to the attention of the person signing this Agreement on behalf of LICENSEE or to the General Manager or Business Manager of Station.

17.   On written notice to LICENSEE, BMI may, effective with such notice, withdraw from the license granted hereunder any musical work as to which any legal action has been instituted or a claim made that BMI does not have the right to license the performing rights in such work or that such work infringes another composition.

18.   This Agreement constitutes the entire understanding between the parties, cannot be waived or added to or modified orally, and no waiver, addition or modification shall be valid unless in writing and signed by the parties. This Agreement, its validity, construction and effect shall be governed by the laws of the State of New York, without giving effect to its law of conflict of laws. The fact that any provisions herein are found to be void or unenforceable by a court of competent jurisdiction shall in no way affect the validity or enforceability of any other provisions. No waiver by BMI of full performance of this Agreement by LICENSEE in any one or more instances shall be deemed a waiver of the right to require full and complete performance of this Agreement thereafter or of the right to cancel this Agreement in accordance with the terms of this Agreement.

IN WITNESS WHEREOF, this Agreement, made at New York, New York, has been duly executed by BMI and LICENSEE on _____.
       (Month)   (Day)   (Year)

BROADCAST MUSIC, INC.

                                            _____
                                             LICENSEE (Legal Name)

By: _____   By: _____
          (Signature)   **(Signature)**

_____   _____
(Print Name of Signatory)   **(Print Name of Signatory)**

_____   _____
(Title of Signatory)   **(Title of Signatory)**

Complete only if in a Local Management Agreement *(Per ¶ 9.A.)*

_____   Date: _____
LOCAL MANAGER (Legal Name)

By: _____   Start Date of LMA: _____
          (Signature)

_____
(Print Name of Signatory)

_____
(Title of Signatory)

8

BMI-03

| BMI-03 | RADIO PER PROGRAM QUARTERLY MUSIC REPORT | SCHEDULE 1 |

BMI

Please mail or fax your completed report forms to:

Broadcast Music, Inc.
Attn: Media Licensing Per Program
10 Music Square East
Nashville, TN 37203-4399
Fax: (615) 401-5797

Date Range Of Week Covered By This Report

From [   ]   To [   ]

Other Station(s) Covered By Report

Station(s) Must Be 100% Simulcast (Indicate AM or FM)

[   ]   [   ]

[   ]   [   ]

Radio Station Covered By This Report

Call Letters [   ]
(Indicate AM or FM)

Account Number [   ]

PART 1   TOTAL WEIGHTED PERIODS COMPUTATION

IF YOU BROADCAST **24 HOURS/DAY, CHECK THIS BOX, SKIP THE TABLE BELOW,** AND **GO TO PART 2.** [ ]

	Time Period (Col. 1)	No. of Hours on Air During Time Period Per Day (Col. 2)	Multiplier (4 Periods Per Hour) (Col. 3)	No. of Periods on Air Per Day (Col. 4)	No. of Weekdays, Saturday & Sundays in Week (Col. 5)	Total No. of Periods on Air During Week (Col. 6)	Applicable Weight (Col. 7)	Total Weighted Periods (Col. 8)
Weekdays:	Midnight to 6:00 AM		X 4 =		X 5 =		X .25 =	
	6:00 AM to 10:00 AM		X 4 =		X 5 =		X 1.00 =	
	10:00 AM to 3:00 PM		X 4 =		X 5 =		X .50 =	
	3:00 PM to 7:00 PM		X 4 =		X 5 =		X .75 =	
	7:00 PM to Midnight		X 4 =		X 5 =		X .50 =	
Weekends:	Saturdays (max. 24 hrs.)		X 4 =		X 1 =		X .25 =	
	Sundays (max. 24 hrs.)		X 4 =		X 1 =		X .25 =	

Instructions if on air less than 24 hours a day:
Col. 2 - Enter the number of hours per day on air during the time period in Col. 1.
Col. 4 - Multiply the entry in Col. 2 by the multiplier in Col. 3.
Col. 6 - Multiply Col. 4 by Col. 5.
Col. 8 - Multiply Col. 6 by Col. 7 and total all entries in Col. 8 and place total in "Total Weighted Periods".

Total Weighted Periods (Add entries in Col. 8) [   ]

PART 2   COMPENSABLE WEIGHTED PERIODS COMPUTATION

A. IF **NO FEATURE MUSIC** WAS BROADCAST DURING THE WEEK, **SKIP B. & C.** AND **CHECK THIS BOX.** [ ]

B. COMPLETE **SCHEDULE 2** TO REPORT **ANY FEATURE MUSIC** BROADCAST DURING THE WEEK.

C. COMPLETE THE TABLE BELOW TO **CONCEDE** ANY 15-MINUTE PERIOD(S) TO CONTAIN PERFORMANCES OF BMI LICENSED FEATURE MUSIC. Schedule 2 does NOT have to be submitted to report conceded periods.

Time Period (Col. 1)	Enter the NUMBER of clock 15-minute programming periods you wish to CONCEDE (Col. 2)							Total 15-minute Periods (Col. 3)	Time Period Weight (Col. 4)	Total Conceded Periods (Col. 5)
	Sunday	Monday	Tuesday	Wednesday	Thursday	Friday	Saturday			
Midnight to 6:00 AM									X .25 =	
6:00 AM to 10:00 AM									X 1.00 =	
10:00 AM to 3:00 PM									X .50 =	
3:00 PM to 7:00 PM									X .75 =	
7:00 PM to Midnight									X .50 =	
Saturdays									X .25 =	
Sundays									X .25 =	

Note: Please reference the instructions to properly complete this section.

Total Conceded Weighted Periods [   ]
(Sum entries in Col. 5)

SUBMITTED BY *[You must also fax your QMR to the RMLC at (212) 754-9286]*   **BMI RECEIVED DATE**

_____   _____
Name (Please Print)   Position/Title

X _____   _____
Signature   Date

If you have any questions, please call (615) 401-2370

BMI-03	RADIO PER PROGRAM QUARTERLY MUSIC REPORT	SCHEDULE 2

BMI

Please MAIL or FAX the completed forms to:

Broadcast Music, Inc.
Attn: Media Licensing Per Program
10 Music Square East
Nashville, TN 37203-4399
Fax: (615)401-5797 Phone: (615)401-2370

Call Letters:

Account No:

Date Range of Week Covered by Report

From:

To:

1	2	3	4	5	6
PERFORMANCE DATA (Specify AM or PM for TIME)		TITLE OF COMPOSITION (Please Do Not Abbreviate)	WRITER(S)/COMPOSER(S) (Please list full name(s) of all writers)	PUBLISHER(S) and/or RECORDING ARTIST	Public Domain (✓)
DATE	TIME				

PLEASE TYPE OR LEGIBLY PRINT ALL COMPOSITIONS IN WHOLE OR IN PART WITHOUT EXCEPTION Page No. ___ of ___ v.10/03

BMI

BMI-03 PER PROGRAM
QUARTERLY MUSIC REPORT
INSTRUCTIONS

Stations licensed under the BMI-03 Radio Station Per Program License are contractually required to submit a Quarterly Music Report for one week per calendar quarter, even if you did not broadcast any BMI-affiliated music during the requested week. BMI will notify your station in writing of the week within the calendar quarter for which your station will be required to submit a Quarterly Music Report. **Quarterly Music Reports must be submitted to BMI within 30 days following the report week**

You can file your Quarterly Music Report electronically via BMI's online service, Radio Select, instead of on the attached paper report forms. To request access to Radio Select, please email your request to radioselect@bmi.com. Be sure to include your name, the call letters of the radio station(s) for which you will be reporting, and your phone number. If you decide to utilize the paper forms and require help with completing the Quarterly Music Report forms, please call **(615) 401-2370** and we will be happy to assist you. Additional blank report forms are available for download on our website at: http://www.bmi.com/licensing/forms/index.asp.

SCHEDULE 1

ACCOUNT INFORMATION
1. **Radio Station Covered By This Report**: Enter your station's call letters (indicate AM or FM) and your station's 7-digit BMI Account Number.
2. **Date Range of Week Covered By This Report**: Enter the first and last day (MM/DD/YYYY) of the report week as indicated in the "Request for QUARTERLY MUSIC REPORT" letter from BMI.
3. **Other Stations Covered By Report (100% Simulcast Stations)**: List the call letters of all other stations (either co-owned or for which you are the Local Manager/Time Broker) that simulcast 100% of your station's programming in the spaces provided. Stations simulcasting less than 100% of your station's programming must complete and submit separate Quarterly Music Reports.

PART 1 - TOTAL WEIGHTED PERIODS COMPUTATION
If your station was ON AIR 24 HOURS A DAY during the report week, check the box at the right, skip the table in **PART 1**, and proceed to **PART 2**. Otherwise, stations that are ON AIR LESS THAN 24 hours a day must complete the steps detailed below:
1. **No. of Hours on Air During Time Period Per Day (Col. 2)**: Enter the number of hours per day your station was regularly on air during the report week for each respective time period.   The maximum number of hours for each time period are as follows:

	Time Period	Maximum No. of Hours
Weekdays:	Midnight to 6:00 A.M.	6
	6:00 A.M. to 10:00 A.M.	4
	10:00 A.M. to 3:00 P.M.	5
	3:00 P.M. to 7:00 P.M.	4
	7:00 P.M. to Midnight	5
Weekends:	Saturdays/Sundays	24

2. **No. of Periods on Air Per Day (Col. 4)**: Multiply the entries in **Col. 2** by the multiplier of **4** in **Col. 3** and enter the results in **Col. 4**.
3. **No. of Weekdays, Sats., and Suns. In Week (Col. 5)**: This represents the number of weekdays (Monday - Friday), Saturdays, and Sundays in the report week.

1

4. **Total No. of Periods on Air During Week (Col. 6)**: Multiply the entries in **Col. 4** by **Col. 5** and enter results in **Col. 6**.

5. **Total Weighted Periods (Col. 8)**: Multiply the entries in **Col. 6** by the respective decimal amounts in **Col. 7 (Applicable Weight)** and enter the results in **Col. 8**.

6. Sum the entries in **Col. 8 (Total Weighted Periods)** and enter the total in the **Total Weighted Periods (Add entries in Col. 8)** box.

PART 2 - COMPENSABLE WEIGHTED PERIODS COMPUTATION

Complete **one** of the following reporting options (**A.**, **B.**, **C.** or **D.**):

A. If your station <u>DID NOT</u> broadcast any feature music during the report week, check the box at the right, omit SCHEDULE 2 and complete the SUBMITTED BY section at the bottom.

B. If your station broadcast feature music during the report week and you elect to report ALL feature performances of music individually on SCHEDULE 2 (elect <u>not</u> to concede any programming periods), you may do the following:
   1. Skip **PART 2 - COMPENSABLE WEIGHTED PERIODS COMPUTATION**.
   2. Complete the steps outlined for **SCHEDULE 2** below.

C. If your station broadcast feature music during the report week and you wish to <u>CONCEDE ALL</u> of the programming periods that contain feature music, you may do the following:
   1. Enter number of CONCEDED clock 15-minute periods by Time Period for each day of the week (Col. 2): Determine the number of 15-minute programming periods you wish to concede for each time period listed in **Col. 1** for each day of the week and enter those numbers in **Col. 2**. To calculate the total number of conceded 15-minute periods for a program or programming block, use the formula detailed in the example below:

   Example 1: A station reporting for a week in January 2004 wishes to concede a 3-hour music program that aired Wednesday from Midnight to 3 A.M. The number of conceded periods would be computed as follows, with the result entered for Wednesday:

Time Period	Program Length		15-min. periods per hour		Total Conceded periods
Weekdays: Midnight-6:00 AM	3 hours	X	4	=	12

   2. **Total 15-Minute Periods (Col. 3)**: Total the entries in **Col. 2** for each time period and enter the results in **Col. 3**.
   3. Multiply the totals in **Col. 3** by the applicable **Time Period Weight in Col. 4**. Enter the results in **Total Conceded Periods in Col. 5**.
   4. Total all entries in **Col. 4** and enter the result in the **Total Conceded Weighted Periods** box.
   5. Omit the **SCHEDULE 2** form (Feature music performance information does not have to be provided when broadcast during conceded periods).

D. If your station broadcast feature music during the report week and you wish to <u>CONCEDE SOME</u> of the programming periods with feature music use <u>AND</u> report feature performances individually for the other programming periods, you may do the following:
   1. Complete all steps for the programming periods with feature performances of music you have chosen to concede on **PART 2 - COMPENSABLE WEIGHTED PERIODS COMPUTATION** (as detailed above in Step C).
   2. Complete all steps to report all non-conceded programming periods with feature performances of music on **SCHEDULE 2** (detailed below).

v.10/03

IMPORTANT:
✓ Please be sure to write your name, title, signature, and date in the SUBMITTED BY section at the bottom-right corner of SCHEDULE 1. The reports cannot be processed by BMI without the appropriate signature.
✓ You must fax a copy of your Quarterly Music Report to the Radio Music License Committee (RMLC) at (212) 754-9286 in addition to submitting your report to BMI.

SCHEDULE 2

You DO NOT need to complete SCHEDULE 2 if:
A. Your station did not broadcast any feature music during the report week and you checked the box next to Step **A** under **SCHEDULE 1, PART 2 - COMPENSABLE WEIGHTED PERIODS COMPUTATION**.
B. You elected to concede ALL programming periods containing feature music in the Step **C** table under **SCHEDULE 1, PART 2 - COMPENSABLE WEIGHTED PERIODS COMPUTATION**.

Please TYPE or LEGIBLY PRINT all entries on this form.

You may report feature performances on forms other than the BMI SCHEDULE 2 form provided that all information requested on the BMI SCHEDULE 2 form is included (e.g. You may submit an output report from your station's traffic or music scheduling software).

You may report feature performances for multiple dates on the SCHEDULE 2 form.

1. **Call Letters**: Enter your station's call letters. Indicate AM or FM.
2. **Account No.**: Enter your station's 7-digit BMI account number.
3. **Date Range of Week Covered By Report**: Enter the first and last day (MM/DD/YYYY) of the week for which you are reporting feature music use.
4. **DATE OF BROADCAST**: Enter the date for each feature performance you are listing.
5. **TIME OF BROADCAST (Specify A.M. or P.M.)**: Enter the time of broadcast for each feature performance you are listing. Please be sure to specify A.M. or P.M.
6. **TITLE OF COMPOSITION**: Enter the full title of every composition, in whole or in part, broadcast during the program. Please do not abbreviate the title(s).
7. **WRITER(S)/COMPOSER(S)**: Enter the full name(s) of the composition's writer(s). *If you are unable to provide the writer(s) or composer(s), please provide the information in Step 9 (Publisher(s)) and/or Step 10 (Recording Artist).*
8. **PUBLISHER(S)**: Enter the name of the composition's publisher(s).
9. **RECORDING ARTIST**: Enter the name of the composition's recording artist.
10. **Public Domain (✓)**: Check this column if the composition is known to be a public domain work. Please indicate the arranger of the public domain work in the **WRITER(S)/COMPOSER(S)** column.
11. **Page No._ of _** : Write the number of each page in the space provided to ensure the pages are kept in the proper order.

BMI®

Local Television Station
Music Performance Per Program License

AGREEMENT, made at New York, N.Y. on _____, 20_____, between BROADCAST MUSIC, INC., a corporation organized under the laws of the State of New York (BMI) with principal offices at 320 West 57th Street, New York, N.Y. 10019, and

_____
(Legal Name of Licensee)

Please Check Appropriate Box And Complete

☐ A corporation organized under the laws of _____

☐ A limited liability company organized under the laws of _____

☐ A partnership composed of _____

☐ An individual residing at _____

_____

(LICENSEE) with offices located at _____

City _____ *State* _____ *Zip* _____ *Telephone No.* _____

and operating the television broadcasting station located at _____

City _____ *State* _____ *Zip* _____ *Telephone No.* _____

and presently designated by the call letters _____ (Station) (the "Agreement").

IT IS HEREBY AGREED AS FOLLOWS:

1.   TERM. The term of this Agreement shall be the period beginning [ ] and ending December 31, 2004, unless earlier terminated as hereinafter provided.

2.   DEFINITIONS. As used in this Agreement, the following terms shall have the following respective meanings:

(a) **"Affiliated Station"** shall mean any free, over the air television broadcasting station licensed by the FCC which is located in the United States, its commonwealth, possessions and territories, that regularly broadcasts Programs transmitted by a television network licensed by BMI during the term hereof.

(b) **"Ambient Uses"** shall comprise the following uses of music in BMI's repertoire:

(1) each use of music in a news or public affairs Program that:

A. does not exceed fifteen seconds' duration; and either

B. has not been inserted by Station or the producer of the Program or Program segment and is audible during:

(i)   coverage of a news story or event;
(ii) news coverage of a sports or athletic event or competition;
(iii) reviews and/or coverage of a live entertainment event;
(iv) previews or reviews of a play, concert or movie;
(v)   interviews (except where the music is performed "live" during the interview by the celebrity/interviewee); or
(vi) teasers or promotions for upcoming news segments used within the news show; or

1

C. is contained in a file clip or footage utilized by Station, or by the producer of the Program or Program segment, which file clip or footage met the criteria of sub-paragraphs B(i), (ii), (iii) or (iv) above at the time the file clip or footage was created;

    (2)   each use of music (without regard to duration) in a sports event Program that has not been inserted by Station or the producer of the Program or Program segment, other than:

A. uses of music that are part of an athletic performance choreographed to music (e.g., figure skating, gymnastics, synchronized swimming); or

B. musical performances that are the subject of sustained, focused coverage during a pre-game or halftime show or event, or during a time out or other break in the action.

    (c) **"Announcement"** shall mean any commercial, promotional, or public service announcement (exclusive of program length "infomercials" of greater duration than 120 seconds), or any producer's or distributor's logo.

    (d) **"BMI Consent Decree"** shall mean the consent decree entered in <u>United States v. BMI</u>, 64 Civ. 3787 (S.D.N.Y.), as amended.

    (e) **"Blanket License Fee"** shall mean LICENSEE's blanket license fee for Station as calculated pursuant to the methodology prescribed in Schedule I of Exhibit A hereto.

    (f) Music that is **"Cleared At The Source"** shall mean music for which LICENSEE has been granted a license to perform publicly by means of television broadcasting (1) directly by the composer(s), author(s), arranger(s), publisher(s) or owner(s) of such music, or licensees thereof, or (2) through the program producer or other authorized licensor of such rights.

    (g) **"COMMITTEE"** shall mean the Television Music License Committee, an unincorporated membership association organized under the laws of the State of New York, which is duly authorized to represent local television stations in music licensing matters.

    (h) **"First-Run Syndicated Television Program"** shall mean any Syndicated Television Program, episodes of which: (1) are currently being distributed in the syndication market for their first season of broadcasts, or (2) were created originally for, and are being transmitted for their first season of broadcasts by, a television network not licensed by BMI at the time such program is broadcast on such network, and broadcast simultaneously or by so-called "delayed" or "repeat" broadcasts (sometimes known as "rebroadcasts") over two or more stations affiliated with such television network not licensed by BMI.

    (i) **"Incidental Use"** shall mean the use of music in the broadcast of Non-Network Announcements.

    (j) **"LMA Operator"** shall mean any person, firm or corporation not under the same or substantially the same ownership, management or control as LICENSEE with whom LICENSEE has entered into a Local Marketing Agreement.

    (k) **"Local Marketing Agreement"** shall mean any arrangement between LICENSEE and an LMA Operator that:

    (1)   authorizes the resale by an LMA Operator of the use of the television broadcasting facilities of Station;

    (2)   permits an LMA Operator to provide Programs for all or substantially all of the time Station is on the air; and

    (3)   provides for the sale by an LMA Operator of all or substantially all Announcements broadcast on Station.

    (l) **"Locally-Produced Television Program"** shall mean any Non-Network Television Program produced by, or expressly for, LICENSEE.

    (m) **"Monthly Base License Fee"** shall mean the base amount used as the starting point for determining LICENSEE's fee pursuant to Paragraph 5(a) hereof. For each of the calendar years 2002, 2003 and 2004, LICENSEE's Monthly Base License Fee shall be equal to one-twelfth (1/12) of its share of the annual industry-wide BMI per program license fee of $98.1 million (or such other amount determined pursuant to Paragraph 1(C) of Exhibit A hereto), as allocated to Station by the COMMITTEE pursuant to the methodology set forth in Schedule I of Exhibit A hereto for such year.

    (n) **"Network Announcement"** shall mean any Announcement transmitted by a television network licensed by BMI as a network at the time such Announcement is broadcast on the network, and broadcast simultaneously or by so-called "delayed" or "repeat" broadcasts (sometimes known as "rebroadcasts") over two or more Affiliated Stations of a network licensed by BMI.

    (o) **"Network Television Program"** shall mean any Program, transmitted by a television network licensed by BMI as a network at the time such Program is broadcast on the network, identified as a Program of the network, and broadcast simultaneously or by so-called "delayed" or "repeat" broadcasts (sometimes known as "rebroadcasts") over two or more Affiliated Stations of a network licensed by BMI.

    (p) **"Non-Network Announcement"** shall mean any Announcement broadcast by Station other than a Network Announcement.

(q) **"Non-Network Television Program"** shall mean any Program broadcast by Station other than a Network Television Program.

(r) **"Otherwise Licensed Split Work"** shall mean a musical work: (1) the copyright in which is owned by two or more individuals or entities, or as to which two or more individuals or entities have the right to collect performing rights royalties, at least one of which is an affiliate of BMI and at least one of which is not an affiliate of BMI, and (2) for which LICENSEE has a valid license to perform publicly the composition by television broadcasting by Station either from another U.S. performing rights organization or from a copyright owner or its licensee who is not an affiliate of BMI.

(s) **"Program"** shall mean all material (visual or otherwise) broadcast by Station other than Announcements.

(t) **"Revenues Attributable to Non-Network Programs"** shall mean, with respect to each Non-Network Television Program broadcast by Station: (1) amounts billed by Station for the sale of commercial or Program time, including for political advertisements; (2) the value of trades and barter (i.e., goods and services, including, without limitation, the Program itself) that Station receives in exchange for commercial or Program time, which value shall be the value Station attributes to such trades and barter in accordance with its established accounting practices; (3) with respect to a telethon, payments to Station by the producer of said telethon; and (4) donations to Station relating to broadcasting activities that are directly attributable to a particular program. For purposes of calculations under subparagraphs (t)(1) and (2) hereof, for any given Program, "Revenues Attributable to Non-Network Television Programs" includes revenue from (i) commercial announcements broadcast within such Program and (ii) commercial announcements preceding such Program which are broadcast after the completion of the prior Program.

(u) **"Station"** shall mean and be restricted to the FCC-licensed commercial television broadcasting station whose ownership and call letters are indicated above.

(v) **"Station Web Site"** shall mean the Web Site operated by or for Station as the Station's Web Site.

(w) **"Syndicated Television Program"** shall mean any Non-Network Television Program supplied to LICENSEE and other television stations by a producer or a distributor, or by a television network which is not licensed by BMI.

(x) **"Television Broadcasting"** shall mean free, unscrambled, point-to-multipoint over-the-air local broadcasting by means of television.

(y) "**Web Site**" shall mean an Internet computer service comprising a series of interrelated web pages registered with a domain name registration service that Station transmits or causes to be transmitted either directly or indirectly to persons who receive the service over the Internet by means of a personal computer or by means of another device capable of receiving Internet transmissions. Station's current Web Site URL is

http://_____.

3. GRANT OF RIGHTS.

(a) BMI hereby grants to LICENSEE, for the term hereof, a non-exclusive license to perform publicly all musical works the right to grant public performing right licenses of which BMI may during the term hereof control:

    (i) by Television Broadcasting in the United States, and its territories, commonwealth and possessions, as part of LICENSEE's Non-Network Television Programs and Non-Network Announcements from Station; and

    (ii) in and as part of a single Station Web Site transmitted or caused to be transmitted either directly or indirectly over the Internet but only in connection with:

    (A) the simultaneous retransmission of the Station's locally produced and aired programming;

    (B) the retransmission of all or a portion of Station's local newscasts and local news based public affairs programming that aired during the Term of this Agreement; and

    (C) other transmissions the primary purpose of which are to promote viewership of Station and its television programming; *provided, however,* that: (1) no single performance licensed under this subsection (C) may exceed thirty (30) seconds in duration; and (2) the total duration of all performances of BMI-repertoire works under this subsection (C) available at any single time for listening on Station's Web Site may not exceed fifteen (15) minutes in duration.

(b) Notwithstanding the foregoing, the license granted herein shall not include transmissions described in subparagraphs 3(a)(ii)(A) and 3(a)(ii)(B) above where such transmissions contain programming which is nationally or regionally aired regularly scheduled series programming (e.g., Regis and Kelly, George Michael's Sports Machine, and Major League Baseball). In the event that Station airs locally-produced programming, and such programming also appears on one or more additional stations (which programming for purposes of this Agreement would not be considered locally produced and aired programming for the additional station(s)), only the Station may retransmit BMI music contained in such programming in the manner described in subparagraphs 3(a)(ii)(A) and 3(a)(ii)(B) above, while the additional station(s) may not.

(c) The license granted herein does not cover transmissions on Station's Web Site of BMI music where members of the public are charged a fee for the right to access such transmissions. Such transmissions shall be subject to appropriate separate licensing. Notwithstanding the foregoing, the fact that a Station may charge members of the public for access to discrete areas of the Station's Web Site other than those areas containing the performances licensed hereunder shall not limit the scope of coverage of this license.

(d) With respect to any portion of the Term prior to January 1, 2002, the Web Site license granted under Paragraph 3(a)(ii) shall be limited to those transmissions of BMI music as described in Paragraph 3(a)(ii)(C) above.

(e) For the rights granted in Paragraph 3(a)(ii) only, the territory shall mean the United States, its commonwealth, territories and possessions and the territories represented by non-U.S. performing right licensing organizations posted as Exhibit C in the licensing section of the BMI web site located at http://www.bmi.com. Such list may be amended by BMI at any time and without notice. Notwithstanding the foregoing, the territorial scope of the grant of rights in Paragraph 3(a)(ii) with respect to any musical works which are affiliated with BMI through a non-U.S. performing rights licensing organization not listed on Exhibit C is limited to public performances in the U.S. Territory.

(f) The performances licensed hereunder may originate at any place whether or not such place is licensed to publicly perform the musical works licensed hereunder, and regardless of the manner, means or method of such origination, but nothing herein shall be deemed to grant a license to such place itself (or to the parties responsible for such performances) for the public performances in such place of any such works.

(g) The license granted herein shall not include dramatic rights, the right to perform dramatico-musical works in whole or in substantial part, the right to present individual works in a dramatic setting or the right to use the music licensed hereunder in any other context which may constitute an exercise of the "grand rights" therein. It is nonetheless expressly understood that nothing contained in this Paragraph shall be construed so as to limit the ability of LICENSEE to perform, by Television Broadcasting, any works contained in Syndicated Television Programs, motion pictures initially produced for theatrical exhibition or music videos which LICENSEE would otherwise have the right to perform under this Agreement.

(h) BMI will, upon specific reasonable written request made by LICENSEE, indicate whether one or more specified musical works listed by LICENSEE are licensed by BMI.   LICENSEE shall provide the title and the writer/composer of each musical work requested to be identified.

(i) Except as expressly herein otherwise provided, nothing herein contained shall be construed as authorizing LICENSEE to grant to others any right to reproduce, retransmit or publicly perform by any means, method or process whatsoever, any of the musical works licensed hereunder or as authorizing any receiver of any television broadcast to publicly perform or reproduce the same by any means, method or process whatsoever.

(j) The license granted herein shall not include the right to adapt the musical works licensed hereunder or to make any other versions thereof.

(k) The license granted herein shall include on a non-precedential, experimental basis the right to engage in such non-dramatic public performances of musical works in BMI's repertoire as may result from Station's free, over-the-air broadcasts of BMI music within its existing geographic market(s) over FCC assigned frequencies, by means of a digital television signal. It is understood that the right to perform works in the BMI repertoire by means of a digital television signal is being included in this Agreement because digital television is a new technology and such grant of rights reflects the experimental character of such broadcasts. Station shall provide BMI, in electronic form, annual reports concerning LICENSEE's digital television signal, using the form attached hereto as Exhibit D. The form shall be filed during the month of October of each of the years 2002, 2003 and 2004.

4.   PAYMENTS FOR APRIL 1, 1999 THROUGH DECEMBER 31, 2001. This Agreement expressly incorporates, and LICENSEE agrees to be bound by, the terms of the letter agreement between BMI and COMMITTEE attached hereto as Exhibit A. LICENSEE agrees to pay BMI, in addition to the interim license fees that were heretofore payable by LICENSEE to BMI in respect of the period from April 1, 1999, through and including December 31, 2001, under the interim BMI Local Television Station Music Performance Blanket or Per Program License for station, such amounts and at such times as are provided in Paragraph 2 of Exhibit A concerning the Settlement Fee. If any such payment is not received by BMI in the twenty (20) days following the date on which such payment is due, BMI may collect a late-payment charge of one percent (1%) per month (simple interest) calculated from the date such payment was due.

5.   PAYMENTS FOR JANUARY 1, 2002 THROUGH DECEMBER 31, 2004.

This Agreement expressly incorporates, and LICENSEE agrees to be bound by, the terms of the letter agreement between BMI and COMMITTEE attached hereto as Exhibit A.

(a) BROADCAST TELEVISION PAYMENTS. In consideration of the license herein granted for the period from January 1, 2002, through December 31, 2004, LICENSEE agrees to pay to BMI for each calendar month of such period the total of the following fees:

(1) A Program Fee. The Program Fee shall be one hundred forty percent (140%) of LICENSEE's Monthly Base License Fee, multiplied by a fraction, the numerator of which shall be "BMI Revenues" computed as prescribed in sub-paragraph 5(a)(1)(A) below, and the denominator of which shall be LICENSEE's total Revenues Attributable to Non-Network Television Programs for the month.

A. For purposes of calculating the Program Fee due BMI hereunder, "BMI Revenues" shall comprise the sum of:

(i) the month's Revenues Attributable to Non-Network Television Programs using music from BMI's repertoire other than those programs whose only uses of music from BMI's repertoire are Cleared At The Source, or consist solely of Incidental Uses, Ambient Uses (subject to Paragraph 5(a)(1)(A)(ii)) or Otherwise Licensed Split Works;

(ii) sixteen percent (16%) of the month's revenues attributable to sports event programs whose

4

only uses of music from BMI's repertoire are Cleared At The Source or consist solely of Incidental Uses, Otherwise Licensed Split Works or Ambient Uses;

(iii) fifty percent (50%) of the revenues attributable to each Syndicated Television Program, other than First-Run Syndicated Television Programs, as to which neither LICENSEE nor BMI can determine whether the music in such Program (other than music Cleared At The Source, Incidental Uses, Ambient Uses or Otherwise Licensed Split Works) is in BMI's repertoire at the time LICENSEE submits its per program license report;

(iv) with respect to each episode of a First-Run Syndicated Television Program for which a cue sheet has not been created or made publicly available at the time LICENSEE submits its per program license report, an amount calculated by multiplying the revenues attributable to such episode by (a) a percentage multiplier (calculated by BMI and verified by COMMITTEE as to the Programs involved and the methodology employed) representing the proportion of the episodes of the specific program containing music in BMI's repertoire (other than music Cleared At The Source, Incidental Uses, Ambient Uses or Otherwise Licensed Split Works); or (b) in the absence of a sufficient number of cue sheets in BMI's or LICENSEE's possession which would enable calculation of such a percentage multiplier for a given First-Run Syndicated Television Program, fifty percent (50%) of the revenues attributable to such Program; and

(v) one hundred percent (100%) of the revenues attributable to each Locally-Produced Television Program as to which neither LICENSEE nor BMI can determine whether the music in such program (other than any Ambient Uses) is in BMI's repertoire at the time LICENSEE submits its per program license report.

(2) An Incidental/Ambient Use Fee. In addition to any payment for Ambient Uses of music in sports event programs as called for under Paragraph 5(a)(1)(A)(ii) hereof, the Incidental/Ambient Use Fee covering LICENSEE's Incidental and Ambient Uses of music in BMI's repertoire shall be fifteen percent (15%) of LICENSEE's Monthly Base License Fee.

(b) WEB SITE PAYMENTS FOR 2002, 2003 and 2004. This Agreement expressly incorporates, and LICENSEE agrees to be bound by, the terms of the letter agreement between BMI and the COMMITTEE attached hereto as Exhibit A. LICENSEE shall pay to BMI for each month during the calendar years 2002, 2003, and 2004, a fee equal to one twelfth (1/12) of LICENSEE's allocated share of the BMI annual Internet fee as set forth in Exhibit A and as determined by the COMMITTEE. Such fee shall be payable to BMI no later than the first calendar day of the month succeeding the month to which the fee is attributable.

(c) For purposes of fee calculations, the length of a Program shall be the length attributed to the Program in the "Program Index" section of the Nielsen report titled "Viewers in Profile" for Station's relevant Designated Market Area ("DMA") (hereinafter, the "VIP Report"), pursuant to Nielsen's then-current "Program Names Guidelines." For Programs not included in the "Program Index" section of the VIP Report, where a question as to Program length occurs and BMI and (1) LICENSEE or (2) COMMITTEE are not otherwise able to agree, a particular period of television broadcasting shall be considered one Program if, with respect to such period, any two of the following questions may be answered in the affirmative:

(1) Is the period referred to by substantially the same title throughout?

(2) Is the dominant personality the same substantially throughout?

(3) Is the period presented to the public as a single show notwithstanding that it may have different parts?

(4) Is the format substantially constant throughout?

(d) (1) LICENSEE shall remit its monthly payment and the monthly report called for by Paragraph 6 hereof to BMI on or before the last day of the month following the month to which they are attributable (e.g., the payment for April 2002 is due the last day of May 2002).

(2) If any such payment is not received by BMI within twenty (20) days following the date on which such payment is due, BMI may collect a late-payment charge of one percent (1%) per month (simple interest) calculated from the date such payment was due.

(3) If LICENSEE fails to submit both its monthly payment and report within sixty (60) days following the date they are due, BMI may collect one hundred fifty-five percent (155%) of LICENSEE's Monthly Base License Fee for that month, representing LICENSEE's maximum per program license fee. If LICENSEE fails to pay such an amount within thirty (30) days of its receipt of said notice of adjustment in fee to the maximum per program license fee from BMI, LICENSEE shall pay to BMI a late-payment charge of one percent (1%) per month (simple interest) on that amount calculated from the thirtieth (30th) day following LICENSEE's receipt of said notice of adjustment in fee to the maximum per program license fee. The payment provisions of this Paragraph shall not apply in circumstances in which LICENSEE is unable to submit its monthly report within the time period reflected in this subparagraph due to "force majeure" (e.g., earthquake, hurricane, fire, flood) and where LICENSEE submits within sixty (60) days of the due date an on-account payment equal to its prior month's per program license fee, which will be credited against the actual fees owing for that month once LICENSEE has submitted its report.

(e) (1) Where any adjusted monthly fee computed by BMI exceeds the fee reported and paid by LICENSEE, LICENSEE shall remit the payment of any such excess fee within thirty (30) days of LICENSEE's receipt of an explanation of the calculation of the adjusted fee.

(2) If any such payment due is not received by BMI within thirty (30) days of LICENSEE's receipt of the appropriate billing statement, LICENSEE shall pay to BMI a late payment charge of one percent (1%) per month (simple interest) calculated from the thirtieth (30th) day following LICENSEE's receipt of said billing statement; provided, however, that if LICENSEE disputes in good faith such an adjustment by BMI pursuant to the procedures provided for in Paragraph 5(g) hereof, such a late payment charge shall be calculated as prescribed in Paragraph 5(g).

(f) (1) Where the monthly fee reported and paid by LICENSEE exceeds any adjusted monthly fee computed by BMI, BMI shall credit LICENSEE's account for the amount of any such excess fee, or, if LICENSEE so elects, and the amount of such adjustment, net of any other amounts owing by LICENSEE to BMI other than any audit claims, exceeds LICENSEE's Monthly Base License Fee, BMI shall, within thirty (30) days of receiving notification from LICENSEE of such election, refund to LICENSEE the amount of any such excess fee.

(2) If any such refund or credit is not received by LICENSEE within thirty (30) days of BMI's receipt of notification by LICENSEE of such election, LICENSEE shall be entitled to receive, in addition to such refund, an additional sum computed at a rate of one percent (1%) per month (simple interest) calculated from the 30th day following BMI's receipt of said election.

(g) (1) If LICENSEE disputes in good faith any adjusted monthly fee computed by BMI under Paragraph 5(e) or 5(f), it shall submit to BMI a post-adjustment review request within thirty (30) days of its receipt of the pertinent billing statement and explanation of the calculation of the adjusted fee. Such post-adjustment review request shall identify the specific Program(s) and episode(s) in dispute, the specific nature of the dispute (including the timely submission of supporting documents which have not already been submitted to BMI). BMI and COMMITTEE shall work together in an attempt to agree upon a format as to allow for a computerized transmission between BMI and its licensees or their representatives.

(2) Within sixty (60) days of its receipt from LICENSEE of a post-adjustment review request, BMI shall provide to LICENSEE a further explanation as to the basis of the disputed adjustment and the modification of said adjusted monthly fee where appropriate (herein, "Post-Adjustment Response").

(3) Upon receipt of a post-adjustment review request from LICENSEE, no late payment charge shall be billed to the account of LICENSEE with regard to that portion of the adjusted monthly fee which is disputed until thirty (30) days after LICENSEE's receipt of BMI's Post-Adjustment Response.

(4) Within thirty (30) days of its receipt of such Post-Adjustment Response, LICENSEE shall pay any remaining portion of the adjusted monthly fee or advise BMI that it still disputes BMI's computation. Absent such notice from LICENSEE, if LICENSEE fails to pay any remaining portion of the adjusted monthly license fee within thirty (30) days of its receipt of BMI's Post-Adjustment Response, LICENSEE shall pay to BMI a late payment charge of one percent (1%) per month (simple interest) calculated from the thirtieth (30th) day following LICENSEE's receipt of such Post-Adjustment Response; provided, however, that if LICENSEE continues to dispute in good faith such fee adjustment, and LICENSEE identifies in writing to BMI the specific nature of the continuing dispute a late payment charge shall accrue on any remaining unpaid portion of the adjusted monthly license fee commencing after the thirtieth (30th) day following the resolution of the dispute.

6. PROGRAM AND MUSIC USE REPORTS.

(a) LICENSEE shall, subject to the provisions of subparagraph (b) below, furnish to BMI on or before the last day of each month reports setting forth on a day-by-day basis, separately for each Non-Network Television Program broadcast by LICENSEE during the prior month (e.g., the April 2002 report is due in May 2002): (1) Program title, including the episode name and/or episode number; (2) date of broadcast; (3) from and to time of broadcast; and (4) the revenues attributable to the Program. LICENSEE shall also identify, on a day-by-day basis, the periods of time during which Station: (i) broadcast Network Programs and (ii) did not broadcast any Programs.

(b) BMI shall provide LICENSEE (or, at LICENSEE's request, LICENSEE's agent) with both: (1) a system, compatible with Microsoft Windows 98 or Windows 2000 to enable LICENSEE to create and transmit, via the Internet using File Transfer Protocol (FTP), its monthly per program reports required to be created pursuant to this Agreement; and (2) computer file specifications to enable LICENSEE to transmit the monthly per program report data to BMI via Internet using File Transfer Protocol (FTP). BMI and one or more representatives designated by COMMITTEE shall agree on the specifications and software to be created by BMI in order to enable LICENSEE to engage in such electronic reporting. LICENSEE must submit its per program reports pursuant to this Agreement employing the agreed upon specifications and means of transmission.

(c) BMI shall provide LICENSEE (or, at LICENSEE's request, LICENSEE's agent) with a searchable database, compatible with Windows 98 or Windows 2000 of the music content of Series, Episodes, and Shows (the "Show Music Database") and BMI will use reasonable efforts to update such a database each month of the term hereafter and shall, in any event, update this database at least once in each calendar quarter of the term hereafter. BMI, however, may adjust LICENSEE's reports and compute LICENSEE's fees based upon the most current music use information available to BMI, whether or not that information has been included in the latest "Show Music Database" provided to LICENSEE. LICENSEE shall endeavor to report Program titles, episode names and/or numbers and music use indicators on its monthly per program reports in exactly the same manner in which such information appears in the

6

"Show Music Database."

(d) Each month LICENSEE shall furnish to BMI a cue sheet, in the electronic form agreed upon by BMI and COMMITTEE with respect to each Locally-Produced Television Program listed in the report in subparagraph 6(a) above.

(e) (1) LICENSEE shall maintain videotapes of all of its Locally-Produced Programs for the later of six (6) months from (A) the due date for the report covering the month in which the Program was broadcast, or (B) the date on which the report was submitted to BMI. LICENSEE shall not be obligated to retain such tapes beyond the prescribed six-month period. LICENSEE shall provide a reasonable number of such videotapes to BMI in response to requests by BMI made within the prescribed six-month period, and subject to the limitation that BMI may request videotapes of no more than one week or the equivalent of one week of Locally-Produced Television Programs per month. Such tapes shall be provided to BMI, with suitable identification of the location on them of the Programs to which BMI's request may be directed. If LICENSEE fails to respond in a reasonable time to a timely request from BMI for a videotape of a Locally-Produced Television Program, LICENSEE shall be required to pay a fee for the Program as if it contained music in BMI's repertoire.

(2) Not more frequently than three (3) times during any consecutive twelve (12) month period, and upon not less than fifteen (15) days' written notice to LICENSEE, BMI may request that LICENSEE provide BMI with either: (A) videotapes of up to one consecutive week of Syndicated Television Programs the music content of which does not appear in the Show Music Database, or (B) videotapes of four consecutive episodes of a Program that airs once a week the music content of which does not appear in the Show Music Database. BMI shall use its best efforts not to request from LICENSEE videotapes of programs for which it has received videotapes from other sources.

(3) If LICENSEE maintains videotapes of Syndicated Television Programs, the music content of which does not appear on the Show Music Database, BMI may request that LICENSEE provide a reasonable number of videotapes to BMI on an as-needed basis.

(4) Any videotapes provided to BMI pursuant to this Agreement are for the exclusive use of BMI in performance of its obligations hereunder. BMI shall not copy, distribute or otherwise make such videotapes available to any entity, other than the COMMITTEE. Upon BMI's completion of its review of such videotapes, BMI shall promptly return such videotapes to LICENSEE or destroy them at LICENSEE's request.

(5) LICENSEE at its option may send BMI a sample videotape strictly for the purpose of allowing BMI to determine if the videotape is of reasonably sufficient quality to enable BMI to determine whether the Programs on it contain music in BMI's repertoire. Within a reasonable period of time following its receipt of such a videotape, BMI shall notify LICENSEE of any perceived problems in the videotape's quality, and thereafter LICENSEE and BMI shall attempt, in good faith, to resolve any such problems.

(f) With respect to any musical work that LICENSEE claims is an Otherwise Licensed Split Work, at the time LICENSEE files its corresponding monthly music report LICENSEE shall identify such claim as well as the performing right organization or copyright holder that has licensed the performing right of said work. If LICENSEE claims that the performing right is licensed under a blanket license from another performing right organization, LICENSEE shall represent that it has such a license in effect and, on BMI's request, shall furnish to BMI a copy of that license (provided that LICENSEE has not previously provided such license to BMI). LICENSEE authorizes BMI to seek to verify from another performing right organization that LICENSEE has a blanket or per program license in effect with that organization. If LICENSEE claims that the performing right is licensed under a per program license from another performing right organization, LICENSEE shall represent that it has such a license in effect and, on BMI's request, shall furnish to BMI a copy of that license (provided that LICENSEE has not previously provided such license to BMI), and shall furnish to BMI a copy of the relevant portion of LICENSEE's monthly report pursuant to that license showing that the performance has been duly reported and the required fee has been paid to the other performing right organization. If LICENSEE claims that the performing right is licensed directly from a copyright holder or its licensee, LICENSEE shall represent that such a license is in effect and on BMI's request, shall furnish to BMI a copy of the license agreement including the name(s) of the work(s) so licensed and the identities of the individual(s) from whom such license was obtained; and the period of time and nature or scope of the rights and performances covered by the license (or if the license was obtained from a music library, the name of the library and such other information contained in the license). Except for the items listed above, LICENSEE, at its option, may remove any financial or other proprietary (material) information from the license agreement.

(g) (1) For any music that is Cleared At The Source, LICENSEE shall furnish to BMI written notice of such clearance at the time LICENSEE submits its corresponding monthly music report. At the time LICENSEE submits such report, LICENSEE shall also endeavor to provide, to the extent it is in existence at that time, a copy of the license agreement between the person or entity (the "Clearing Entity") pursuant to which LICENSEE has obtained such clearance (the "Source License"), from which LICENSEE may, at its option, remove any financial or other proprietary (material) information. LICENSEE shall submit a copy of the license agreement by sending it to BMI via certified mail or by some other means by which confirmation of delivery may be proved. In the event that more than seven (7) months have passed since the monthly music report containing the musical work is due or submitted, whichever is later, and LICENSEE has not yet submitted to BMI a copy of its agreement with

7

the Clearing Entity or LICENSEE failed to provide BMI with notice of the clearance at the time LICENSEE submitted its monthly music report, LICENSEE may no longer claim that such musical work was Cleared At The Source and one hundred percent (100%) of the revenues from the Program containing such music shall be BMI Revenues for purposes of calculating the Program Fee under Paragraph 5.

(2) With respect to each Source License obtained from a person or entity who is not a writer, composer or publisher affiliate of BMI, LICENSEE shall additionally furnish to BMI such information as may be in the possession of LICENSEE as will enable BMI to determine the names of the works licensed and the authors, composers, arrangers or publishers of the works licensed. In this regard, if the Clearing Entity is a "music library," this obligation shall be satisfied by LICENSEE's identification of the title of the specific track of a compact disc, or other recording containing music from the library, performed by LICENSEE. If the Clearing Entity is a program producer or other authorized licensor of such rights, such obligation shall be fulfilled by LICENSEE's furnishing of a cue sheet for the program in which the licensed works appear when BMI does not already possess the cue sheet and makes a request of LICENSEE to provide same. If LICENSEE is unable to supply, or BMI is otherwise unable to obtain, the music use or other information required by this subparagraph, the parties shall have the same rights and obligations as may otherwise be available to them regarding payment and reporting in circumstances in which a program contains unidentified music, as set forth in Paragraphs 5, 6 and 7 hereof.

(h) For any music that is Cleared At The Source, the parties agree that the following procedures shall apply:

(1) If BMI believes that the Source License furnished by LICENSEE pursuant to the provisions of subparagraph 6(g) is or may be legally insufficient to convey music performing rights to LICENSEE, BMI shall so advise LICENSEE within sixty (60) days of BMI's receipt of a Source License in connection with reports covering the period commencing January 1, 2002. In such case, BMI shall communicate with the Clearing Entity by means of a letter or other writing, the content of which shall be agreed upon by BMI and COMMITTEE, and BMI shall furnish LICENSEE and COMMITTEE with copies of all such correspondence. If, following such written communication, the Clearing Entity disputes that it intended to convey music performing rights to LICENSEE, the parties shall have the same rights and obligations as may otherwise be available to them regarding payment and reporting in circumstances in which a Program contains unidentified music, as set forth in Paragraphs 5, 6 and 7 hereof.

(2) In circumstances in which the Clearing Entity is not a writer or publisher affiliate of BMI, BMI shall have thirty (30) days after having identified the affiliates of BMI whose works are covered by the Source License, to communicate in writing with such affiliates to determine if the Clearing Entity owns, or has been granted, the right to convey music performing rights to LICENSEE, and BMI shall notify LICENSEE, COMMITTEE and the Clearing Entity of such communication. BMI shall notify LICENSEE and the Clearing Entity within sixty (60) days following such written communication, if an affiliate or affiliates of BMI dispute that the Clearing Entity owns, or has been granted, the right to convey music performing rights to LICENSEE, and the basis for any such dispute. If BMI and LICENSEE or the Clearing Entity are not able to resolve such dispute, the parties shall have the same rights and obligations as may otherwise be available to them regarding payment and reporting in circumstances in which a Program contains unidentified music, as set forth in Paragraphs 5, 6 and 7 hereof.

(3) In circumstances in which the Clearing Entity is not a writer or publisher affiliate of BMI and in addition, the Clearing Entity asserts it has been granted the right to convey music performing rights to LICENSEE from a third party other than a writer or publisher affiliate of BMI, BMI shall have thirty (30) days after receipt of the Source License to communicate with such third party, by means of a letter or other writing, the contents of which shall be agreed upon by BMI and COMMITTEE, to determine if such third party has granted the right to convey music performing rights to the Clearing Entity, and BMI shall notify LICENSEE, the COMMITTEE and the Clearing Entity of such communication. BMI shall notify LICENSEE, COMMITTEE and the Clearing Entity within sixty (60) days following such written communication, if such third party disputes that the Clearing Entity owns, or has been granted, the right to convey music performing rights to LICENSEE, and the basis for any such dispute. If BMI, LICENSEE, the Clearing Entity and such third party are not able to resolve such dispute, the parties shall have the same rights and obligations as may otherwise be available to them regarding payment and reporting in circumstances in which a program contains unidentified music, as set forth in Paragraphs 5, 6 and 7 hereof. If such third party shall fail to respond to BMI's written communication within sixty (60) days following such written communication, BMI shall so notify LICENSEE and the Clearing Entity and the parties shall have the same rights and obligations as may otherwise be available to them regarding payment and reporting in circumstances in which a Program contains unidentified music, as set forth in Paragraphs 5, 6 and 7 hereof.

(4) The disposition of a given dispute pursuant to subparagraphs (h)(1), (2) and (3) hereof for purposes of determining the license fees payable under this Agreement shall be without prejudice to the respective rights of LICENSEE and the Clearing Entity arising out of the disputed Source License itself.

(5) LICENSEE shall have seven (7) months from the time it is notified of a dispute pursuant to subparagraphs (h)(1), (2) and (3) hereof in which to resolve such dispute. Notwithstanding the provisions of Paragraphs 5, 6 and 7 hereof regarding the timing of adjustments to LICENSEE's monthly

8

187

per program license report, if within this seven (7) month period, it is determined that LICENSEE was in fact granted the right to perform the music which was the subject of the dispute, BMI shall adjust LICENSEE's report for the month in which such music was performed and shall issue a refund or credit to LICENSEE for the amount of any fees previously paid in error on account of such performances.

(i) Music Performance Reports.

(1) BROADCAST TELEVISION REPORTS. LICENSEE, upon written request from BMI made on notice of not less than four (4) weeks specifying the period of time to be covered, agrees to furnish (on forms to be supplied by BMI) reports of LICENSEE's performances by Station of all musical works indicating the works performed by title and composer or by such other convenient method as may be designated by BMI. In no event shall such reports be furnished for more than one (1) week of each year of the term. It is expressly understood that, with respect to any Syndicated Television Programs, LICENSEE's obligation to report music data to BMI under this subparagraph shall be limited to providing BMI with the title and episode name or number of such Syndicated Television Program(s); if no cue sheet is available, LICENSEE shall cooperate with BMI in attempting to obtain such cue sheets and/or in providing BMI with access to a tape or recording of the Syndicated Television Program involved. In addition to these reports, LICENSEE shall provide a copy of a list of its Non-Network Announcements for the week (*e.g.*, traffic reports); LICENSEE may redact any revenue or financial information from this list, provided that the list includes the name of the commercial, the dates and number of times it was broadcast and the ISCI code number for the commercial.

(2) WEB SITE REPORTS. LICENSEE shall notify BMI in writing, using the form attached hereto as Exhibit B, reasonably promptly after beginning to stream its over-the-air broadcast television signal or to distribute a Web Site licensed pursuant to this Agreement. Thereafter, upon written request from BMI made on notice of not less than four (4) weeks specifying the period of time to be covered, LICENSEE shall provide to BMI, in electronic form, a music use report for a period specified by BMI not to exceed one month for each calendar year during the Term of the Agreement using the form attached hereto as Exhibit C. BMI reserves the right to request from LICENSEE information sufficient to identify the title(s) of any Program(s) promoted on individually retrievable archived promotional announcements on the Web Site as part of such reports.

7.   ADJUSTMENTS FOR UNIDENTIFIED MUSIC.

(a) If, within seven (7) months from the date on which LICENSEE's per program reports are due or submitted, whichever is later:

(1) BMI or LICENSEE obtains a cue sheet for a specific episode of a Syndicated Television Program for which such cue sheet previously had not been created or made publicly available, BMI shall adjust LICENSEE's report, and compute, and advise LICENSEE of any additional fees owing or credit due, based upon the music use reported in such cue sheet;

(2) BMI obtains information that a Syndicated Television Program series has a theme in BMI's repertoire, BMI, subject to verification by COMMITTEE as to the sufficiency and accuracy of the information upon which BMI is relying in this regard, shall adjust LICENSEE's per program report in accordance with such information; or

(3) Neither BMI nor LICENSEE has obtained a cue sheet or other music content information for a specific episode of a First-Run Syndicated Television Program, the fee for which was originally calculated using a percentage multiplier as set forth in Paragraph 5(a)(1)(A)(iv) above, BMI will adjust LICENSEE's report, and compute, and advise LICENSEE of, any additional fees owing or credit due, by substituting (except in the circumstances described in subparagraph (4) below) in the numerator of the Program Fee fraction set forth in Paragraph 5(a)(1)(A) above, the amount calculated by multiplying the revenue attributable to the relevant First-Run Syndicated Television Program by fifty percent (50%) for the amount which previously had been calculated for the Program under Paragraph 5(a)(1)(A)(iv).

(4) Neither BMI nor LICENSEE has obtained a cue sheet for a First-Run Syndicated Program produced by LICENSEE, LICENSEE's parent or by an affiliated company in which LICENSEE or its parent is a majority owner, BMI shall adjust LICENSEE's report, and any fees owing to BMI by LICENSEE, by substituting in the numerator of the Program Fee fraction, set forth in Paragraph 5(a)(1)(A) above, one hundred percent (100%) of the revenue attributable to the relevant First Run Syndicated Program for the amount which previously had been calculated for the Program under Paragraph 5(a)(1)(A)(iv).

(b) Subject only to the audit rights described in Paragraph 8 below, BMI shall complete its review of LICENSEE's monthly per program report, and any adjustments thereto, within eight (8) months from the date it is due or submitted, whichever is later. At the request of BMI, LICENSEE shall furnish to BMI a copy of those portions of such program and music use reports or other records as are required for BMI to review the accuracy of information contained in LICENSEE's per program license reports. If BMI has not completed its review and adjustment of LICENSEE's per program report within this eight (8) month time period, all Program and music content identifications contained therein shall be treated as accurate.

8.   AUDITS.

9

(a) Upon at least ten (10) business days' written notice to LICENSEE, BMI shall have the right to examine, at any time during customary business hours, the Program logs, books and records of account, and all other records of LICENSEE only to such extent as may be necessary to verify any of the financial information contained in LICENSEE's per program reports, including ASCAP blanket and per program license fees. The records subject to examination shall include any documents pursuant to which LICENSEE has obtained the performing right to music that is Cleared At The Source, except to the extent that such documents may have previously been provided to BMI by LICENSEE. BMI shall consider all data and information coming to its attention as a result of any such examination of logs, books and records as confidential.

(b) BMI shall complete any audits of the financial information contained in LICENSEE's per program reports by no later than two (2) years after the date upon which this Agreement expires or is otherwise terminated.

(c) Upon BMI's request, LICENSEE shall furnish to BMI a description of the methodology used by LICENSEE to attribute a value to trades and barter in accordance with its established accounting practices. LICENSEE shall thereafter furnish to BMI a description of any changes to such methodology which may occur during the term of this Agreement. Should BMI believe that the methodology utilized by LICENSEE does not comport with generally accepted accounting principles (or otherwise believe that LICENSEE's reporting practices under this Paragraph warrant it), BMI shall have the right, upon notice to COMMITTEE, to refer this matter to the BMI Rate Court for determination pursuant to Article XIV of the BMI Consent Decree.

(d) In the event that BMI's audit of LICENSEE discloses that LICENSEE has underpaid license fees due BMI:

(1) LICENSEE shall pay a finance charge on such additional license fees of one percent (1%) per month (simple interest) with respect to any additional license fees owing, computed: (a) in circumstances in which under-payments for the audited period exceed seven and one-half percent (7½%) of the total fees owing, from the date(s) such fees should have been paid pursuant to this agreement, or (b) in circumstances in which underpayments for the audited period are less than or equal to seven and one-half (7½%) percent of the total fees owing, beginning thirty (30) days after the date BMI bills such additional license fees to LICENSEE.

(2) If LICENSEE disputes all or part of BMI's claim for additional fees pursuant to an audit, LICENSEE shall, within thirty (30) days from the date BMI bills such additional fees, (i) advise BMI, in writing, of the basis for such dispute and (ii) pay to BMI any fees indisputably owed together with any applicable finance charges on additional fees indisputably owed in accordance with subparagraphs (1) and (2) above. If LICENSEE, in good faith, disputes all or part of the additional fees BMI has billed pursuant to this Paragraph, no finance charges shall be billed with respect to such disputed fees for the period beginning on the date BMI bills such disputed fees and ending sixty (60) days from the date BMI responds to LICENSEE's written notification of the existence of a dispute.

(3) Finance charges computed in accordance with this Paragraph and pertaining to additional fees which LICENSEE disputes in accordance with subparagraph (2) above shall be adjusted pro-rata to the amount agreed upon by LICENSEE and BMI in settlement of the dispute with respect to additional fees due.

9.   LOCAL MARKETING AGREEMENT.

(a) If LICENSEE is, or becomes, a party to a Local Marketing Agreement, LICENSEE and the LMA Operator shall execute a letter to BMI, in the form attached as Exhibit E and made a part of this Agreement, requesting amendment of this Agreement to add LMA Operator as a party. When such a letter has been fully executed by LICENSEE, the LMA Operator and BMI, this Agreement shall be deemed amended accordingly.

(b) BMI shall be entitled to receive, upon request, a copy of the entire Local Marketing Agreement or, if LICENSEE so requests, a copy of the portion of the agreement which sets forth the respective obligations of LICENSEE and the LMA Operator regarding the payment of BMI fees, accountings, record keeping and administrative responsibilities. An officer of LICENSEE shall certify that it is a true and correct copy of the agreement.

10.   INDEMNIFICATION. BMI agrees to indemnify, save and hold harmless and to defend LICENSEE, its advertisers and their advertising agencies, and its and their officers, employees and artists, and each of them from and against all claims, demands and suits that may be made or brought against them or any of them with respect to the performance licensed under this Agreement of any works in the BMI repertoire that are licensed hereunder; provided, however, that such indemnity shall be limited to those claims, demands and suits that are made or brought within the United States, its territories, commonwealth and possessions, and provided further that this indemnity shall not apply to broadcasts of any musical work performed by LICENSEE which is not contained in the BMI repertoire at the time of performance by Station or which is the subject of a written notice of withdrawal in accordance with Paragraph 11 hereof. LICENSEE agrees to give BMI immediate notice of any such claim, demand or suit and agrees to deliver immediately all papers pertaining thereto. BMI shall have full charge of the defense of any such claim, demand or suit, and LICENSEE shall cooperate fully with BMI therein. LICENSEE, however, shall have the right to engage counsel of its own at its own expense who may participate in the defense of any such action. The provisions of this Paragraph shall survive termination of this Agreement, but solely with respect to performances broadcast by Station during the term of this Agreement.

11.   WITHDRAWAL OF WORKS. BMI reserves the right upon written notice to LICENSEE to withdraw from the license granted hereunder any musical work as to which any legal action has been instituted or a claim made that BMI

10

does not have the right to license the performing right in such work or that such work infringes another work. BMI shall notify LICENSEE as promptly as reasonably possible of any such withdrawal and shall attempt to determine and advise LICENSEE at the time of such notice of any Syndicated Television Program in which any such withdrawn work may be contained.

12.   ASSIGNMENT. This license shall be non-assignable except to the person, firm or corporation acquiring the Federal Communications Commission license of Station, and upon assignment to the acquiring person, firm or corporation and upon the acceptance by BMI in form approved by BMI of the application of LICENSEE hereunder, LICENSEE shall be relieved of future liability under this Agreement as long as all statements have been submitted by LICENSEE and all fees due BMI under this Agreement have been paid to BMI. Nothing herein is intended to limit the new owner's entitlement to a license pursuant to Article XIV of the BMI Consent Decree.

13.   ARBITRATION.

(a) With the specific exception of disputes which may be within the jurisdiction of the United States district court having jurisdiction under the BMI Consent Decree, all disputes of any kind, nature or description arising in connection with the terms and conditions of this Agreement shall be submitted to the American Arbitration Association in New York, New York for arbitration under its then prevailing rules, the arbitrator(s) to be selected as follows: Each of the parties shall, by written notice to the other, have the right to appoint one arbitrator. If, within ten days following the giving of such notice by one party, the other shall not, by written notice, appoint another arbitrator, the first arbitrator shall be the sole arbitrator. If two arbitrators are so appointed, they shall appoint a third arbitrator. If ten days elapse after the appointment of the second arbitrator and the two arbitrators are unable to agree upon the third arbitrator, then either party may, in writing, request the American Arbitration Association to appoint the third arbitrator. The award made in the arbitration shall be binding and conclusive on the parties and judgment may be, but need not be, entered thereon in any court having jurisdiction. Such award shall include the fixing of the reasonable costs, expenses and attorneys' fees of arbitration, which shall be borne by the unsuccessful party, subject to the provisions of subparagraph (b) below.

(b) If, during the term of this Agreement, any dispute arises between BMI and LICENSEE concerning the interpretation of any of the provisions of this Agreement, the resolution of which, in the judgment of BMI or COMMITTEE, either jointly or severally, has or may have industry-wide impact, BMI and COMMITTEE shall first endeavor to resolve such dispute, failing which either party may refer the matter to arbitration (unless the parties agree on some alternative mechanism for dispute resolution); and LICENSEE agrees to be bound by the results of all of such arbitrations involving BMI and COMMITTEE. In the event of such a reference, each party shall bear its own costs, expenses and attorneys' fees. In the event of such a reference, either party, as a preliminary matter, shall be entitled to assert that the dispute between the parties is not properly dealt with under the terms of this subparagraph.

14.   TERMINATION BY LICENSEE. LICENSEE shall have the right to terminate this Agreement, upon ten business days' notice to BMI, in the event of: (a) the termination or suspension of the governmental licenses covering LICENSEE, or any substantial alteration or variation of the terms and conditions thereof; or (b) the suspension of operations by Station for a substantial period of time.

15.   BREACH OR DEFAULT. Upon LICENSEE's breach or default of any payment, accounting or substantive reporting obligation required under the terms of this Agreement, BMI may give LICENSEE thirty (30) days' notice in writing to cure such breach or default. In the event that such breach or default has not been cured within thirty (30) days of said notice, BMI may then terminate this Agreement.

16.   NOTICE. Any notice of termination given hereunder shall be given by registered or certified mail or delivery service for which there is proof of delivery to, and receipt by, the addressee. Any other notice required or permitted to be given under this Agreement shall be in writing and shall be deemed duly given when sent by ordinary first-class U.S. mail to the party for whom it is intended, at its office address hereinabove stated, or any other address which either party hereto may from time to time designate for such purpose, and when notice is so mailed, it shall be deemed given upon the mailing thereof. Any notice sent to BMI shall be to the attention of S.V.P. Media Licensing Department. Any notice sent to LICENSEE shall be to the attention of the person signing this Agreement on behalf of LICENSEE or such other person as LICENSEE may advise BMI.

17.   INTERFERENCE IN OPERATIONS. In the event that any law hereafter enacted of the state, or political subdivision thereof, in which LICENSEE is located shall result in major interference with the operations of BMI in that state or political subdivision, or in a substantial increase of the cost to BMI of operating within that state or political subdivision, BMI shall have the right, upon notice to COMMITTEE and upon a showing that the matters referred to affect the licensing of performing right under this Agreement, to apply to the judge with supervisory authority over the BMI Consent Decree for whatever relief BMI deems appropriate, including termination of this Agreement.

18.   BLANKET LICENSE. LICENSEE acknowledges that the BMI Local Television Station Blanket License for the term commencing January 1, 2002 and ending December 31, 2004 (the "Blanket License") is being offered to LICENSEE simultaneously with this Agreement and LICENSEE is entering into this Agreement instead thereof. During the term of this Agreement, LICENSEE may hereafter elect to change from a per program to a blanket license as of the first day of a month, prospectively on prior written notice to BMI (an "Election"). By making an Election, LICENSEE agrees to all the terms of the elected agreement. Thereafter LICENSEE may switch back to the Per Program License in accordance with the provisions of the Blanket License. An Election to change between this Agreement and the

11

Local Television Station Blanket License may be made by LICENSEE not more than twice in any calendar year 2002, 2003 or 2004.

19.   CONFIDENTIALITY.

(a) BMI shall treat as confidential, and shall not disclose to any third party (other than its employees, directors and officers, in their capacity as such, on a need-to-know basis, and other than as set forth in subparagraph (b) below), any financial or other proprietary documents or information provided to BMI by LICENSEE in connection with this Agreement.

(b) BMI is hereby authorized to provide to COMMITTEE such of LICENSEE's financial or other proprietary documents or information, provided to BMI pursuant to this Agreement, as COMMITTEE may request in connection with its representation of the local television industry in future negotiations with BMI, future rate court proceedings, litigation or disputes over the implementation or interpretation of this Agreement, unless LICENSEE notifies BMI in writing to the contrary. As reflected in Exhibit A hereto, COMMITTEE has agreed to treat as confidential any financial or other proprietary documents or information provided to it by BMI pursuant to this Paragraph.

20.   WITHOUT PREJUDICE. The parties are entering into this Agreement without prejudice to any arguments or positions they may assert in any future rate proceeding concerning what constitutes reasonable blanket and per program license fees and terms for the local television industry, or, in BMI's case, as to any other licensee. The definition of Ambient Uses is for purposes of this Agreement only and is being agreed to without prejudice to any positions either party may take in any future litigation or negotiation, including positions with respect to whether or which specific uses of music constitute "fair uses" under 17 U.S.C. § 101 *et seq.* The inclusion of donations in the definition of Revenues Attributable to Non-Network Programs is for purposes of this Agreement only and is being agreed to without prejudice to any positions either party may take in any future litigation or negotiation. The information that LICENSEE has agreed to provide under Paragraph 6(i)(2) shall not prejudice any position either party may take in future negotiation, proceeding or litigation as to the relevance or necessity of such information in licensing musical performances over the Internet.

21.   RESERVATION OF RIGHTS. The license granted in Paragraph 3(a)(ii) is experimental in nature. BMI and LICENSEE recognize that the license granted herein covers certain transmissions originating from and/or received in certain territories outside of the United States, its commonwealth, possessions and territories pursuant to experimental agreements with certain non-U.S. performing rights licensing organizations around the world, and is broader in geographical scope than BMI's previous licenses. Notwithstanding, BMI is offering the license in Paragraph 3(a)(ii) on an experimental and non-prejudicial basis for the purpose of evaluating such international licensing initiatives. Accordingly, the removal during the Term of any or all of the territories listed on Exhibit C in the licensing section of the BMI web site located at http://www.bmi.com from the scope of coverage provided for in Paragraph 3(a)(ii) shall have no impact on the fees due hereunder. The Parties hereby expressly reserve their right to re-evaluate the appropriateness of the fees and terms herein with respect to all transmissions licensed under Paragraph 3(a)(ii), including, but not limited to, the reasonable value of a license that covers transmissions beyond the United States, its commonwealth, possessions and territories, for periods following the Term.

22.   MISCELLANEOUS. This Agreement, and all Exhibits hereto, constitutes the entire understanding between the parties and cannot be waived or added to or modified orally, and no waiver, addition or modification shall be valid unless in writing and signed by the parties. This Agreement, its validity, construction and effect shall be governed by the laws of the State of New York. The fact that any provisions herein are found to be void or unenforceable by a court of competent jurisdiction shall in no way affect the validity or enforceability of any other provisions.

IN WITNESS WHEREOF, the parties hereto have duly executed this Agreement the day and date hereinbefore set forth.

BROADCAST MUSIC, INC.

	LICENSEE (Legal Name)

By: _____   By: _____
        (Signature)   *(Signature)*

_____   _____
    (Print Name of Signer)   *(Print Name of Signer)*

_____   _____
        (Title of Signer)   *(Title of Signer)*

12

TELEVISION MUSIC LICENSE COMMITTEE

EXHIBIT A

May 17, 2002

Broadcast Music, Inc.
320 West 57th Street
New York, N.Y. 10019

Attention: Mr. John Shaker

Re: <u>BMI – Local Television Station Blanket and Per Program Licenses</u>

Dear Mr. Shaker:

This letter sets forth the agreement reached between Broadcast Music, Inc. ("BMI") and the Television Music License Committee (the "COMMITTEE") concerning certain additional terms of the BMI – Local Television Station Blanket and Per Program License Agreements covering the periods April 1, 1999 through December 31, 2004 (herein "Blanket Licenses" and "Per Program Licenses", and collectively referred to as "Licenses"). This letter agreement is expressly incorporated in paragraph 4 of the Blanket and Per Program Licenses, respectively, and is binding upon the parties hereto and upon the signatories to the Licenses and their successors and assigns.

The parties agree as follows:

1. For the years 2002, 2003 and 2004, domestic commercial television stations that were licensed by BMI in 2001 pursuant to interim licenses agreed to between BMI and the COMMITTEE ("Existing Television Stations") shall pay license fees to BMI as follows:

(a) Existing Television Stations entering into the Blanket License with BMI, or switching thereto, shall each pay BMI each year their allocated share of the annual industry-wide BMI blanket license fee of $85 million, at such times and in such manner as provided therein for such years (or portions thereof) that they have elected to be bound by a Blanket License. The methodology for the allocation of blanket license fees among Existing Television Stations for each of those calendar years is set forth in Schedule I hereto.

(b) Existing Television Stations entering into Per Program Licenses with BMI, or switching thereto, shall each pay BMI such fees, and at such times and in such manner, as are provided therein. Per Program License Fees for Existing Television Stations shall be computed based upon each station's Monthly Base License Fee. For each calendar year 2002, 2003 and 2004, each Existing Television Station's Monthly Base License Fee shall be equal to one-twelfth of its share of the annual industry-wide BMI per program license fee of $98.1 million, subject to subparagraph (c) hereof.

(c) In the event that during the term of the Licenses, the COMMITTEE negotiates with the American Society of Composers, Authors and Publishers ("ASCAP") an annual industry-wide per program license fee, or the ASCAP rate court establishes an annual industry-wide per program license fee for ASCAP in a proceeding no longer subject to appeal, different from $98.1 million, then the parties agree that the ASCAP amount will be substituted for the $98.1 million figure in paragraph (b) prospectively from the effective date of such ASCAP fee change for any period remaining in the term of the Licenses; provided, however, that substitution of the base fee shall only occur if the material non-fee terms and conditions of the ASCAP per program license are similar to the terms and conditions of the BMI Per Program License.

9 East 53rd Street, 5th fl., New York, NY 10022 phone: (212) 308-9040 fax: (212) 754-9286

13

(d) Each Existing Television Station shall pay to BMI its allocated share of the annual industry-wide BMI Internet blanket license fee of $558,333.33 in each of the years 2002, 2003 and 2004. An Existing Television Station's allocated share of the industry-wide BMI Internet blanket license fee shall be calculated by multiplying $558,333.33 times a factor representing the percentage of the industry-wide BMI blanket license fee that is allocated to the station in a given year pursuant to Schedule I to this letter agreement. For example, a station with an annual blanket license fee of $850,000 (or 1% of the industry-wide blanket license fee for the year 2003) shall be allocated 1% of the industry-wide BMI Internet blanket license fee (or $5,583.33).

2. For the period from April 1, 1999, through December 31, 2001 (the "Settlement Period"), BMI and the COMMITTEE agree that Existing Television Stations shall pay to BMI their allocated share of the industry-wide lump-sum settlement fee of $12 million (the "Settlement Fee"), which payments will represent, when combined with the interim fees payable to BMI under the interim BMI Blanket and Per Program Licenses agreed to by BMI and the COMMITTEE for that period, the final license fees payable for the Settlement Period. The COMMITTEE shall allocate the Settlement Fee among the Existing Television Stations, and shall provide BMI prior to February 15, 2002 with a schedule that details the amounts to be billed to each station. The stations' shares of the Settlement Fee shall be billed in equal monthly installments over a 36 month period commencing January 1, 2002, separately from the stations' monthly payments as calculated pursuant to Paragraph 1(a) above and Schedule I to this letter agreement.

3. Subject to paragraph 7 below, if for any part of the term of this letter agreement, BMI enters into a License with a television station that is not an Existing Television Station (a "New Television Station"), the New Television Station shall pay BMI license fees, whether under the Blanket License or the Per Program License, as the case may be, as follows:

(a) if the New Television Station was previously licensed by the FCC and operating as a broadcast television station for more than twelve (12) months prior to entering into a License with BMI, then the fees payable by all stations in the New Television Station's local market as of the effective date of the New Television Station's license agreement shall be reallocated under Schedule I hereto as if such station were an Existing Television Station and without any increase in the total fee amount otherwise allocable to the relevant local television market. The New Television Station and all other licensees in its local market shall thereafter be obligated to pay such re-allocated fees; or

(b) if the New Television Station was not previously licensed by the FCC and operating as a broadcast television station for more than twelve (12) months prior to entering into a License with BMI, such station shall pay the minimum monthly fee of forty-five dollars ($45.00) for the remainder of the calendar year following the effective date of its license agreement. Thereafter, the fees payable by all stations in the New Television Station's local market shall be reallocated under Schedule I hereto as if such station were an Existing Television Station and without any increase in the total fee amount otherwise allocable to the relevant local television market. The New Television Station and all other licensees in its local market shall thereafter be obligated to pay such re-allocated fees.

(c) BMI shall be obligated to notify licensees in writing as to any adjustment in their fees resulting from the reallocation procedures set forth in Paragraphs 3(a) and (b) within ten (10) days of the determination of such reallocated fees. In the event an Existing Television Station's fees are reduced as a result of any such reallocation, BMI shall credit such licensee's account for the amount of any such excess fees which have already been paid by such licensee as of the effective date of reallocation, or, if such licensee so elects, BMI shall, within thirty (30) days of receiving notification of such election, refund to licensee the amount of any such excess fees.

4. If, during the term of this Agreement, BMI licenses any entity agreed or determined to be a broadcast television "network" previously unlicensed by BMI (such as FOX, UPN, or The WB), whose network programs are carried by local television stations licensed by BMI pursuant to the Licenses, the industry-wide amounts set forth in Paragraph 1 above pertaining to the periods of such third party license agreements shall be adjusted downward in an appropriate amount. BMI shall have the ultimate responsibility for re-allocating industry-wide blanket license fees to reflect any such reduction, following consultation with the COMMITTEE. BMI and the COMMITTEE will confer and attempt to reach agreement concerning the appropriate amount of any such fee adjustments and such agreement shall be binding on all licensees. If BMI and the COMMITTEE shall fail to agree on such fee adjustments, either party may refer the matter to the federal judge with supervisory authority over the BMI Consent Decree for determination.

5. BMI shall provide to the COMMITTEE or its designated representative for verification, by no later than forty-five (45) days before its scheduled dissemination to licensees, a copy of each list of Syndicated Television Programs prepared pursuant to Paragraph 6(c) of the Per Program License. The COMMITTEE shall notify BMI of any suggested revisions or corrections to this list no later than three weeks from the date it was received.

6. If, for any part of the term hereof, a station previously licensed by BMI under a separate agreement changes its format and elects to be licensed pursuant to a License, such station's blanket and per program license fee allocations shall be determined pursuant to the methodology set forth in Schedule I as though it were an Existing Television Station, except that: (a) such station's allocated blanket or per program license fee shall be in addition to the industry-

14

wide blanket or per program license fees set forth in Paragraph 2 above; and (b) blanket or per program license fees allocated to other stations in the same market shall be determined as if such station were not licensed pursuant to a License, and thus shall remain unchanged.

7. The COMMITTEE shall treat as confidential any financial or other proprietary information or documents provided to it by BMI pursuant to the Local Television Station Per Program License Agreement ("Confidential Information"). The COMMITTEE shall limit access to Confidential Information to the COMMITTEE's staff, representatives and counsel, and shall not disclose Confidential Information to any third party or to any COMMITTEE member, other than a COMMITTEE member who is employed by the station group which provided Confidential Information to BMI.

8. BMI and the COMMITTEE are entering into this Agreement without prejudice to any arguments or positions they may assert in any future rate proceeding concerning what constitutes reasonable blanket and per program license fees and terms for the local television industry or, in BMI's case, as to any licensee.

Please indicate your agreement to the above by signing on the line provided below.

Very truly yours,

s/ Chuck Sennet

Co-Chair

Television Music License Committee

s/ Catherine Nierle

Co-Chair

Television Music License Committee

AGREED TO:

s/ John Shaker

Senior Vice President/Licensing

Broadcast Music, Inc.

15

Television Music License Committee
Methodology for Industry-Wide BMI License Fee Allocation for the Period From January 1, 2002 through December 31, 2004

STEP 1: Allocation of Industry-Wide Fee Among DMA Markets

In a given year, each television market is to be assigned its allocable share of the $85 million industry-wide blanket license fee based on a weighted, three-year average percentage of the total U.S. television households it represents.[1]

1. For each of the years 2002 through 2004 ("Contract Years"), the number of TV households in each of the roughly 210 DMA markets as measured by Nielsen[2] is to be "weighted" as follows:

Markets 1 - 10	Multiply by 1.19
Markets 11 - 25	Multiply by 1.05
Markets 26 - 50	Multiply by 0.92
Markets 51 - 75	Multiply by 0.85
Markets 76 - 100	Multiply by 0.85
Markets 101 - 125	Multiply by 0.85
Markets 126 plus	Multiply by 0.80

The purpose of the weighting is to reflect, within broad parameters, that a household in the 150th market does not represent the same value as a household in the New York market.

2. For each Contract Year, each market is to be assigned its share of the industry's overall $85 Million blanket license fee by the following procedure: Each market's three-year households average (based on the three prior years) will be computed. The multiples set forth in Paragraph 1 above will next be applied to these market rankings resulting from computation of the three-year averages to produce a weighted average households figure for each market. Thus, for example, the top ten markets in terms of three-year households average will receive a 1.19 multiple. Each market's weighted average households figure is to be divided by the total U.S. average weighted households to derive a percentage of U.S. weighted TV households for each market. This weighted percentage is then applied to the industry-wide blanket license fee. Thus, if the weighted percentage of total U.S. TV households for market "x" is one percent, market x's share of the Contract Year 2002 industry-wide blanket license fee would be $85 Million x 1%, or $85,000.

STEP 2: Allocation of Blanket License Fees to Stations Within Each Market[3]

A series of computations will be undertaken to apportion a given market's allocated blanket license fee in relation to each station in that market's viewing households (with an allowance for a portion of the prime-time audience reached by network-affiliated stations). [4]

1. For Contract Year 2002, the process will begin with Nielsen's Market Ratings Reports for the "sweeps" months assigned for these purposes to each of 1999, 2000 and 2001. Within each market, each station's average DMA quarter-hour viewing households, Sunday through Saturday, 9 a.m. through midnight, is to be computed for each of the sweeps months for each of 1999, 2000 and 2001. The same methodology is to be utilized for Contract Year 2003 (employing comparable Nielsen viewership data for the three years 2000, 2001 and 2002) and Contract Year 2004 (employing comparable Nielsen viewership data for the three years 2001, 2002 and 2003).[5]

2. To make allowance for the fact that a portion of a network affiliate's 9 a.m. to midnight schedule constitutes BMI licensed network programming, the following computations, which lead to each station's "qualifying" viewing households, are to be made for each sweeps month:

---

1. In addition, in a given year, each television market is to be assigned its allocable share of the industry-wide base per program license fee (as set forth in paragraphs 1(b) and (c) of Exhibit A to the BMI Local Television Station Music Performance Blanket and Per Program Licenses) pursuant to the methodology described in this Step 1.

2. The number of television households in television markets located in: Alaska and Hawaii shall be determined based upon data collected by Nielsen; Virgin Islands and Guam shall be determined based upon data collected by the United States Census; and Puerto Rico shall be determined based upon data collected by Media Fax. For purposes of assigning an allocable share of the industry-wide blanket license fee to television markets in Alaska, Hawaii, Virgin Islands, Guam and Puerto Rico, the number of television households in each of these markets is to be given the same weight as the Nielsen DMA that most closely approximates the number of television households in these markets.

3. The computations described in this Step 2 will also be used to apportion a given market's allocated base per program license fee among the stations within that market.

4. Network-affiliated stations are defined as those affiliated with the ABC, CBS, and NBC television networks and those affiliated with, but not owned by, the Univision Television Network

5. For purposes of these calculations, the sweeps months for a given year comprise the November sweeps period of the prior year, and the February and May Sweeps period of that year. For example, the designated sweeps months for 2000 are November 1999 and February and May 2000.

16

(a) multiply each station's average DMA quarter-hour viewing households by 420 (the number of quarter-hour units between 9 a.m. and midnight in one week). For independent stations, the result of this computation constitutes those stations' qualifying viewing households.

(b) with respect to the allocation of fees for network-affiliated stations, arrive at "qualifying" viewing households by subtracting from the totals generated by step (a) 100 percent of a prime-time viewing households figure, which figure (prior to application of the 100 percent factor) is calculated by taking a station's average DMA quarter-hour households in prime-time, and multiplying this figure by 88 (the number of quarter-hour units in prime-time in one week.[6])

3. The nine separate months of DMA viewing households data thus derived for each independent and affiliated station in a market are next aggregated as to each station to arrive at its total qualifying viewing households. This is done for each station in the market. The qualifying viewing households data for all stations in the market are then aggregated to get a base for the entire market. Each station's percentage share of the allocated market blanket license fee (derived through the process described in Step 1, above) is computed by dividing its qualifying viewing households number by the base qualifying viewing households number for that market.

4. A station's blanket license fee is computed by applying the resulting percentage applicable to that station to the market blanket license fee.

5. In those markets having stations which receive no rating in the Nielsen reports and which are not separately licensed by BMI, the following methodology will be employed. Each such station will be assigned a blanket license fee equal to 0.25 percent of the allocable blanket license fee for that market or $540 annually, whichever is higher. The remaining stations will be allocated blanket license fees based on the methodology set forth in Step 2 hereof, except that the allocable blanket license fee for the market for purposes of those computations shall be reduced by the amount payable by those stations in the market not listed by Nielsen. If, by way of example, the blanket license fee allocated to market "k" is $300,000, and there are operating in market "k" two stations not listed by Nielsen, each of those stations would be assigned a blanket fee of $750 ($300,000 x .0025). The remaining stations in market "k" would pay their appropriate percentages, not of $300,000, but of $298,500.

6. The minimum blanket license fee for a given station shall be the greater of 0.25 percent of the allocable blanket license fee for its market or an annual blanket license fee of $540 (or $45 per month for partial years) ("Minimum Blanket License Fee").

7. If, during a given Contract Year, BMI enters into a license agreement with a television station that was not previously licensed (a "New Television Station"), the New Television Station shall be assigned blanket license fees as follows:

(a) if the New Television Station was previously licensed by the FCC and operating as a broadcast television station for more than twelve (12) months prior to entering into a license with BMI, then the fees payable by all stations in the New Television Station's market as of the effective date of the New Television Station's license agreement shall be reallocated pursuant to paragraphs 1 - 6 above without any increase in the total fee amount otherwise allocable to the relevant market; or

(b) if the New Television Station was not previously licensed by the FCC and operating as a broadcast television station for more than twelve (12) months prior to entering into a license with BMI, such station shall pay the minimum monthly fee of forty-five dollars ($45.00) for the remainder of the Contract Year following the effective date of its license agreement. The fees payable by all stations in the New Television Station's market in the following Calendar Year shall be reallocated under paragraphs 1 - 6 above without any increase in the total fee amount otherwise allocable to the relevant market.

6.　　*E.g.,* on the East Coast, prime-time occupies Monday-Saturday 8:00-11:00 p.m. and Sunday 7:00-11:00 p.m.

17

BMI®   **EXHIBIT B**

Broadcast Music, Inc.
320 West 57ᵗʰ Street
New York, NY 10019
ATTN: BMI Local TV Web Site Licensing

Re: Launch of Local TV Station Web Site

To Whom It May Concern:

Please be advised that, on _____ *(day, month)*, _____ *(year)*, local television
station _____ *(call letters)* began distributing a web site known as _____
and located at the Uniform Resource Locator (URL) http:// _____
pursuant to the 1999-2004 BMI Local Television Music Performance Agreement.

WEB SITE REPORT CONTACT:
NAME:_____
TITLE:_____
EMAIL:_____
TELEPHONE:_____

Sincerely,

_____
            (Signature)

Print Name: _____
Company: _____
Address: _____
                      _____
Telephone: _____
Fax: _____
Email: _____

18

197

BMI®

EXHIBIT C

LOCAL TV STATION WEB SITE
MUSIC USE REPORT

Music use report for the period from _____, _____ through _____, _____.
Month/Day,   Year   Month/Day,   Year

Legal Name: _____

Call Letters: _____

Address:_____

_____

URL: _____

WEB SITE TRAFFIC INFORMATION:

Total number of page impressions on the web site during the period:

Total number of streamed transmissions during the period:

LIVE STREAMING: the simultaneous transmission of station's locally produced and aired programming *(see Paragraph 3(a)(ii)(A) of the Agreement):*

☐ Please check here if the TV Station Web Site engaged in the simultaneous retransmission of locally produced and aired programming during the period. Please identify such programming below (e.g., if all, write 'all'; if local newscasts only, write 'local newscasts'; if other programming, write the title(s) of such other programming).

_____

_____

ARCHIVED STREAMING: the transmission of station's local newscasts and/or local news based public affairs programming *(see Paragraph 3(a)(ii)(B) of the Agreement):*

☐ Please check here if the TV Station Web Site engaged in the retransmission of local newscasts and/or local news based public affairs programming during the period. Please identify such programming below.

    ☐ Local Newscasts
    ☐ Local News Based Public Affairs Programming

PROMOTIONAL CLIPS TO PROMOTE VIEWERSHIP OF STATION AND ITS TELEVISION PROGRAMMING *(see Paragraph 3(a)(ii)(C) of the Agreement):*

☐ Please check here if the TV Station Web Site contained individually retrievable, archived promotional announcements to promote viewership of station and its television programming during the period.

    Please check the appropriate box(es) to indicate the type(s) of programming:

    ☐ Syndicated Programs
    ☐ Network Programs
    ☐ Local Programming

I hereby certify on this _____ day of _____, _____ that the above is true and correct.

By: _____

    (SIGNATURE)

_____

    (PRINT NAME OF SIGNER)

_____

    (TITLE OF SIGNER)

19

BMI®   **EXHIBIT D**

DIGITAL SIGNAL QUESTIONNAIRE

This questionnaire should be filled out and e-mailed to BMI
during the month of October 2002, 2003 and 2004.

Legal Name of Licensee: _____

Analog Signal Call Letters: _____

Station's Address: _____

City: _____   **State:** _____

---

1. **Is the station currently broadcasting a digital signal?**

   ☐ Yes

   ☐ No (Skip all remaining questions)

2. **What are the call letters of your digital signal?** _____-DT

3. **What are the current weekly hours of on-air operation of your digital signal?** _____

4. **Does your digital signal programming consist completely of simulcasts of your analog signal programming?**

   ☐ Yes (Skip the last question)

   ☐ No

5. **If your digital signal programming differs from your analog signal programming, or if you have multicast programming in your digital signal, please identify all non-simulcast programming broadcast in your digital signal, including broadcast dates and times. (Please add additional sheets as necessary.)**

   _____

   _____

   _____

20

199

EXHIBIT E

Local Marketing Agreement Amendment to Local
Television Station Music Performance License Agreement

WHEREAS, _____ ("LICENSEE") has entered into a Local

Marketing Agreement ("LMA") with _____ ("LMA OPERATOR") for the

television station _____ (the "STATION") for the period

_____through _____; it is hereby agreed to as follows:

1. LICENSEE and LMA OPERATOR add LMA OPERATOR as a party to the BMI Local Television Blanket [Per Program] License Agreement, including all extensions, schedules and exhibits thereto, in effect between LICENSEE and BMI ("the License"), and LMA OPERATOR shall assume, with LICENSEE, all of the rights and obligations of LICENSEE set forth in the License for the full period of the LMA with respect to the STATION.

2. LICENSEE/LMA OPERATOR (circle one) shall be responsible in the first instance for the payment of any fees owing to BMI and for the submission to BMI of any reports or other information pursuant to the License for the full period of the LMA with respect to the STATION.

3. LICENSEE remains fully liable for all its obligations under the License. Even if the LMA OPERATOR is responsible in the first instance for the payment of fees and submissions of reports or other information to BMI as set forth in Paragraph 2 above, if LMA OPERATOR defaults in any way on those obligations, LICENSEE remains responsible for fulfilling those obligations.

4. LICENSEE and LMA OPERATOR jointly designate the following single address for billing, and other regular correspondence, and the following single address for any notices in accordance with the License.

Billing Address: _____   **Notice Address:** _____

_____   _____

_____   _____

In the event that the LMA between LICENSEE and LMA OPERATOR terminates, both LICENSEE and LMA OPERATOR shall notify BMI of the termination within 30 days, and submit all required statements, reports and payments through the date of said termination. In the event that both LICENSEE and LMA OPERATOR fail to notify BMI of the termination of the LMA, then both LICENSEE and LMA OPERATOR shall remain obligated under this agreement for all statements, reports and payments.

Dated: [   ]   [   ]

                                        LICENSEE

                            By: [   ]

                            Title: [   ]

Dated: [   ]   [   ]

                                        LMA OPERATOR

                            By: [   ]

                            Title: [   ]

Broadcast Music, Inc. hereby consents and agrees to the amendment of the above-mentioned License Agreement.

BROADCAST MUSIC, INC.

Dated: [   ]   By: [   ]

                            Title: [   ]

soundexchange   1330 CONNECTICUT AVE, NW, SUITE 330, WASHINGTON, DC 20036
P: 202.828.0120 F: 202.833.2141
WWW.SOUNDEXCHANGE.COM

SOUND RECORDING COPYRIGHT OWNER AUTHORIZATION LETTER

Dear Sound Recording Copyright Owner:

SoundExchange®, an independent nonprofit performance rights organization, ("SoundExchange") invites you (the "Copyright Owner" identified below) to participate in the SoundExchange Performance Right Program ("the Program") if you own the exclusive right under the U.S. Copyright Act to perform publicly by means of a digital audio transmission one or more copyrighted sound recordings or have the right to license the public performance of one or more copyrighted sound recordings by means of a digital audio transmission.

If you choose to participate in the Program, then, pursuant to the authority granted by Section 114(e)(1) of the Copyright Act, you hereby grant SoundExchange the nonexclusive right to license the public performance of all of your sound recordings by means of digital audio transmissions subject to statutory licensing under Section 114(d)(2) and the making of phonorecords of all of your sound recordings, or any part thereof subject to statutory licensing under section 112(e) of the Copyright Act (including the making of multiple such phonorecords of a single sound recording), and authorize SoundExchange to receive and distribute royalties on your behalf, for the term set forth in, and otherwise in accordance with, the attached "SoundExchange Performance Right and Ephemeral Recording Program Terms and Conditions" dated August 5, 1999. The person countersigning this letter on behalf of the Copyright Owner represents and warrants that he or she has the authority to grant such right and authorization on behalf of the Copyright Owner.

If you agree to the attached SoundExchange Performance Right Program Terms and Conditions and choose to participate in the Program in accordance with those terms and conditions, please provide the information requested in the spaces provided below, countersign a copy of this letter, and return the signed copy to SoundExchange.

Sincerely,

John L. Simson
President/Executive Director
SoundExchange, Inc.

(Rev. 5.06.04)

201

Accepted and Agreed to:

Name of Copyright Owner:

_____

By: _____

            (Signature of authorized representative)

Name of person signing: _____

Title: _____

Date: _____

SOUNDEXCHANGE® PERFORMANCE RIGHT AND
EPHEMERAL RECORDING PROGRAM TERMS AND CONDITIONS

This document sets forth the terms and conditions of the agreement ("Agreement") between a sound recording copyright owner (the "Copyright Owner") and SoundExchange, an independent nonprofit performance rights organization ("SoundExchange") pursuant to which SoundExchange will, among other things, negotiate licenses and agree to royalty rates and terms and conditions for the performance of sound recordings and the making of certain ephemeral recordings, and receive royalty payments, on the Copyright Owner's behalf, on a nonexclusive basis.

1. <u>Representation and Warranty</u>. The Copyright Owner represents and warrants to SoundExchange that the Copyright Owner, either alone or jointly with others, including its affiliates listed in Exhibit A, owns, or has the right to license, the rights under the U.S. Copyright Act to perform one or more copyrighted sound recordings publicly by means of a digital audio transmission and to reproduce phonorecords of such sound recordings.

2. <u>Right to License</u>. Subject to the reservation of rights in Paragraph 3, the Copyright Owner, including on behalf of its affiliates listed in Exhibit A, hereby grants SoundExchange, for the term of the Agreement, the nonexclusive right to license (i) the public performance of the "Licensed Recordings," or any part thereof, by means of digital audio transmissions subject to statutory licensing under Section 114(d)(2) of the Copyright Act, and (ii) the making of phonorecords of the "Licensed Recordings," or any part thereof, subject to statutory licensing under Section 112(e) of the Copyright Act (including the making of multiple such phonorecords of a single sound recording). For purposes of the Agreement, the term "Licensed Recording" means each and every sound recording with respect to which the Copyright Owner at any time during the term of the Agreement either (a) owns, alone or jointly with others, the right under the Copyright Act to perform the sound recording publicly by means of a digital audio transmission and to reproduce phonorecords of such sound recording, (b) has the power to cause another person or entity to grant the foregoing right to license, through ownership, management, employment or other working control over such person or entity, or (c) otherwise has the authority to grant the foregoing right to license or the power to cause such right to be granted. For purposes of the Agreement, the terms "public performance" and "digital audio transmission," and other terms of art in copyright law, shall have the meaning given those terms under copyright law. The foregoing right to license shall be deemed granted to SoundExchange when a Sound Recording Copyright Owner Authorization Letter ("Authorization Letter") is signed by the Copyright Owner. With respect to each Licensed Recording, the right to license shall apply as soon as (x) the Authorization Letter is signed, (y) the sound recording first is commercially released, and (z) rights therein first are acquired by the Copyright Owner or the sound recording otherwise first satisfies the foregoing definition of "Licensed Recording."

3. <u>Reservation of Rights</u>. The Copyright Owner retains all rights with respect to the Licensed Recordings not specifically granted herein. The right to license provided in Paragraph 2 is granted on a nonexclusive basis. Thus, the Copyright Owner retains the right

SoundExchange
3

203

to license the public performance and reproduction of Licensed Recordings independent of SoundExchange. However, the Copyright Owner shall not authorize any other person or entity to license public performance of the Licensed Recordings, or the making of phonorecords of the Licensed Recordings subject to statutory licensing under Section 112(e) of the Copyright Act, collectively with other sound recordings. The parties acknowledge that the Agreement does not cover the licensing of digital audio transmissions not subject to statutory licensing under Section 114(d)(2) of the Copyright Act or the licensing of reproductions not subject to statutory licensing under Section 112(e) of the Copyright Act.

4. Authority to Negotiate. Pursuant to Sections 112(e)(3) and 114(e)(1) of the Copyright Act, the Copyright Owner, including its affiliates listed in Exhibit A, hereby authorizes SoundExchange, during the term of the Agreement, to negotiate licenses with third parties and agree to royalty rates and terms and conditions for the performance of the Licensed Recordings by means of digital audio transmissions subject to statutory licensing under Section 114(d)(2) of the Copyright Act and the making of phonorecords of the Licensed Recordings subject to statutory licensing under Section 112(e) of the Copyright Act, and to receive royalty payments, on the Copyright Owner's behalf on a nonexclusive basis. Without limiting the generality of the foregoing, the Copyright Owner authorizes SoundExchange to represent the Copyright Owner in connection with voluntary negotiation proceedings and arbitration proceedings as described in Sections 112(e) and 114(f) of the Copyright Act and otherwise to represent the Copyright Owner in (i) licensing the public performance of the Licensed Recordings by means of digital audio transmissions subject to statutory licensing under Section 114(d)(2) of the Copyright Act and the making of phonorecords of the Licensed Recordings subject to statutory licensing under Section 112(e) of the Copyright Act, and (ii) other related proceedings, administrative actions, hearings, litigation, and appeals. The Copyright Owner shall not similarly authorize any other person or entity to undertake such activities on a collective basis for the Copyright Owner and other owners of copyrights in sound recordings.

5. Collection of Royalties. SoundExchange shall deposit all royalties received by SoundExchange from the licensing of the Licensed Recordings in interest-bearing accounts for distribution to copyright owners. In its discretion, SoundExchange may audit the royalty payments made and records kept by licensees.

6. Payment to SoundExchange. From the royalties collected by SoundExchange from the licensing of the Licensed Recordings and other sound recordings and from any amounts recovered by SoundExchange through enforcement of sound recording copyrights as to activities subject to licensing under the Agreement, SoundExchange shall deduct SoundExchange's actual, reasonable expenses of its performance right and ephemeral recording program, including administrative expenses, attorneys' fees and any other amounts paid by SoundExchange in connection with its performance right and ephemeral recording program. SoundExchange's royalty distribution system described in Paragraph 7 shall be intended to distribute such expenses equitably among all copyright owners participating in SoundExchange's performance right and ephemeral recording program. At the Copyright Owner's request, SoundExchange shall provide reasonable access to SoundExchange's records concerning the calculation of expenses allocated by SoundExchange to its performance right and ephemeral recording program.

SoundExchange
4

7. <u>Distribution of Royalties</u>. During the term of this Agreement, SoundExchange shall distribute the royalties that SoundExchange obtains from the licensing of the Licensed Recordings and sound recordings of other copyright owners, as well as any amounts recovered by SoundExchange through enforcement of sound recording copyrights as to activities subject to licensing under the Agreement, less SoundExchange's expenses as described in Paragraph 6, in accordance with the system of classification and distribution determined in accordance with the Governance documents of SoundExchange for this purpose, as such system may be modified from time to time. SoundExchange shall notify the Copyright Owner at least sixty days before any change in such system becomes effective. The Copyright Owner authorizes SoundExchange to establish and implement a program of monitoring to acquire data on which to base distributions. In addition, the Copyright Owner shall provide to SoundExchange such accurate and timely information concerning the Copyright Owner's entitlement to royalties, and SoundExchange's distribution thereof, as SoundExchange may reasonably require, including without limitation titles of sound recordings included in the Licensed Recordings, proof of rights with respect thereto, release dates, configuration types and royalty distribution information. In order to make distributions, SoundExchange may from time to time adopt systems for classifying sound recordings or copyright owners participating in SoundExchange's performance right and ephemeral recording program. The Copyright Owner may appeal SoundExchange's classifications made with respect to the Copyright Owner in accordance with the process established by the aforesaid committee or panel. However, at the conclusion of any such appeal, SoundExchange's classifications shall be final, conclusive and binding.

The Copyright Owner hereby grants to SoundExchange the following rights in the Copyright Owner's share of any royalties: If SoundExchange is unable to distribute the Copyright Owner's share of any royalties (e.g., because the Copyright Owner does not provide necessary information or SoundExchange is unable to locate the Copyright Owner at the time a distribution is to be made), SoundExchange shall retain the Copyright Owner's royalties, and solicit such information or try to locate the Copyright Owner, for a period of three years from the date the royalties shall have become payable. At the end of such period, all right, title and interest to such royalties shall fully and absolutely vest in SoundExchange, which may use the unclaimed funds to distribute to all copyright owners and to pay expenses as described in Paragraph 6, and the Copyright Owner will have no further right, title, interest or claim to such royalties.

8. <u>Enforcement</u>. During the term of the Agreement, with the consent of the Copyright Owner, SoundExchange shall be authorized to enforce and protect the rights under the Copyright Act to perform the Licensed Recordings publicly by means of a digital audio transmission and to reproduce phonorecords of the Licensed Recordings under circumstances subject to statutory licensing under Section 112(e) of the Copyright Act, either standing in the name of the Copyright Owner or others, and regardless of whether the copyrights in the Licensed Recordings are in the name of the Copyright Owner or others. Without limiting the generality of the foregoing, once SoundExchange has obtained such consent, SoundExchange may, in SoundExchange's sole judgment, (i) commence and prosecute litigation, in the name of SoundExchange or the Copyright Owner or in the name of others in whose name the copyrights may be held, to collect and receive damages arising

from infringement of the foregoing rights, (ii) join the Copyright Owner or others in whose names the copyrights may be held as parties plaintiff or defendant in any litigation involving such rights, or (iii) release, compromise, or refer to arbitration any claims or actions involving infringement of such rights, in the same manner and to the same extent as the Copyright Owner could. Subject to SoundExchange's obtaining the Copyright Owner's consent as provided above, the Copyright Owner hereby makes, constitutes and appoints SoundExchange or its successor as the Copyright Owner's true and lawful attorney, irrevocably during the term of the Agreement, to do all acts, take all proceedings, and execute, acknowledge and deliver any and all instruments, papers, documents, process and pleadings that may be necessary, proper or expedient to restrain infringements and recover damages relating to the infringement or other violation of such rights and to discontinue, compromise or refer to arbitration any such proceedings or actions, or to make any other disposition of the differences in relation thereto, in the name of SoundExchange or its successor, or in the name of the Copyright Owner or otherwise. Any amounts recovered by SoundExchange through enforcement activities authorized pursuant to this Paragraph 8 shall be allocated and distributed in accordance with Paragraphs 6 and 7.

9. Further Assurances. The Copyright Owner agrees from time to time to execute, acknowledge and deliver to SoundExchange such assurances, powers of attorney or other authorizations or instruments as SoundExchange may deem necessary or expedient to enable it to exercise, enjoy and enforce, in its own name or otherwise, all rights and remedies described above; provided that this Paragraph 9 shall not allow SoundExchange to require the Copyright Owner to grant or assign to SoundExchange any greater rights with respect to the Licensed Recordings than the rights otherwise specifically granted in the Agreement.

10. Term. The term of the Agreement shall commence when the Copyright Owner has signed an Authorization Letter, provided that the Copyright Owner promptly delivers the signed Authorization Letter to SoundExchange, unless SoundExchange notifies the Copyright Owner within thirty days after receiving the signed Authorization Letter that SoundExchange does not accept the Authorization Letter. Thereafter, the term of the Agreement shall continue unless either party gives the other party thirty days notice of termination, which notice shall be in writing and be delivered by certified mail, reputable overnight courier, or other means resulting in proof of receipt. Upon the termination of the Agreement, each party's rights and obligations under the Agreement shall cease, except that (i) any licenses granted by SoundExchange with respect to Licensed Recordings shall remain in effect for the duration thereof in accordance with their terms; (ii) for so long as SoundExchange receives royalties from the licensing of Licensed Recordings, such royalties shall be subject to the provisions of Paragraph 5, and SoundExchange shall distribute such royalties to the Copyright Owner in accordance with Paragraphs 6 and 7; and (iii) SoundExchange shall continue to be authorized under Paragraph 8 to continue any litigation commenced before the date of termination.

11. Changes to Terms. In order to maintain flexibility in administering SoundExchange's performance right and ephemeral recording program, SoundExchange may change these terms and conditions by giving the Copyright Owner sixty days written notice. However, no change will apply retroactively, and if the Copyright Owner does not agree with any change, the Copyright Owner may terminate the Agreement in accordance

SoundExchange
6

with Paragraph 10. The Agreement otherwise may be modified or amended only by written agreement of the parties to the Agreement.

12. <u>Limitation of Liability</u>. SoundExchange will undertake its responsibilities under this Agreement in accordance with its sound business judgment and a reasonable standard of care. However, SoundExchange shall not be liable to the Copyright Owner for any direct, indirect, incidental, special or consequential damages arising from this Agreement, except in the event of gross negligence or willful misconduct on the part of SoundExchange.

13. <u>Assignment</u>. Neither party shall assign any of its rights under this Agreement without the written consent of the other party, which consent shall not be withheld unreasonably. Notwithstanding the foregoing, SoundExchange may assign its rights and delegate its obligations under this Agreement to a corporation or other legal entity formed for the purpose of carrying on SoundExchange's performance right and ephemeral recording program. SoundExchange shall give the Copyright Owner sixty days written notice of any proposed such assignment, and if the Copyright Owner does not agree with such proposed assignment, the Copyright Owner may terminate the Agreement in accordance with Paragraph 10. If SoundExchange makes such an assignment, the Copyright Owner waives any claims against SoundExchange arising under the Agreement after the date of the assignment. The Copyright Owner's sole recourse with respect to such claims shall be against SoundExchange's assignee.

14. <u>Additional Provisions</u>. The Agreement constitutes the entire agreement between the parties concerning the subject matter of the Agreement and supersedes all prior agreements between the parties concerning the subject matter of the Agreement. The Agreement shall be binding upon and inure to the benefit of the parties, their successors, permitted assigns and legal representatives. The Agreement shall be governed by and construed in accordance with the laws of the District of Columbia, without regard to its conflict of laws principles.

August 5, 1999

SoundExchange
7

NOTICE OF ELECTION TO PAY ROYALTIES AS AN ELIGIBLE SMALL WEBCASTER

For All or Any Portion of Period January 1, 2007 – December 31, 2007[1]

(must be filed by no later than the first date on which royalty payments are due for the relevant period)

I. ELECTION

In accordance with the authority granted to SoundExchange under the Small Webcaster Settlement Act of 2002 (the "SWSA"), Pub. L. No. 107-321, 116 Stat. 2780, and pursuant to Sec. 6 of The Copyright Royalty and Distribution Reform Act of 2004, the transmission service named below hereby files with SoundExchange its notice of election to pay royalties and comply with the terms adopted pursuant to the SWSA and published in the Federal Register on December 24, 2002, 67 Fed. Reg. 78510 (the "Eligible Small Webcaster Rates and Terms") for the making of ephemeral phonorecords or digital audio transmissions of sound recordings, or both, under the statutory licenses set forth in sections 112(e) and 114(d)(2) of title 17 of the United States Code, respectively, for the period commencing on January 1, 2007, or the date of the first digital audio transmission of a sound recording under statutory license after such date, and ending on December 31, 2007.

II. BINDING NATURE OF ELECTION

The service acknowledges that this election to pay royalties in accordance with the Eligible Small Webcaster Rates and Terms is in lieu of any different rates and terms that may be available to such service. Upon the filing of this notice of election, and for so long as the service qualifies as an "eligible small webcaster," as such term is defined in Section 8 of the Eligible Small Webcaster Rates and Terms, the service acknowledges that it cannot opt out of these Rates and Terms in order to elect different rates arrived at by a CARP except in the limited circumstance set forth in Section 1(d) of the Eligible Small Webcaster Rates and Terms. See http://www.soundexchange.com/Rates_Terms.pdf.

[REMAINDER OF PAGE INTENTIONALLY LEFT BLANK]

---

[1] There is currently a rate adjustment proceeding before the Copyright Royalty Board ("CRB") of the Library of Congress to establish statutory royalty rates for webcasters for the period January 1, 2006 through December 31, 2010. We expect those rates to be established near the end of the first quarter of 2007 and apply retroactively to January 1, 2006. Depending upon the CRB's determination, a licensee may be required to file an amendment to this notice.

III.   INITIAL STATEMENT OF QUALIFICATION TO MAKE PAYMENTS AS ELIGIBLE SMALL WEBCASTER IN 2006.

The service hereby states that it and its "affiliates" "gross revenues," plus "third party participation revenues" and revenues from the operation of a new subscription service, have not exceeded $1,250,000 in any calendar year prior to 2007, and that the service expects to be an "eligible small webcaster" during 2007. "Affiliate," "gross revenues," "third party participation revenues" and "eligible small webcaster" shall have the meanings set forth in Section 8 of the Eligible Small Webcaster Rates and Terms. The service acknowledges that the filing of this notice of election does not guarantee the service the right to pay statutory royalties under the Eligible Small Webcaster Rates and Terms if and when the service no longer qualifies as an eligible small webcaster.

IV.   DATE OF FIRST DIGITAL AUDIO TRANSMISSION UNDER STATUTORY LICENSE

The service hereby states that the date it first made a digital audio transmission of a sound recording under the statutory license set forth in 17 U.S.C. § 114(d)(2) after December 31, 2002 is _____ (enter date).

V.   IDENTIFYING INFORMATION FOR ELIGIBLE SMALL WEBCASTER

Please provide the requested information for each item.

1. Name of service _____

2. Mailing address _____

_____

3. City/State/Zip _____

Note: A post office box is acceptable only if it is the only address that can be used in that geographic location.

4. Telephone number _____

5. Fax number _____

6. Website address of service   http://_____

7. Contact person for questions _____

8. Telephone number for contact person _____

9. E-mail address for contact person _____

VI.   CERTIFICATION

The undersigned hereby states, under penalty of perjury, that the information provided in this notice of election is accurate and that the undersigned is authorized to act on behalf of the service electing to pay royalties as an eligible small webcaster. The undersigned further acknowledges that he/she has reviewed the Eligible Small Webcaster Rates and Terms and that the service agrees to be bound by the same and the provisions of the statutory licenses and any applicable provisions of regulations adopted thereunder.

Officer or authorized representative of eligible small webcaster

Signature   _____

Name   _____

Title   _____

Date   _____

VII.   DELIVERY

A completed notice of election must be delivered to the following address: SoundExchange, ATTN: Royalty Administration, 1121 14th Street, N.W., Washington, DC 20005.

hfa

The Harry Fox Agency, Inc., 711 Third Ave., New York, NY 10017

APPLICATION FOR HFA MECHANICAL LICENSING ACCOUNT

This form is to create a licensing account with HFA for the manufacture and distribution of CDs, Audio Cassettes, LP's, etc. within the U.S. **Domestic** license request forms can be downloaded at www.harryfox.com/docs/m-license_laccountapp.pdf; however, if you'd like to apply for licenses online, see option #4 on the reverse of this page. If you plan to license songs for **digital uses** as ringtones, downloads, streams, Digital Phonograph Delivery, etc., you will need to submit a New Media Application, which is available at www.harryfox.com/newmediareg/ nmrForm1.html.   If you plan to **import** into the U.S. recordings manufactured outside of the country, you will need to complete a Request Form for Phonorecord Importation, which is available at www.harryfox.com/docs/Importation_Request_Form.pdf.

1. GENERAL CONTACT INFORMATION

Name of Company: _____   Contact Person: _____

Address: _____ City: _____ State: _____ Zip: _____
(No P.O. Boxes; must be a street address. If a rural address, we still need a street address in addition to P.O. Box)

Telephone #: _____   Fax#: _____

E-mail: _____   Website: _____

2. PRELIMINARY RELEASE INFORMATION

Anticipated Quantity of Units: ___ over 2,500 (See section 3 below)
                                      ___ 501- 2,500 (You will be invoiced; payment is due before licenses will be issued)
                                      ___ 1- 500 (HFA does not issue licenses for fewer than 500 units. Your non-refundable
                                               advance payment will be calculated for 500 units, and you will receive license
                                               authority to make up to 500 copies, even if you plan to make less.)

Signature: _____   Title: _____   Date: _____

Print name: _____

3. ADDITIONAL INFORMATION ON ACCOUNTS RELEASING 2,500+ UNITS

Have you ever done business with HFA before? If "Yes," under what account name? _____

Check the category which best applies to you:

___ Corporation ___ Partnership ___ LLC ___ Individual ___ School ___ Church ___ Military Organization

If incorporated, please supply State and Date of Incorporation _____

If an individual, please supply Social Security Number _____

Years at Present Address _____

Annual U.S. Gross Receipts (check one) ___ $5,000 or less ___ $5,001 to $50,000 ___ $50,001 to $100,000 ___ Over $100,000

Bank Name: _____   Bank Address: _____

Type of Account: _____   Bank Telephone: _____

(over)

12-6-05   1

4. HFA ONLINE LICENSING TOOLS

Licensees with an HFA account can have access to our online licensing system, eMechanical, and to online reports of licensing activity. These tools are described further below. If you would like to use HFA Online, you must designate an Administrator(s) responsible for overseeing user accounts for your company's employees as described below. You may designate more than one person with Administrator duties; if your company elects to do this, please send a separate copy of the form for each Administrator.

eMechanical is a web-based mechanical licensing application, which will allow you to apply for licenses for physical and digital products online. Licensees can submit and track the progress of license requests in real time; research their entire licensing account online, not just transactions submitted through the application; and request licenses for digital permanent download singles and albums. Please note that this is not a bulk license request tool; if you are interested bulk licensing, please inform an HFA Licensing agent.

Online Licensing Reports give licensees the ability to view all their licensing transactions online and download this data to their own systems. In addition, these reports will help to identify trends or analyze problems using a set of business analytical tools. The data used by the reporting application is now refreshed on a monthly basis with plans to move to weekly updates. The following reports are available in both Adobe PDF and Microsoft Excel formats: Download of License Transactions, Reports of License Transactions by Status Summary; Status Detail; Release Detail; and Song, and Notice of Song Ownership Changes. The reports may be customized using a series of prompts, or filters. The filters for licensing transactions include transaction type (such as digital), transaction status (such as unsigned), and the reporting period.

If you would like to use the HFA Online Licensing tools, please complete the following:

Request for Administrator Account and Password for HFA Online Systems

The organization(s) identified on the reverse of this page hereby request(s) HFA to open an account for and assign a password to the employee identified below, who will act as an Administrator to oversee access within our organization(s) to HFA's online systems. It is understood that the Administrator will be subject to all applicable terms governing use of HFA's online systems and will be responsible for supervising the access of our employees to HFA's online systems in accordance with such terms.

Administrator Name: _____

Administrator Title: _____ Administrator Dep't: _____

Administrator Postal Address: _____

(if different than company's) _____

_____

Administrator Email: _____

Administrator Phone: _____ Administrator Fax: _____

In signing below I represent that I am authorized by the organization(s) identified above to designate the person identified above as an Administrator to oversee our employees' access to HFA's online systems.

By:_____ Print Name: _____

 Authorized Signature

Dated: _____ Title: _____

Return with License Request (attached) to: Licensing Department
                                                     The Harry Fox Agency
                                                     711 Third Ave. 8th Floor
                                                     New York NY 10017
                                                     Fax: 646-487-6746

HFA Internal Use ONLY: Approved by: _____ Acct # _____

12-6-05   2

Sony/ATV Music Publishing
SYNCHRONIZATION REQUEST

Thank you for your interest in a Sony/ATV Music Publishing copyright. We require the following information in order to process your request:

Synchronization Request Form
Please print and complete the attached form (below). Be sure to include: a synopsis of your project, a detailed description of the relevant scene, and nature of use of the song (e.g., "Song is playing on the radio while main characters are driving their motor home through a snow storm," or "Song will be used over the end credits of the film," etc.) Also include the media rights you require (e.g., film festivals, videocassette, TV, advertising, etc.). If you are requesting music for a video production, game or consumer product, we need to know how many units will be manufactured. Your request will be processed upon receiving the required information. We will notify you in writing as soon as possible.

Submission of this **Synchronization Request Form** does not constitute or imply an agreement of any kind between the person or company submitting same and Sony/ATV Music Publishing LLC.

Sony/ATV Music Publishing LLC
2120 Colorado Avenue, Suite 100
Santa Monica, CA 90404

SYNCHRONIZATION REQUEST FORM
FAX: 310 449-2541

Your Name: _____
Company: _____
Address: _____

_____

Phone: _____
Fax: _____
Email: _____
Song Title: _____
Writer(s): _____
Publisher(s): _____
Artist: _____
Label: _____
Name of Production: _____
Cast: _____
Distributor/Production Co: _____
Production Budget: _____
Music Budget: _____
Brief Synopsis: _____

Detailed Scene Description: _____

_____

Nature of Use: _____

_____

Duration of Use: _____
Media: _____
Term: _____
Territory: _____
Miscellaneous: _____

Sony/ATV Music Publishing LLC
2120 Colorado Avenue, Suite 100
Santa Monica, CA 90404

Index